P9-APG-489

Praise for *50 Reasons to Buy Fair Trade*

"A lively, accessible and inspiring survey of how fair trade is bringing new hope to poor producers around the world."

Paul Chandler, Chief Executive, Traidcraft

"The best and most comprehensive guide around to the principles and practice of fair trade."

Joanna Blythman, food writer and campaigner

"A wonderfully inspiring and uplifting book, which demonstrates the power of the personal choices we make as consumers. *50 Reasons to Buy Fair Trade* not only offers 50 powerful reasons to choose fairly traded goods, but also tells us some of the compelling stories behind the products. And while each of the stories is very different, the message remains the same: fair trade changes lives. The fair trade movement is one of the great success stories of our time – and this book bears witness to its growing strength and importance."

Dr Caroline Lucas, Green Party MEP for South-East England

"This well-researched, balanced and inspiring book is a great guide to how and why the empowered individual can make a difference. ... This book educates and empowers – the WTO board should read it and learn from it."

Craig Sams, founder of Green & Black's

"This book captures the spirit of our times. We live in a risky and divided world and though as an individual you can't do everything, you can do something – or, as this book shows, 50 things. This book is a celebration of social justice."

Ed Mayo, Chief Executive, National Consumer Council

"Want that really pithy example to convince a sceptic you are right when it comes to the way the world is headed for oblivion but doesn't have to be? It's here. Want to be surprised by how much you can make

THE UNITED LIBRARY
2121 Sheridan Road
Evanston, IL 60201

a difference? Try this book. Eloquent voices from around the world will compel and provoke you, reason by reason, to act differently!"

Pauline Tiffen, founder of Cafédirect and the
Day Chocolate Company

"*50 Reasons to Buy Fair Trade* is a extensively researched piece of work that defies all myths that fair trade doesn't work."

Wendy Martin, Editor, New Consumer magazine

"Buying fair trade goods is one of the most direct ways a consumer in the North can help some of the poorest people in the world to get a decent price for their products. As *50 Reasons to Buy Fair Trade* shows, fair trade's impact goes much wider, forcing governments and corporations to rethink the way they do business."

Duncan Green, Head of Research, Oxfam

"Quietly, against the odds, fair trade has emerged as a powerful social force. But there are even more powerful forces against it: not just nasty, thoughtless companies or people, but all of us desiring things on the cheap. Sometimes we don't know what lies behind the goods; sometimes we bury our heads, denying the hidden costs, pretending we don't know. This book gives powerful reasons why that tension in modern consumer culture cannot go on and why the fair trade movement is not about being 'worthy' or wallowing in guilt, but about changing what we do and injecting justice into what otherwise easily becomes a brutal world."

Tim Lang, Professor of Food Policy, City University, London

"Buying fair trade is one of the most practical actions consumers can take against exploitation by the multinationals. This highly readable book shows how and why."

Patricia Barnett, founder and Director, Tourism Concern

"Fair trade allows people to act – to use their power as consumers to make a difference. *50 Reasons to Buy Fair Trade* will encourage many more to join them, and that's good news for producers in developing countries, the partners they work with in the UK, and their growing legion of customers."

James Niven, Triodos Bank

"Provides a lively and important reminder that fair trade provides consumers with a way to take individual positive action in solidarity with the poor."

Benedict Southworth, Director, World Development Movement

"While fair trade is complex, *50 Reasons to Buy Fair Trade* has untangled the issues and lays them out clearly in excellent easy-to-read chapters."

Stefan Durwael, Executive Director, International Fair Trade Association

"This book is illuminating, accessible, and above all, empowering."
Jeremy Seabrook, author of Consuming Cultures: Globalisation and Local Lives
"This timely and well-researched publication confronts those doubtful of the effectiveness of fair trade as an instrument for sustainable development with substantiated evidence. Litvinoff and Madeley's extensive overview of the advantages inherent to the logic of fair trade contributes dearly to the cause of increased justice in international trade."

Dr Frithjof Schmidt MEP, European Parliament Rapporteur on Fair Trade

"Fresh and clear as a see-thru mint. If this doesn't persuade you to support fair trade, nothing will."

Anuradha Vittachi, OneWorld.net

"In showing how buying fair trade products can support a range of social and environmental goals, *50 Reasons* reminds us that trade is simply the interaction between all of us and reflects our level of consciousness as humans today. Litvinoff and Madeley show us a range of reasons for thinking, living and, yes, shopping, as one people on one planet. Those of us who have the knowledge and opportunity to do something about the fragmentation between people and nature that exists in mainstream commerce no longer have any option but to change it, and ourselves."

Dr Jem Bendell, Senior Strategic Advisor, World Wide Fund for
Nature

"A first-class guide, without ducking the issues, to why being a smart consumer makes sense. Whether you're a fair trade fanatic or wondering whether to start, this book will give you lots of new reasons to be a smart consumer. Buy it and help change the world through the way you shop."

Richard Bennett, General Secretary, BOND;
former Chair, Make Poverty History

Miles Litvinoff and John Madeley have done a service in writing this book. It will, I hope, make a contribution to a world where the people who produce goods that enhance our lives receive a return that also enhances theirs.

Wendy Craig, actor

HF
1713
.L48
us

50 Reasons to Buy Fair Trade

Miles Litvinoff and John Madeley

Pluto Press
London • Ann Arbor, MI

For

Gillian and Stephen

Cecilia

and fair trade producers around the world

First published 2007 by Pluto Press
345 Archway Road, London N6 5AA
and 839 Greene Street, Ann Arbor, MI 48106

www.plutobooks.com

Copyright © Miles Litvinoff and John Madeley 2007

The right of Miles Litvinoff and John Madeley to be identified as the authors of this work has been asserted by them in accordance with the Copyright, Designs and Patents Act 1988.

British Library Cataloguing in Publication Data
A catalogue record for this book is available from the British Library

Hardback
ISBN-13 978 0 7453 2585 9
ISBN-10 0 7453 2585 8

Paperback
ISBN-13 978 0 7453 2584 2
ISBN-10 0 7453 2584 X

Library of Congress Cataloging in Publication Data applied for

10 9 8 7 6 5 4 3 2 1

Designed and produced for Pluto Press by Curran Publishing Services, Norwich
Printed and bound in the European Union by Antony Rowe Ltd, Chippenham and Eastbourne, England

Contents

CONTENTS

CONTENTS

CONTENTS

Goods produced under conditions which do not meet a rudimentary standard of decency should be regarded as contraband and not allowed to pollute the channels of international commerce.

President Franklin D. Roosevelt,
message to US Congress, 1937

Acknowledgements

We are grateful to the following for their help and advice:

Sergio Allard, Richard Armstrong, Tricia Barnett, Simon Billing, Felicity Butler, Paul Chandler, Mark Cherrington, Atif Choudhury, Tony Cook, Maria José Cordoba, Wendy Craig, Barbara Crowther (special thanks for enhancing the accuracy of the text), Cathi Davis, Chris Davis, Janixce Florian, Heather Gardner, Christine Gent, Xavier Gomez, Dave Goodyear, Colin Hopkins, Regina Joseph, Silver Kasoro-Atwoki, Harriet Lamb, Jamie Lloyd, Bente Madeira, Tatiana Mateluna Estay, Blanca Rosa Molina, Terry Mollner, Maranda St John Nicolle, Veronica Pasteur, Shailesh Patel, Abi Pettit, Andy Redfern, Craig Sams, Kate Sebag, Issaka Sommande, Arsene Sourabie, Annabel Southgate, Joel Uribe, Luis Villaroel, Nicola Ward, Helen Yuill, Roger van Zwanenberg.

Any errors or omissions in the book are of course our own.

We and the publishers would also like to thank the various fair trade organisations for permission to use the trademarks, logos and symbols that appear on the cover of the paperback edition of this book

Miles Litvinoff and John Madeley

About the authors

Miles Litvinoff writes and edits on human rights, sustainable and international development, and corporate responsibility. His *Earth-scan Action Handbook for People and Planet* and *Young Gaia Atlas of Earthcare* were shortlisted for awards, and he was general editor of the *World Directory of Minorities*. He is also a manager in the NGO sector and has worked in Africa, Asia, Eastern Europe and Latin America. He previously taught environment studies with the Open University and has supported fair trade for 20 years.

John Madeley is the author of eight books and many other publications and articles on economic and social development issues, especially international trade, transnational corporations, food and agriculture, and human rights. His interest in fair trade spans three decades. He was a member of the Council of Reference of Traidcraft when it was set up in 1979. He has travelled in over 50 developing countries and seen some of the poverty of people who produce for the mainstream trading system.

Introduction

> When we arise in the morning ... at the table we drink coffee which is provided for us by a South American, or tea by a Chinese, or cocoa by a West African; before we leave for our jobs we are already beholden to more than half the world.
> Martin Luther King

We are beholden to people across the world – many of them the very poorest – who supply products that we value so highly. Yet how much do they receive for them? In most cases, it's a pittance, and most of us feel that's not right. Those sandals we picked up for a fiver – well, that made us feel uneasy. How much could the woman or man who made them have earned?

We don't want the poor to get screwed like this. The question is, how to put it right? More and more of us want to know how we can buy goods which have given the producer a fair return. And in the mid to late 1990s we increasingly began to buy food, drink, craftwork and other products which do that – goods that have been traded fairly.

Fair trade is a success story of our time. In the first five years of this millennium the number of fair trade products we could buy increased by over 15-fold. Originally it was just handicrafts. Then it spread to coffee and chocolate, and on to include a widening range of foodstuffs. Today we can buy far more. Fair trade clothes, bedlinen, shoes, furniture, flowers, carpets, footballs, wine and fruit juice are all available – and they are great quality!

WHAT IS FAIR TRADE?

Fair trade is trade with a difference. It's a way for us to help the world's poor every time we shop. With fair trade, producers in poor countries receive a decent return – a fair and stable price or wage for their products. And also in many cases they get extra money – a premium – to invest in their business or community. Buying fair trade products is a way of taking practical action to bring about a better, more generous world. It can help make poverty history.

Many fair trade products carry the Fairtrade Mark. This is awarded by an organisation called Fairtrade Labelling Organisations (FLO) International to products that meet internationally agreed fair trade standards. FLO is the umbrella organisation of "national initiatives" in 21 countries across Europe, Japan, North America, Mexico, Australia and New Zealand. The Fairtrade Foundation is its UK member.

Fair trade products also come from fair trade organisations like Traidcraft and People Tree that belong to the International Fair Trade Association (IFAT). This is a network of 270 fair trade organisations in more than 60 countries, from every continent, which adhere to fair trade principles.

There are other initiatives that are close to fair trade in spirit, such as Rugmark carpets and community-based tourism. Our book covers these too.

The need for fair trade is clear. The mainstream international trade system is failing the world's poor. Since 2001, and the launch of the Doha Development Round of world trade negotiations, member countries belonging to the World Trade Organization (WTO) have talked about changing world trade to benefit the poor. But wealthy countries, notably European Union countries and the United States, have refused to make the changes needed. The poor are left to wait. All this makes fair trade more crucial than ever.

The poor cannot eat talk. They need real, lasting benefits. The fair trade system can provide these benefits. The great thing about fair trade is that it works for poor people. Fair trade provides a viable alternative to the mainstream trading system.

As dramatic as the growth of fair trade has been, and for all its increasing influence, it still represents only a small fraction of world trade. Most producers of fair trade coffee, for example, still have to sell a lot of their crop on non-fair trade terms.

Fair trade has huge potential. It can influence and change the world trade system and help poor people and communities work their way out of poverty. But for this to happen, it needs to keep on grow-ing. The more fair trade goods we buy, the more people can sell under a fairer system. *50 Reasons to Buy Fair Trade* gives 50 powerful and different reasons for buying these products. The Reasons show, very directly, how fair trade works for the benefit of children, women and men in developing countries and what people in developed countries can do to give it more impact.

HEAR PEOPLE TALKING

In most of the Reasons in this book, we hear people in the fair trade system doing the talking. They tell us in their own words about the difference that fair trade makes to them, to their families, to their communities. Many of them are poor, some very poor. But they are all clear that fair trade means a better life.

Nicaraguan coffee grower Blanca Rosa Molina tells us that the fair trade system "makes the difference between whether my family eats or does not eat".

Cecilia Mwambebule, who grows tea in Tanzania, tells us that with fair trade "we have been able to do many things. We have primary schools, secondary schools. ... Our schools are very important. Now we have tables and chairs, and real floors and windows to keep the wind and dust out."

For Dominican banana farmer Amos Wiltshire, fair trade "has made a huge difference to the families, the farmers concerned and to the economy as a whole. ... Fairtrade is a shining light."

And Shailesh Patel, fair trade cotton project manager for Agrocel in India, tells us that "Fair trade saves farmers' lives. It prevents suicides."

Did you know that around three-quarters of the world's footballs are made in and around the city of Sialkot in Pakistan? We hear of how fair trade footballs have made a big difference to the families who stitch them.

We hear of how the "social premium" included in the price of Fairtrade-certified products helps small-scale farmers and other low-income producers raise the quality of their produce, make the land more productive, improve the local environment, support community education, health services and women's rights, and deliver a host of other benefits.

Whether it's fair trade mangos from Burkina Faso, one of Africa's poorest countries, Rugmark-labelled carpets from Pakistan, or fair trade wine from Chile, this book shows the many connections between buying fair trade and helping low-income people all over the world.

WIDER ISSUES

Our book also looks at wider issues. Fair trade alone will not solve all the world's poverty, although its growth could make a significant contribution for many people. We talk about the need for trade justice, the importance of respect for human rights, and achieving the Millennium Development Goals. And we highlight how fair trade has helped trigger a wave of consumer awareness. How it has even led to transnational corporations making some improvements.

The role of the transnational corporations in fair trade is controversial. There is a big debate about whether a product from a company such as Nestlé should be awarded Fairtrade certification. We look at both sides of the argument.

Some transnationals talk about ethical trade. But fair trade goes further. Ethical trade means companies trying to ensure that workers or farmers in developing countries who make or grow their products have decent working conditions. Fair trade goes beyond ethical trade, because it guarantees fair terms of trade and fair prices, supports and encourages workplace democracy and co-operatives, and enables people to take more control over their own lives.

Today there's an important debate about food miles and climate change, about global versus local, the environmental costs of air transport, and the negative impacts that big supermarkets can have on local economies. For a more sustainable world, we need to buy local produce where we can, and have supply chains that are less oil dependent. What sense is there in flying apples across the world when we can grow them in the UK? Fair trade does not address these issues – and it's not intended to.

Where fair trade does contribute to sustainable development is in those goods that cannot easily be, or are not currently, produced locally in the global North. Most fair trade produce comes from tropical regions that Western countries have exploited for so long, and most people living in those regions need our solidarity. So if we're buying their tea, coffee, cocoa or bananas, we can make it fair trade every time.

THE FUTURE

There are growing doubts as to whether the mainstream international trading system – dominated by corporations whose overwhelming concern is to make big profits – can change enough to help the poor. By contrast, the verdict on fair trade is loud and clear. Shah Abdus Salam, executive director of the non-governmental organisation Development Wheel in Bangladesh, puts it like this:

> Only Fair Trade can ensure better and sustainable livelihoods for the marginalized artisans in the world. [The] Fair Trade movement can enhance market access for the southern poor and distress[ed] producers and [help] to establish ethics in the business in the world.

Harriet Lamb, director of the UK's Fairtrade Foundation, says the first ten years of the Fairtrade Mark have proved that consumer choice, "once derided as trivial, individualistic and apolitical, can wield positive power".

It's people like us buying the products that has made fair trade a success – and will make it even more so. Fair trade products are for everyone. Most compete on price and are widely available in supermarkets. Recognition of the Fairtrade Mark is growing. One in every two people in the UK now recognises the Mark across all age groups from 16 to 64. It's especially encouraging that recognition has grown fastest among younger people aged 16 to 34.

When you buy fair trade, your purchases can help to redress the income balance. You can help change the world. We end the book with a look into the future – a future where there can be more hope for poor people.

This book does not pretend to be an exhaustive list of reasons to buy fair trade. You may have others. If so, please write to us c/o Pluto Press, 345 Archway Road, London, N6 5AA, or email: 50reasons@phonecoop.coop. We would be delighted if readers can help us turn our 50 reasons into 100.

In the Appendices at the back of this book, we give information about where to buy fair trade (shops and suppliers), the Fairtrade Towns movement, and leading UK and international fair trade organisations and campaigns.

We feel excited about the future of fair trade. If you are new to fair trade, a whole new world awaits. If you're an old hand, we hope that in these pages you will discover even more reasons to buy the goods that help poor people.

Miles Litvinoff and John Madeley
August 2006

1. Back a system that benefits the poor

The mainstream trading system is failing the poor. Fair trade offers partnership in place of exploitation.

Trade is as old as humankind itself. At its most basic, trading takes place because people have different skills and abilities and find it worthwhile to exchange with people who have other skills and resources. Nations began to trade for much the same reason.

International trade has enabled people to enjoy a vast range of goods and has raised the living standards of many communities. But it has long been marked by greed, indifference and the oppression of those whose trading skills, resources and circumstances are relatively poor. Trading skills in an unfettered "free" market have led to the amassing of wealth for some, who gain a dominant position over others. The mainstream trading system is today failing the poor. While some gain, many lose.

The trade that has increased living standards has also caused people to go hungry and starve. During Ireland's famine of 1845–9, for example, which killed almost a million people, large landowners routinely exported food to Britain as poor peasants dropped all around them. Today food is still being exported from countries where there is gross hunger and people are dying as a result.

Substitute developing countries for Ireland, transnational corporations for large landowners, and the Western world for Britain, and little has changed. The system continues to fail the poor.

As international trade widened, economists developed the theory of comparative advantage. This holds that output will be maximised and all will gain if each country specialises in producing those goods and services for which it is best suited, and then trades them with other countries. For a variety of reasons a country may be able to produce something at a lower cost than another country. It may have a better climate, or its workforce may have special skills, for example.

[7]

But the theory is deeply flawed. Clearly, not all countries have gained from international trade. Countries that produce industrial goods – notably Western nations – have fared better than those specialising in primary produce, notably developing countries. Divisions between industrialised and primary-producing countries are widening rather than narrowing. Some 300 years ago, there was little difference in income levels across countries. At the start of the twenty-first century the difference across countries was 100 to 1.

The economists' theory has failed. Whereas people in Western countries buy more manufactured goods as incomes increase, many developing countries are less and less able to earn enough from selling their commodities to buy the manufactured goods they need.

"FREE" TRADE TODAY

In the last 20 years of the second millennium, international trade went even more severely wrong. Trade liberalisation – the reduction of barriers to trade to bring about "free" trade – began to work against millions of the poor, intensifying their poverty. The liberalisation had been underway for manufactured goods since the late 1940s, but the big move came under the structural adjustment programmes of the World Bank and International Monetary Fund, introduced in the early 1980s. Developing countries had to agree to these programmes if they wanted aid, investment and, more recently, debt relief. Trade liberalisation was a central feature.

More recently the World Trade Organization, set up in 1995, has given a further push to liberalisation. The Geneva-based WTO makes the rules that govern trade. With 149 member countries (in July 2006) the WTO has the task of enforcing the agreements that emerged from the Uruguay Round of world trade talks which ended in 1993. There are four main agreements – the Agreement on Agriculture, the General Agreement on Trade in Services, and agreements on Trade-Related Intellectual Property Rights (TRIPs) and Trade-Related Investment Measures (TRIMs).

The WTO presents itself as a forum for members to negotiate over trade liberalisation. In practice it is a trade liberalisation juggernaut which has been ceded enormous power by its members. It uses that position to further the cause of liberalisation, chiefly to the benefit of those who stand to gain most from that process – in practice, transnational corporations. The WTO's first director-general, Renato Ruggiero, said in 1998:

> We stand at the very beginning of a whole new phase of internationalism. We are living through a time of deep and rapid transition towards a very different world. [We have] an opportunity to reaffirm our political will to move towards a better system of global governance ... shaping the institutions of an increasingly borderless economy. The great promise of the new global age demands nothing else.

The vision is therefore one of a borderless world economy, of global governance, based on the "free" trade system. A snapshot of what has happened to developing countries since the early 1980s and the coming of significant trade liberalisation is revealing. Developing countries were growing at about 3 per cent between 1960 and 1980, but they grew at only about 1.5 per cent between 1980 and 2000, as University of Cambridge economist Ha-Joon Chang points out. He says:

> During the last 20 years, African economies have been shrinking (at a rate of about 0.8 per cent per year versus a 1.6 per cent growth rate before), while Latin America has been basically stagnant (growing at 0.3 per cent vs 2.8 per cent before).

Only in parts of Asia, notably South Korea, Taiwan, Indonesia and China, has there been any significant reduction in poverty, and those countries have made extensive use of trade restrictions. They have not followed the classic trade liberalisation route.

There is clear evidence from developing countries that the poorest peoples and communities have lost ground under trade liberalisation. Small-scale farmers are an example. The last 20 years have seen a huge increase in food imports into developing countries.

Millions of small-scale farmers have been unable to compete and have been driven into bankruptcy. "The relentless pursuit of trade liberalisation, privatisation and deregulation", said the Make Poverty History campaign, "has continued in the face of mounting evidence that they entrench and do not overcome poverty. The impact on poor people and our collective environment has been disastrous."

A world without barriers may sound a good idea, but the reality is that in today's economic world there are huge disparities of power. In the twenty-first century, it is companies not countries that trade. In a "free" trade, no-barriers system, the poor swim in the same economic stream as the corporations. Putting a tiddler into the same stream as a shark can have only one outcome – and it's not good for the tiddler. The poor cannot be expected to survive, let alone gain, in a system where they have no say, control, power or influence.

The corporations have been described as "instruments of a market tyranny that is extending its reach across the planet like a cancer ... destroying livelihoods, displacing people, rendering democratic institutions impotent, and feeding on life in an insatiable quest for money". The worst aspect of this is that it hits hardest at the most vulnerable people. Throughout the developing world people are working in poor countries for less than a dollar a day to make goods such as clothes and toys for the Western world. Often these goods carry prestigious brand names and sell for high prices. But wages for the people who make them are rock bottom and working conditions are often appalling. "Free" trade does not free the poor from poverty. In the mainstream trading system, the poor lose.

Fair trade, which helps the poor rather than reinforcing their poverty, is gaining support the world over and offers important hope to millions of impoverished people. In the fair trade system, the poor gain.

The rest of this book will show just how much.

2. Pay small-scale farmers a fairer price

Fair trade raises incomes of small-scale farmers and boosts local economies. The fair trade farm-gate price is the key to a better life for hundreds of thousands of families.

Agriculture is the biggest economic sector in most developing countries, and hundreds of millions of people earn a living as small-scale farmers. For decades there has been an oversupply on world markets of widely traded agricultural commodities like coffee, sugar and tea – and often an undersupply of more varied local produce for local needs. This market glut has resulted in falling prices and dwindling incomes for Southern growers. Variations in the weather, crop diseases and other factors also make farm-gate prices rise and fall unpredictably.

Twenty-five million farmers in 50 developing countries depend on coffee as their main or only crop, roughly half of them operating small family farms. Many small-scale coffee growers are geographically isolated or lack transport to take their produce to market, so they have to sell to traders and moneylenders (see Reason 21). In the case of exported coffee, the middlemen often sell to a mill for processing first, and the costs at each stage cut part of the price paid to the original grower. In addition, having to hire seasonal labour at harvest time can easily double a coffee grower's production costs.

When we buy coffee in a supermarket, only a small fraction of the retail price goes to the producer. No surprise, then, to hear from Oxfam that two-thirds of the world's coffee growers live in absolute poverty. With the international coffee agreement's collapse in 1989, prices fell below the cost of production for many farmers. Supermarkets, coffee shops and large transnational brands like Kraft and Nestlé carried on making big profits, while many debt-burdened growers could hardly scratch a living. In the words of Nicaraguan coffee farmer Mario Perez: "We practically had to give away our harvest."

Low and unstable coffee prices have had a terrible impact on the lives of small-scale farmers and their communities. There have been reports of increasing social unrest, robberies, suicides, mounting household debt, children withdrawn from school by parents, families unable to afford hospital fees – and in Colombia and Haiti growers turning in desperation to illegal drugs cultivation. In Nicaragua thousands of coffee workers held a "March of the Hungry" to the capital in mid 2003. It's said that 14 of the marchers died on the way.

Prices have been falling for banana producers too. The world banana trade – worth more than £5 billion a year – is dominated by five transnationals: Dole, Del Monte, Chiquita, Fyffe's and Noboa. They have driven down costs by sourcing supplies from large Latin American and West African plantations that pay rock-bottom wages, where working conditions are abusive and the fruit is drenched dangerously with pesticides. The smaller independent banana growers – such as hillside farmers in the Caribbean – have been unable to compete on price and have lost market share. As Dominican grower Amos Wiltshire puts it: "The economy went down to zero. ... Everything was going haywire: increasing crime, youth violence, ... delinquency. ... Husbands couldn't maintain their families."

Faced by this downward price spiral, "free" trade seems to have nothing to offer small-scale Southern farmers except more of the same. But fair trade does have an answer: a fair minimum price.

BETTER INCOMES FROM FAIR TRADE

Fairtrade certification guarantees minimum prices for producer organisations. The minimum price is based on local economic conditions and covers production costs, plus provision for household members to enjoy a decent living standard, and the cost of farm improvements and compliance with fair trade standards, including the cost of belonging to a farmers' co-operative.

Fair trade buyers pay this "floor price" – plus, for all Fairtrade-certified produce, a "social premium" (Reason 4) – when world market prices are low. But they pay the going world market rate when it rises above the "floor". In recent years the floor price paid to producers for Fairtrade-certified arabica coffee has averaged $1.21 per pound, compared with an average world market price of 70 cents a pound.

The fair trade market for bananas – second in retail value worldwide only to coffee – works similarly. The floor price takes account of the fact that smaller-scale banana growers use fewer pesticides than large plantations, and so have higher production costs because more handwork is needed, and that they have higher organisational and transport costs. In 2005 the minimum fair trade export price for Ecuadorian bananas was $0.13 per pound – roughly double the non-fair trade market rate.

The additional benefit to producers for Fairtrade-certified produce worldwide was an estimated $100 million in 2004–05. Every study made has found income higher for producers who sell to fair trade markets than for those who don't. Fair trade farmer co-operatives are estimated to earn between 25 and 60 per cent more than they would without fair trade.

How do the producers feel about it? Nicaraguan fair trade coffee grower Bertilda Gamez Peres says:

> There are big advantages. ... We get more money for our crop. We didn't make enough money to live on before. Now we get a better price and the money comes directly to us. I can buy more food. I can help support my daughter at university ... and take care of my son.

Costa Rican farmer Guillermo Vargas, who visited the UK in 2002, recalled:

> For my grandfather and my father, both coffee farmers, nothing changed. Between 1950 and 1988, nothing got better. We knew we had good coffee, but working on our own, trading as individuals, we could do nothing. Then, in 1988, we decided to form a co-operative. It gave us strength to negotiate a better price and we were able to sell to Fairtrade. When we found that one thing had gone well by acting together, we tried other things.

For Amos Wiltshire, a Dominican banana producer, fair trade "has made a huge difference to the families, the farmers concerned and to the economy as a whole. ... Fairtrade is a shining light ... the saviour of the farmers in Dominica."

Fair trade farmers and their families benefit by being able to invest in their smallholdings and homes and pay for schooling and health services (rarely entirely free in developing countries). But the wider community also gains from the "multiplier" effect of more money earned and spent locally. New jobs get created, and local governments have more tax to spend (Reason 48).

On a broader scale, influenced by the success of fair trade in raising coffee producers' incomes, banana companies like Fyffe's and Dole are looking into ways to source and market fair trade or other forms of "socially responsible fruit".

3. Buy products you can trust

There are now over 2,000 Fairtrade-certified products – and even more fair trade goods besides!

When you buy a fair trade product, you want to know that it's the genuine thing. You want to know that it's a product you can trust. There are two main ways you can do this.

PRODUCTS THAT CARRY THE FAIRTRADE MARK

The Fairtrade Mark is your guarantee that a product has been carefully checked and certified. It's an independent label that appears on products as a guarantee that disadvantaged producers are getting a better deal.

Coffee was the first product to be certified Fairtrade – in the Netherlands in 1989. The Dutch label is called Max Havelaar, after a best-selling nineteenth-century book about the exploitation of Javanese coffee plantation workers by Dutch colonial merchants (see

Reason 11). After this first initiative, other national labelling initiatives soon followed, some using the same name, others introducing new ones like TransFair, Fairtrade Foundation and Rättvisemarkt. They all started individually, and each chose for its market the Fairtrade consumer label it wanted on the products.

In 1997, 17 national initiatives together founded a worldwide organisation, Fairtrade Labelling Organisations International (FLO). And they recognised the need for a single mark. This came into being in 2002 as the "International Fairtrade Certification Mark". FLO is responsible for setting international fair trade standards, for certifying production and auditing trade according to these standards, and for the labelling of products. Its Fairtrade Mark is both a certification mark and a registered trademark. FLO is now made up of members in 20 countries (Appendix 3).

A product qualifies for the Mark when FLO standards and procedures are met. They need to be met by producer groups, traders, processors, wholesalers and retailers. There are two sets of standards for producers, one for small farmers and one for workers on plantations and in factories. The first set applies to smallholders organised in co-operatives or other organisations with a democratic, participative structure. The second applies to organised workers whose employers pay decent wages, guarantee the right to join trade unions and provide good housing where relevant. This applies, for example, to plantation workers (Reason 7). The FLO standards stipulate that traders have to:

- pay a price to producers that covers the costs of sustainable production and living
- pay a premium that producers can invest in development
- partially pay in advance, when producers ask for this
- sign contracts that allow for long-term planning and sustainable production practices.

Fair trade is ultimately about development, so FLO's standards distinguish between minimum requirements, which producers must meet to be certified Fairtrade, and "progress requirements" that encourage producer organisations to continuously improve working conditions and product quality. Progress requirements also include improving the environmental sustainability of activities and investment in organisational and producer or worker development.

FLO gives credibility to the Fairtrade label by providing independent, transparent and competent certification of social and economic development. The four main aspects of certification are:

- ensuring the producer groups conform to the standards
- ensuring that Fairtrade benefits are used for social and economic development
- auditing FLO-registered traders to make sure that the fair trade price reaches the producers
- ensuring that the label is used only on products coming from Fairtrade-certified producers.

To ensure that producer groups comply with fair trade standards, FLO works with a network of independent inspectors who regularly visit all producer organisations to monitor traders' and retailers' compliance with Fairtrade conditions. A specially developed trade auditing system checks that every Fairtrade-labelled product sold to a consumer has genuinely been produced by a certified producer organisation which has been paid the fair trade price. Finally, there are specific fair trade standards for each product that determine such things as minimum quality, price, and processing requirements that have to be complied with.

FLO guarantees that products sold anywhere in the world with a Fairtrade label marketed by a "national initiative" conform to fair trade standards and contribute to the development of disadvantaged producers and workers.

The Fairtrade Mark therefore gives you a fivefold guarantee. It guarantees:

- a fair and stable price to farmers for their products
- extra income for farmers and estate workers to improve their lives
- a greater respect for the environment
- a stronger position for small farmers in world markets
- a closer link between consumers and producers.

There are now over 2,000 Fairtrade-certified products on the market. They include coffee, tea, chocolate, cocoa, sugar, bananas, apples, pears, grapes, plums, lemons, oranges, satsumas, clementines, lychees, avocados, pineapples, mangoes, fruit juices, quinoa, peppers, green beans, coconut, dried fruit, rooibos tea, green tea, ice cream, cakes and biscuits, honey, muesli, cereal bars, jams, chutney and sauces, herbs and spices, nuts and nut oil, wine, beer, rum, flowers, sports balls, rice, yoghurt, babyfood, sugar body scrub, cotton wool and cotton products.

And these are only some of the fair trade goods available. There are a great deal more beyond the certified range.

PRODUCTS FROM IFAT MEMBERS (INTERNATIONAL FAIR TRADE ASSOCIATION)

You can also buy fair trade goods from organisations that you trust: registered members of the International Fair Trade Association (IFAT). IFAT is made up of over 270 organisations in 60 countries (see Reason 11). Many of its members date back to the 1960s and 1970s, and they started to meet in 1985. To qualify for membership, organisations have to meet the requirements of IFAT standards, and to be registered they have to have completed the assessment process.

In January 2004 IFAT launched the "Fair Trade Organization Mark". This is an organisation mark rather than a product mark, and recognises that a whole organisation produces, imports, distributes or sells fair trade, and has poverty reduction at its core. It is used equally in both South and North. The FTO Mark recognises and unites fair trade organisations, enabling them to campaign for trade justice with greater power.

The FTO Mark guarantees that the organisation using it is registered with IFAT, and all such organisations must prove that they:

- trade honestly
- pay a fair price
- work with people who are marginalised
- exchange and build skills

- promote greater equality and empowerment for all
- protect children's rights
- respect the environment.

IFAT registration involves a three-part monitoring process: self-assessment, peer review and then external review. There is one standard for both North and South, developed and developing countries. This was established by the members and is constantly revised by them. It is not only a standard but also a tool for each FTO to ensure that it is reaching its own poverty-reducing objectives.

IFAT-registered organisations must generate the majority of their income through the sale of fair trade products. In addition, fair trade networks – such as the British Association of Fair Trade Shops (BAFTS) – and support organisations such as Shared Interest, a bank dedicated to fair trade (Reason 47), also qualify to join IFAT.

IFAT is a democratic organisation, with a majority of members from the South. It holds a global conference every two years, alternating in venue between the North and South. In the UK there are 18 members, including Bishopston Trading, Café Direct, Day Chocolate Company, People Tree, Shared Earth, Tearcraft, Traidcraft, Tropical Wholefoods and Twin Trading. Products from FTOs include clothing, jewellery, giftware, homeware, baskets, rugs, furniture, tablecloths, bedding, packaging, glassware, ceramics, embroidery, essential oils, tea, coffee, mangos and many other food products.

Among the best known UK IFAT members is People Tree, which sells "fair trade fashion" via mail order and online. People Tree clothes are made by fair trade producers at every stage – from the cloth to the final product. The company buys from farmers who grow natural fibres such as organic cotton, from handloom weavers who work in small-scale co-operatives, and from artisans who make and stitch the clothes. It is committed to supplying customers with "healthy, safe and attractive products with good service, together with information about the background of the products, producers and lifestyle alternatives".

Another major IFAT member is Traidcraft, which describes itself as "the UK's leading organisation dedicated to fighting poverty through trade". Established in 1979, Traidcraft is "a pioneering and successful trading company (Traidcraft plc), offering the widest range of fairly traded products available in the UK". These include food, wine, fashion and crafts. It also has a development charity (Traidcraft Exchange) specialising "in making trade work for the poor" (Reason 46). The company has almost 300 different products, sourced from more than 100 producer groups in some 30 developing countries. The products are sold through a mail order catalogue, online (which is growing in popularity), and through a nationwide network of around 5,000 "fair traders" – volunteers who sell fair trade products from stalls at their church, school, university or at local events.

Products sold by IFAT member organisations can be bought with the confidence that producers receive a fair return. Consumers can trust these organisations – challenging poverty is their purpose.

4. Help producers believe in tomorrow

The "social premium" included in the price for Fairtrade-certified products may be small. But it makes a major difference when the rural poor put the money to work. And it benefits both young and old.

Millions of small-scale farmers and plantation workers in the global South are trapped in a cycle of poverty. With just enough money coming in to survive today – sometimes not enough – they are unable to think about tomorrow. Many are burdened with debt and saddled with despair.

There may not be any quick fixes. But fair trade has a medium-term remedy: the social premium. This is the extra money – on top of the guaranteed price or fair plantation worker wage – that goes to the producer community when you buy Fairtrade-certified produce. Year on year, social premium spending on community projects helps give rural producers a better future.

How much is it worth? For coffee, the current fair trade price of US$1.26 per pound paid by coffee importers includes a social premium of 5 cents. For the consumer, the premium represents about 2 per cent of the shelf price – say 5p on a £2.30 227g pack of Café-direct medium-roast ground coffee. With Fairtrade bananas it's more. For most produce the premium averages about 10 per cent of the price the importer pays.

For the producers, who spend it with great care, this money can go a long way. The Mabale Growers Tea Factory, for example – jointly owned by 1,000 small-scale Ugandan tea farmers – earns about US$30,000 a year by way of the premium. And this is based on selling only 5 per cent of its output to Teadirect and other fair trade brands. "Fair trade is significantly contributing towards the social improvement of our community and providing a better future for our youngsters," says Silver Kasoro-Atwoki, Mabale director and board member.

Under fair trade rules, the premium is saved or invested by the growers' co-operative or the plantation "joint body" of elected workers' representatives and management. It's paid directly into a special bank account, and there's a collective decision on how to use it.

Producer co-ops and plantation workers invest their premiums in a host of social projects: from building and equipping schools, clinics and community centres to paying school or medical bills; from installing water supplies, toilets and electricity to financing organic conversion; from small start-up business loans for income diversification to funding workers' pension schemes; from tree planting to women's empowerment projects.

PUTTING THE PREMIUM TO WORK

Here's how fair trade banana growers are making the most of the premium.

Leneff Hector, a St Vincent grower, told the Fairtrade Foundation: "We decided, before we use the premium for anything else, to help our schools – our producers, nurses and teachers of tomorrow." Besides supporting local schools and providing education scholarships, Windward Islands growers have invested in supporting health clinics, refurbishing community centres, upgrading local roads and small loans for on-farm improvements.

Ghanaian banana growers have used the premium to reduce herbicide use – providing more work in manual weeding – and to pay year-end bonuses. They plan to invest future premiums in organic production and a social and environmental action plan. Costa Rican growers have used the premium to pay for advice from an agronomist and environmental specialists, and for repairs to housing. "Before when it rained we couldn't transport our bananas from our fields. With the improved roads, we can," says fair trade banana farmer José Alama, who belongs to the Valle del Chira co-operative in Piura, Peru. His association of 182 small-scale growers are using the premium to improve the roads around their smallholdings and to pay for an office computer, desks, accounts books and a phone line.

Tea and coffee producers make equally good use of the premium. Tea pickers in Herkulu, Tanzania, who supply tea for Teadirect, are building a maize mill. This will save local women a 15 km walk. Their ideas for future use of the premium include paying school fees, buying sewing machines and building a technical college to train local youngsters in vocational skills. Sivapackiam, a Sri Lankan tea picker, represents fellow workers on the workers' and managers' "joint body" that decides how to use the premium on her estate: "A year ago, we didn't have any electricity in our houses," she recalls:

> All the members of the joint body got together and discussed how we could pay to install it. Some money came from the Fairtrade premium and we each took out a loan. With electricity, my children can study at night. In the morning I can iron their clothes and we can use a hotplate for cooking. I am happy that fair trade helps me support my family.

The Nilgiris tea estate in the West Ghats mountains, southern India, employs more than 3,000 people. Here workers used the premium to start a pension fund. Jointly run by estate workers and managers, the scheme is a rarity in India, where few manual workers can retire with any financial security. Workers like Manickam – who picked tea for 41 years – can retire when they are 58 and receive a pension of up to 1,200 Rupees (£15) per month for the next 15 years. This can be crucial, because retired tea pickers usually have to leave the plantation where they were living and rarely receive any social security payments.

At Mabale in Uganda, the premium has been invested in training and plant husbandry. Growers are steadily producing more and better-quality tea, obtaining higher prices for the tea that they have to keep selling to non-fair-trade markets until fair trade demand grows larger.

More than 3,500 small-scale coffee growers belonging to Costa Rica's Coocafé co-operative association supply fair trade coffee to Europe and the United States. The foundation they set up with the social premium in the mid 1990s supports soil restoration, tree planting and environmental education. They have also used the money to maintain local primary schools and to fund secondary school and university scholarships for hundreds of farmers' children, as well as to provide plots to landless families.

5. Make trade more democratic

International trade is mostly undemocratic, controlled by large corporations. Fair trade spreads power and enables more people to have control over their lives.

Countries don't trade, companies do. Especially large companies. Around two-thirds of international trade is between transnational corporations (TNCs). Defined by the United Nations as "an enterprise with activities in two or more countries with an ability to influence others", transnational corporations are mostly public companies owned by their shareholders. The corporations are large, powerful and unaccountable to anyone but their shareholders. They are unelected and undemocratic and they make the mainstream trading system undemocratic.

TNCs are large. In 1999, 51 of the world's 100 largest economies were corporations, 49 were governments. To put this in perspective, General Motors is bigger than Denmark and over three times the size of New Zealand. The top 200 corporations' combined sales are bigger than the combined economies of all countries except the largest ten.

Their numbers are increasing rapidly. In the early 1990s there were an estimated 37,000 TNCs with 170,000 foreign affiliates. "By 2004", says UNCTAD, "the number of TNCs had risen to some 70,000 transnational corporations with at least 690,000 foreign affiliates." The foreign affiliates therefore increased fourfold in little over a decade.

TNCs are widespread, involved in every sphere of economic activity in virtually every country, and they are powerful. Their size, usually with the protection afforded by company law and governments, gives corporations power to make the rules. They can dictate terms to national governments – dangling jobs and foreign earnings as the carrot – and have taken full advantage of the move towards privatisation to influence government policy. TNCs have also used their power to influence international trade negotiations, often secretly. Although they work locally in developing countries, key decisions affecting what they do may be taken thousands of miles away in their head office in New York, London, Paris or other capital cities.

TNCs are not subject to international regulation. The United Nations tried for 17 years, from 1975 to 1992, to draw up a code of conduct for them. It had to abandon the attempt. The corporations were powerful enough to stop it.

TNCs dominate markets. Several million small-scale coffee farmers sell into a market where just four companies buy 40 per cent of global output, and similar structures apply in cocoa, bananas, soya and many other products.

In most developed markets, retailing has also become extremely consolidated. In Britain the "Big Four" supermarket chains account for over 70 per cent of all food sales. Globalisation offers buying companies operating at this scale huge benefits as they can seek the best deals from anywhere in the world, whereas producers, especially smallholders, are limited in their ability to find new customers.

TNCs resist attempts to make them more democratic. In mid 2006, for example, Parliament debated a Bill to reform company law. Campaigners urged that the Bill should include a clause that would hold company directors accountable for the social and environmental impact of their company's activities. They also pressed for a clause that would require companies to monitor and report on their social and environmental impacts. The Confederation of British Industry, the main UK business lobby group, were successful in persuading the government not to support such changes. The Bill does however strengthen some aspects of company reporting requirements and directors' duties.

While they make noises about sustainable development, TNCs fail the sustainable development tests. Their interest lies in maximising profits in the short term, not necessarily sustaining them over the long term. TNCs have to make good profits for their shareholders, otherwise they will be judged to be underperforming and be ripe for take-over. Shareholders want their dividends, this year and TNCs have to deliver. In terms of accountability to the wider public, they are deeply undemocratic. But it does not have to be like this.

THE DEMOCRATIC ALTERNATIVE

The fair trade system is a viable and proven economic alternative. Fair trade is democratic, decentralised and transparent. Fairtrade Labelling Organisations International – the Fairtrade Foundation is the UK member – awards the Fairtrade Mark to products that qualify. For food products, one of the conditions is that the farmers democratically organise into small-farmer groups such as co-operative organisations under terms that include the following:

- The majority of the members of the organisation must be small-scale producers.
- The organisation must be an instrument for the social and economical development of the members, and in particular the benefits of Fairtrade must come to the members.
- The organisation must therefore have a democratic structure and transparent administration, which enables an effective control by its members and its board over the management, including the decisions about how the benefits are shared. There must be no discrimination regarding membership and participation.
- An organisational structure is in place which enables control by the members.
- There is a general assembly with voting rights for all members as the supreme decision taking body, and an elected board. The staff answers through the board to the general assembly.
- The organisation holds a general assembly at least once a year.
- The annual report and accounts are presented to and approved by the general assembly.
- The organisation works towards transparent planning of the business plans. Such plans will be approved by the General Assembly.
- The participation of members in the organisation's administration and internal control is promoted through training and education.
- The organisation establishes or improves internal mechanisms of members' control over the administration, such as a control committee with rights to review the administration.
- Increasingly, the organisation's policies are discussed in member meetings.
- Management actively encourages members' participation in meetings.
- There is improvement of the flow of information from board to members about the business and the organisation's policies.

Organisations are encouraged to make annual business plans, cash flow predictions and longer-term strategic plans.

In the case of products such as tea which are grown on plantations, there are of necessity differences. One of the conditions for the Fairtrade Mark for plantation-grown tea is the development of "joint bodies" which enable workers to engage in decision-making processes with management and influence social development projects on plantations (see Reason 7).

Other fair trade organisations, such as IFAT, Traidcraft, People Tree and Oxfam Trading, have requirements about democratic structures. All are a big improvement on the structure and practice of the transnational corporation.

Fair trade is democratic trade.

6. Put a human face on development

There's a lot of debate about "development". Fair trade puts many of the best ideas into practice. This small-scale Chilean honey-producers' co-operative provides a perfect example.

The setting is the small provincial town of Santa Bárbara in southern Chile. Sitting in their wooden one-storey office in a corner of the tranquil *plaza*, Joel Uribe and Luis Villaroel talk about their beekeepers' co-operative, COASBA, with quiet pride. It was Joel, an engineer by training, who founded the association in 1994 and built it up from next to nothing, using his home as an office and working unpaid to get COASBA on its feet. More recently Luis, who used to drive lorries for a living, took over from Joel as president.

Early on, COASBA's members – families who kept bees and produced honey on a small scale – were all part-timers. "Very few of us owned any land, so most had to rent a *parcela* [small plot] for their hives. None could earn a decent livelihood as honey producers," Joel and Luis recall.

Today most of COASBA's 35 members, including two women, practise beekeeping full time. Honey and bee serum are their main source of income. After years of effort invested in developing their skills and processes, Joel and Luis claim the taste, cleanliness and nutritious quality of their honey are among the best in the country. They feel they are raising standards in their industry for the whole of Chile's BioBío region.

Too often, so-called "development" has involved huge transnational companies arriving in developing countries, plundering their raw materials, undermining the local economy, wrecking the environment and people's lives – and then getting the hell out of there.

But there's another way. It's been called "people-centred development" or "development with a human face". Examples can be found all over the world, and increasingly they're linked to fair trade.

FROM DEBT TO DEVELOPMENT

COASBA has come a long way. At first, co-op members were often in debt to local moneylenders. They had to use the cheapest low-quality bulk containers to transport the honey. There was little time to spend on hygiene, pest and disease control, or breeding. Plus they had no way of knowing when they would make their next sale. That was before COASBA was introduced to fair trade by a Chilean church-based development organisation supported by the European Union.

COASBA's honey has been Fairtrade-certified for the past five years. The most obvious benefit, say Joel and Luis, is better incomes: "Co-op members get 20 per cent more for their honey under fair trade than when they sell through other channels."

All COASBA members – who between them now keep several thousand beehives, producing roughly 130 tonnes of honey a year – allocate some of their produce to be bulked up in modern stainless steel drums and sold to Apicoop, a large fair trade exporter co-operative based on the coast. Apicoop exports the honey to fair trade buyers in Germany, Switzerland, France, Italy, Spain, Belgium and the UK. In the UK it's an ingredient in Traidcraft's popular Geobars.

Joel and Luis believe they could not have developed COASBA

without fair trade. "Fair trade has helped raise earnings for beekeepers all round – not just for co-op members," they claim. Freed from moneylenders and exploitative middlemen, each COASBA member has a regular guaranteed income. The co-op pays them a decent lump sump once a year, which enables people to plan. COASBA itself retains a percentage of sales income to invest in improving production processes and for administration. This has created several new jobs, such as for Maria-José Cordoba, the young woman who runs the small office in the *plaza*.

Co-op households have raised their standard of living. Many have bought their own plot of land and improved their homes. Several now own a vehicle for transporting the honey. Some of their children are among the first from this rural community to go to university. In a region where poverty is widespread, family finances are far better than before. Crucially, the younger generation can see a future in beekeeping and in running a co-operative enterprise, rather than joining the exodus of young rural unemployed to the bigger towns and cities.

COASBA has earned a reputation for paying off its debts promptly and won respect from such bodies as the Agriculture Ministry's Institute for Agriculture and Livestock Development. Among the members there is increasing trust and mutual support. When necessary COASBA lends members money to buy equipment or medicines for their bees, with more time to repay than before. It has supported member households through periods of hospitalisation.

Professional development, advice and training are another major benefit. Maintaining and improving production standards are all important to COASBA. The co-op is a member of Chile's national network of beekeepers and prides itself on high technical and sanitary standards. Joel and Luis sense they are gaining national recognition for their produce. COASBA has recently begun to provide advisory services for local beekeepers outside the co-op, along with programmes in basic beekeeping for the local municipality.

Though it is not certified organic, Joel and Luis claim their honey is organic in all but name. They see beekeeping as essentially an ecological activity and are determined to help protect the diverse native flora of the beautiful BioBío river valley.

HONEY FROM SANTA BÁRBARA

COASBA's confidence is growing. At the heart of their future plans lies the small yet ultra-modern honey processing plant and laboratory they are building just outside the town. The new one-storey building will house facilities that, they intend, will be second to none in the whole country. Initial support for the project, begun in 1999, came from a regional non-profit foundation.

The building is almost ready and will enable the co-op to add far more value to their product. Here they will not only bulk up their honey for export but also bottle it in jars for domestic retail markets, proudly labelled "Honey from Santa Bárbara". At the front gate will be a shop selling to passers-by.

The laboratory they are installing will enable co-op members to diagnose and control diseases among their bee colonies far more swiftly than at present. Currently they have to send samples away for analysis. The laboratory will serve not just co-op members but beekeepers throughout the region. Genetic improvement and training programmes are being planned in partnership with two Chilean universities.

Joel and Luis's ambition is for COASBA to become an independent honey exporter. They foresee a day when jars labelled "Honey from Santa Bárbara" will be on sale in food shops throughout Chile, Europe and even the Middle East.

7. Ensure plantation workers earn a living wage

Plantation workers can be among the poorest of the poor. With fair trade they receive a proper wage and decent conditions.

Plantation workers. The people who work on large farm estates toil for long hours often under the hot sun. Their working conditions may be unsafe, and they are usually paid a pittance for the work they do. And when work is finished for the day their low wages cause them to live in conditions that may be an affront to human dignity. Too often they lack the freedom to join a union to defend their rights and the opportunity to participate in decisions that affect their lives on the plantation.

Under the fair trade system a proper wage is paid to workers on plantations (estates, as they are sometimes called). And there are other benefits too.

TEA

Tea is the UK's most popular drink. We sip an average of three and a half cups a day. Only in Ireland and Poland do people drink more tea.

Most tea is plucked on plantations, notably in India, Sri Lanka, China and Kenya. Tea plantations are labour-intensive, with planting, maintenance and harvesting usually carried out by hand. The crop is picked year-round in tropical areas, mostly by women with baskets or bags on their backs to carry the leaves plucked from the growing tips of the shrubs. The leaves are taken to a collection point to be weighed then transported to a nearby processing plant, as they need to be processed on the same day to retain freshness and flavour. At these plants the leaves are withered, rolled, fermented, dried and sorted.

Working under a scorching sun, lugging heavy baskets and sacks estate employees are normally paid on a piece rate system. The amount they earn depends on how much they pluck. Often they earn the statutory minimum wage – where one exists – and receive some of the lowest wages in their countries. Taking into account the fact that entire families may have to survive on one or two incomes, the per capita wage in many cases is below US$1 a day. And that is the daily income that the World Bank defines as the acute poverty line.

Workers on tea plantations often do not earn enough to have any reserve. If they lose their jobs, their very survival can be at stake. In March 2004, for example, around 800 tea workers in India were reported to have died of starvation, "with several surviving on wild roots and rats, because the closure of uneconomic plantations rendered a million labourers jobless". The report by the Indian People's Tribunal on Human Rights and the Environment, a civil rights group based in Mumbai, said that the deaths resulted from a combination of starvation, malnutrition, general debility and diseases among workers.

In many Asian plantations entire families of men women and children work together. In India, Sri Lanka and Viet Nam women account for over 50 per cent of the plantation labour force, and in Pakistan and the Philippines it is around 35 per cent. Women usually pluck the tea whereas men are responsible for preparing the land, spraying pesticides, pruning and supervision. In most cases female workers are also responsible for the majority of household tasks, such as fetching water, which can take hours.

Although the fact is usually officially denied, child labour is also common in many of the poorer tea-producing regions due to the economic conditions of the household and lack of schools. Even where it is illegal for children to work on plantations, as in Sri Lanka, their situation may not be much better as children of tea workers are sometimes sent off to the cities to work as domestic servants, leaving them even more vulnerable. A survey by the Malawi Congress of Trade Unions found that the use of child labour is a very serious problem on many tea plantations.

India's Plantations Labour Act (of 1951) sets the legal framework for the tea industry in India but has one serious omission. It does not cover occupational health hazards and safety measures for field workers. In Assam and West Bengal, pesticides are usually sprayed by untrained casual daily wage workers, mostly children and adolescents, who are illiterate and unable to read the warnings on the containers. They often use bare hands to mix these chemicals, some of which are banned, yet workers are not provided with masks, goggles, gloves, rubber boots, polythene aprons or other protective gear. Usually they are unaware of the risks, and no compulsory medical check-ups are conducted. When they sustain injuries, their medical care is highly inadequate.

The tea industry in India relies on insecticides, pesticides, herbicides and fungicides to protect the tea crop from various diseases and maintain yields. Evidence shows that workers have developed poisoning of the cardiovascular and nervous systems as well as the kidneys and liver, blindness, memory loss and premature senility. Research in Sri Lanka has shown that deaths due to the use of pesticides are common. The International Labour Organization has identified a high incidence of accidents relating to chemical exposure.

FAIRTRADE ESTATE TEA

The need for a better deal is clear. Some tea estates now qualify under the fair trade system. To qualify for Fairtrade certification for their tea, estate employers must pay decent wages, guarantee the right to join trade unions and provide good housing when relevant. Minimum health and safety as well as environmental standards must be complied with. No child below the age of 15 can be employed. Forced labour is not allowed. A premium of €0.50 to €1.00 per kg must also be paid to be invested in social, economic or environmental programmes for the benefit of the workers (see Reason 4).

"Joint bodies" must be developed which enable workers to have a say in decisions that affect them, allowing them to influence the social development projects on plantations. This means that Fairtrade tea estate workers can negotiate directly with owners and management and have a direct input into the decision-making process. The joint bodies decide how the Fairtrade premium can be invested in projects that benefit the estate community. They proportionately include women and members of minority groups.

Business development services also have to be available to help build the commercial capacity of producers. And sustainable farming methods must be implemented that are safer for humans and the environment.

Most tea gardens have received the equivalent of a few thousand or perhaps a few tens of thousand of pounds, but some in India and Sri Lanka have earned several hundred thousand pounds in Fairtrade premiums. This money is making a significant contribution to empowering workers and improving their livelihoods. An analysis of how the premium money has been allocated shows that funds are spent on a variety of projects. Some joint bodies have decided to construct schools or health centres with the help of this money. Others have acquired computers and other equipment for schools or awarded scholarships. Electricity has been installed, cattle bought, pension and loan funds established, vaccination programmes set up or forests replanted. Village roads have been improved, playgrounds built, and flushing toilets and solar lighting installed. Pensioners, orphans and people with disabilities have received financial support.

Fairtrade-certified tea is making big difference to the lives of plantation workers.

8. Empower women and girls

Women produce most of the food and craftwork and make most of the clothes in developing countries. But they're still often treated as second-class citizens. Buying fair trade is a great way to support the fight for gender equality.

Of the world's 1.2 billion people living on less than $1 a day, 70 per cent are women and girls. Women everywhere work longer hours than men for less pay and in worse jobs. When they do the same job they earn on average two-thirds of a man's wage. And they do many extra hours of unpaid work in the home, providing food, shelter, health care, education and clothing for their families, especially in rural areas.

Most women in developing countries work in the "informal" sector. Many support their families through subsistence farming or small-scale crafts production. Often with little or no land, capital, credit or technology, they have to toil all the harder. In traditional communities, women's tasks are often treated as less important than men's.

To makes ends meet, Southern women increasingly need to work outside the home. In agriculture they are often hired on low-paid seasonal contracts, working long hours and exposed to hazardous chemicals. In manufacturing, women are less likely than men to demand better working conditions. Hours of unpaid overtime may be enforced to meet just-in-time orders from international big-name companies.

Among the world's most exploited women are millions of garment workers in countries like Bangladesh, Honduras and Morocco. Oxfam says they are "burnt out by working harder, faster and over longer hours, and with few heath, maternity or union rights".

Women's poverty goes hand in hand with widespread disempowerment. Widowed, divorced or separated women may lose their home, family or means to survive. Millions of women and girls are trafficked into the sex trade.

Yet women are so much more than victims. They often offer the best solutions for poverty reduction. Their income has been shown to provide more family and community benefits than men's, with a greater proportion spent on nutrition, health and education. Women's empowerment is crucial to improving the lives of the poorest, and fair trade is an effective way to help.

HOW FAIR TRADE HELPS WOMEN

One of fair trade's main goals is to promote women's development opportunities by valuing and rewarding their work fairly and empowering them in organisations. According to internationally agreed fair trade standards, women should have the same opportunities as men to train, develop skills, apply for job vacancies and seek leadership roles, and their gender-specific health, safety and cultural needs must be taken into consideration. This all means better opportunities for uneducated, widowed and divorced women and for single mothers.

Fair trade rules also require women workers to be well represented on the "joint bodies" and committees that decide how the fair trade social premium is spent (see Reason 4). This often gives women a chance to speak in public for the first time. Greater self-reliance and participation in a co-operative or committee enhance women's self-esteem and social standing. They gain leadership skills and a greater sense of freedom and security. Says Punjiben, who grows fair trade cotton in Gujarat, India, "Our voices are equally important in the committee. Our voices are strong in the decision-making process."

[34]

Traidcraft, one of the UK's biggest and longest-established fair trade companies, supports a range of women-centred projects in Bangladesh. Among its suppliers of arts and crafts products are: Aarong, 85 per cent of whose rural artisans are women; Eastern Screen Printers, which employs 30 women in printing designs onto handmade paper and jute and cotton fabrics; Jahanara Cottage Industries, which trains rural women in painting, weaving, knitting, wood-carving and basket weaving; and CORR-The Jute Works, working since 1973 with war-widowed and war-affected rural women.

In Africa, Traidcraft's food and drink supply chains also clearly benefit women. Sugar from Malawi used in GeoActive bars comes from the Kasinthula Cane Growers' Association, whose income paid for a borehole for Kapasule village, saving women a 1.5 kilometre daily trek for water. Juliet Ntwirenabo, of Igara Growers, Uganda, whose tea is sold by Teadirect and Traidcraft, chairs the growers' committee that decides how to spend their social premium. Juliet says: "Since we became Fairtrade farmers our women no longer die in childbirth being carried down the mountain to the hospital. From our Fairtrade proceeds we have built two maternity wards."

In 2005 the BBC reported on one of the women-only fair trade coffee co-operatives that have sprung up in Rwanda, where many women were widowed in the 1994 genocide. One member explained that now she could afford family health insurance, her children could see a doctor, and there was money to send even girls to school.

Nicaraguan agronomist and community organiser Janixce Florian tells a similar story. Janixce works with fair trade coffee co-operative SOPPEXCCA and visited the UK during Fairtrade Fortnight 2006. Of the co-op's 650 members, 190 are women, and fair trade has enabled many of them to participate in workshops for the first time.

Women have proved excellent quality coffee growers, Janixce says, in one case winning a national prize three years running. Some women members so impressed visiting US buyers that their women-only coffee is now marketed under the brand name "Las Hermanas" (The Sisters). Some of the husbands have become jealous, but the women know how to handle them.

Kuapa Kokoo, the large and well-known co-operative in Ghana that supplies cocoa to the Day Chocolate Company (Reason 44) and Traid-craft, runs a range of women's income generation projects. These include production and marketing of vegetables, soap and palm oil.

Just as deprivation gets passed down across generations, so does empowerment. Women strengthened by fair trade bring up daughters with higher expectations. Teenager Rijayatu Razak, daughter of Kuapa Kokoo members, is an example of how fair trade is changing girls' outlook. Able to go to secondary school only as a result of fair trade's social premium, Rijayatu won an essay competition and visited the UK one Fairtrade Fortnight. She says:

> At school I have started my own co-operative for girls only. We think that it is not fair that the girls have to do all the housework while the boys can ride around the village on their bicycles and play football. We think the work should be equal between the girls and the boys.

9. Bring hope to coffee growers

An expansion of the market for Fairtrade-certified coffee offers hope for coffee growers – not least the basic hope of eating.

When Nicaraguan coffee grower, Blanca Rosa Molina is asked about the difference that selling through the fair trade system makes, her reply is both simple and devastating. "It makes the difference between whether my family eats or does not eat," she says.

Blanca farms three hectares of land in the Matagalpa region in the north of Nicaragua. The country is one of the world's main coffee growing countries and coffee is its primary export crop. Blanca is president of the Cecocafen co-operative of some 1,200 coffee producers. Like other members of the co-operative, she sells about a third of her coffee in the Fairtrade-certified system.

Now 47, life for Blanca began the hard way, as it did for many other generations in Nicaragua. Her parents were workers on a large coffee plantation in Matagalpa. At the age of six, Blanca joined her parents at work in the fields. Aged 11, she left home to work as a maid in Managua, the capital city.

But things were to change dramatically when the Nicaraguan revolution was won in 1979. Agricultural reform laws were introduced and land was redistributed to the landless. A new phase of hope began for Blanca's family and many of her neighbours when they started to grow coffee on their own land in Matagalpa. Things were good for a while.

But the volatility of coffee prices on the world market began to make their lives precarious. Throughout the 1990s prices fluctuated, but were often too low for growers to make a decent living. In the early 2000s the collapse of coffee prices continued to undermine the security of peasant farmers, and gradually eroded Nicaragua's export earnings.

In 2002, the crisis reached catastrophic proportions. Coffee prices plummeted to 30-year lows, with the result that many of the big commercial farmers could no longer afford to harvest their crop and laid off full-time and seasonal labour. It was a price fall that hit workers very hard. Thousands of out-of-work coffee workers and their families were reduced to setting up makeshift roadside camps. They only survived thanks to food donations from concerned local people and businesses.

"Most people who worked on large coffee plantations lost their jobs," said Blanca. She was fortunate. The Cecocafen co-operative had by then obtained the Fairtrade mark for its coffee. Blanca points out:

> The fair trade price allows us to eat, to keep our land. It means our children can stay in school and that we can have the basic health provisions. The price has enabled me to

send my daughter to university and build my house bit by bit. It's a very humble house and I am still building. I took a loan from the co-operative which has to be paid back within a year. But small producers, if they are not supplying the fair trade market, could hardly afford a house, and they have no access to credit.

Blanca has also been able to diversify production on her land, "which has given us greater food security".

EMPHASIS ON QUALITY

"We hope that fair trade increases because there are many more coffee farmers in our region who would like to sell some of their crop through this system," Blanca says. "We know the importance of producing top-quality coffee so that the market keeps growing. Only the best quality goes into Cecocafen coffee. The emphasis on quality starts at the point of selection of the seeds."

Coffee from Cecocafen goes into Cafédirect's 5065 and Percol's Nicaragua coffee. The Cecocafen co-operative distributes and markets coffee for its 1,200 members, who decide at general assembly meetings how to use the Fairtrade premium they receive.

Of the US$1.26 cents a pound that growers receive for their coffee in the Fairtrade certification system, 5 cents is the Fairtrade premium that is used for business or community development programmes (see Reason 4).

"Fair trade is not just to benefit the individual farmers," stresses Blanca. "It's to benefit the community as a whole. Fairtrade isn't only about buying and selling. It has a very important social aspect." The co-operative has used the premium for social improvements, ensuring that children are going to school, for example, and that women are included in decision-making processes. The premium has also been invested in social projects such as water supply services, road building and buying medicines for the community. A scholarship fund has paid for further education for 70 children of co-operative members. A general credit scheme has been set up as a savings and loan programme for women. This is benefiting over 200 female members and non-members.

Blanca goes on:

> We don't just want to see farmers who are selling under the fair trade system improve their own standard of living, we want the community as a whole to benefit. So our co-operative is teaching literacy skills to both adults and children, and we have done lots of primary health education.

Community improvements are happening, she says. One community has used the premium to pay for a teacher. Others have ensured that young children receive nutritious food.

The Fairtrade premium has also been invested in processing facilities and a quality control laboratory. This has helped Cecocafen to develop and market its own roast and ground and organic coffee brands. The investment has created a new source of income for Cecocafen members, as the facilities are also hired to other producers.

When farmers become part of the fair trade system, says Blanca:

> It is easier for them to convert to organic, chemical-free production, because they have support in terms of training, advice on organic methods and so on. The coffee premium allows farmers to carry out soil and water conservation activities and helps to protect the environment.

She would like to sell more of her coffee through the Fairtrade system, "but that depends on the market expanding". Asked what her message is to people who buy coffee, Blanca says: "Buy our coffee because it is the best quality, not because we are poor farmers."

Coffee prices on the world market have recovered since the bleak days of the early 2000s, but in late 2006 were still low and fluctuating. This gives most growers an uncertain future. An expansion of the market for Fairtrade-certified coffee offers hope for an increasing number.

10. Save a cotton farmer's life

Buying fair trade pyjamas can help prevent suicides among Indian cotton farmers. Sounds far-fetched? Read on and decide for yourself.

Small-scale farmers the world over are more likely to commit suicide than many other occupational groups. Even in a rich country with all kinds of safety nets, such as the UK, farming can be an isolated, debt-burdened and stressful business. Crises like foot and mouth, added to uncertain or falling farm-gate prices, can easily lead to financial difficulties, anxiety and depression.

In developing countries the problems are usually worse. For many Southern smallholders, the global trading system and a collapse in government support have made it virtually impossible to earn a decent living on the land. Falling prices, rising costs, increasing reliance on expensive agrochemicals and irrigation, alongside years of worsening drought, crop failure, environmental problems and ill-health, have led millions of small-scale farmers into debt and despair.

Small-scale cotton farmers have had particularly severe problems – not least because cotton is unusually pest-prone and uses more insecticides than any other crop. In recent years world cotton prices have been undercut by heavily subsidised cotton from the EU (grown mainly in Greece, Portugal and Spain), the USA and China, and through increasing competition from synthetic fibres like nylon and polyester. India's cotton farmers have been among the worst hit, and suicides among them are common. The online newspaper *India Together* reported in 2005:

> The spell of suicides continues even in the harvest. The last two years have seen inadequate rainfall. The irrigation scenario is frustrating, and water resources are fast drying up. ... An unregulated open market and private usurers have tightened their noose around the debt-ridden cotton farmers.

Aged just 30, for example, Maharashtra state cotton farmer Lokeshwar Keshavrao Bhoyar took his life by jumping into his dried-up well in October 2005. Lata, his widow, is now a day labourer cotton picker, earning 2 Indian rupees (3 pence) per kilo.

Farmer suicides have been reported across the country – in Andhra Pradesh, Karnataka, Kerala, Maharashtra, Punjab and Rajasthan. And not only farmers are at risk, but their sons and daughters too. In November 2005, 19-year-old cotton farmer's daughter Neeta Pundalikrao Bhopat, a BA student, committed suicide, leaving a note that read: "My family can't make even a thousand rupees a month. And I have two younger sisters ... we don't have enough to eat. So I am ending my life."

VILLAGES AND KIDNEYS FOR SALE

Since 2001, when the trend began, whole Indian villages have been reported as being up for sale. In December 2005, villagers of Dorli in Maharashtra state put up signboards announcing: "Dorli village is for sale." Each of the village's 270 residents, including all its children, was said to be carrying a debt of 30,000 rupees (£380).

Not long afterwards, the people of Chingapur village, also in Maharashtra, announced a "human market for the sale of kidneys" and sent invitations to India's President, Dr Abdul Kalam, and Prime Minister Manmohan Singh to witness the proceedings. The villagers saw this as the only way to raise money to repay their debts.

"This village is ready to be auctioned. Permit us to commit mass suicide," read banners displayed by people living in another village, Shivani Rekhailapur, nearby.

MEET SHAILESH

If you ask Shailesh Patel, project manager at Indian fair trade cotton producers Agrocel Industries, what the main benefits of fair trade are, he replies: "Fair trade saves farmers' lives. It prevents suicides. ... Working alone, volatile prices and continuing worries are among the main causes of farmer suicides," he says.

Fairtrade-certified in 2005, Agrocel is co-owned by the Gujarat government and several small companies, and works with small-scale cotton growers in three Indian states. Shailesh's visit to London for Fairtrade Fortnight 2006 coincided with a high-profile launch of fair trade cotton by Marks & Spencer, followed by fair trade jeans later in the year.

Ganesha, Gossypium, Hug, People Tree, Traidcraft and other suppliers in the UK sell goods made from Agrocel's fair trade cotton, along with retailers and brands in continental Europe, North America and India. The range is wide: trousers, shirts, blouses, jackets, skirts, pyjamas, baby clothes, hats, bags, duvets, cushions, bed linen, soft toys, tableware, t-shirts, hoodies, yoga wear, crew tops, shorts and underwear. All Agrocel's cotton is grown by environmentally sensitive methods, and the farmers increasingly seek organic certification. The company pays producers 8 per cent above prevailing market prices. And there are plenty of other advantages for cotton farmers apart from a fair and steady price.

"With fair trade, each farmer belongs to an association," Shailesh points out. "And fair trade also brings the social premium and community development." Agrocel offers a range of support services. Its twelve centres across India support thousands of farmers by selling them good quality inputs at fair prices, providing advice and training in sustainable and organic production, arranging farmer-to-farmer skill-share programmes and seminars, and running demonstration plots.

One Agrocel programme involves encouraging cultivation of the neem tree, whose natural oil and leaves are a rich source of biological pesticide and fertiliser. Working with the neem tree, farmers can reduce their dependence on costly bought-in chemicals, as well as providing themselves with valuable off-season employment. Another Agrocel scheme is training women in handicrafts production, enabling them to improve family income. Agrocel farmer households – and others in surrounding communities – also benefit from a veterinary service for their livestock.

Agrocel began supporting organic fair trade cotton production in 1998 and currently works with 20,000 growers. It is expanding steadily as more and more farmers come to appreciate the difference its support, and fair trade, can make.

Indian cotton farmers are not the only ones to benefit. Cameroon, Mali, Peru and Senegal also supply Fairtrade-certified cotton for goods on sale in the UK.

11. Be part of a growing global movement

Link up with one of the most exciting developments for years!

The fair trade movement today is a world-wide success story. Over a million small-scale producers and workers in 580 certified producer groups in 58 countries are actively involved in the system. And the products are increasingly being used in workplaces, and sold in restaurants and hotels. They are sold in thousands of "world shops" or fair trade shops, supermarkets and many other sales points in the North and, increasingly, in sales outlets in the Southern hemisphere. Fair trade unites producers with millions of consumers in Europe, North America, Australasia and Japan with people in developing countries.

THE START

The first formal "fair trade" shop opened in 1958 in the USA, selling goods from Puerto Rica and other poor communities in the South. The earliest traces of fair trade in Europe date from the late 1950s when Oxfam UK started to sell crafts made by Chinese refugees in Oxfam shops. In 1964 it created the first fair trade organisation, Oxfam Trading. Parallel initiatives were taking place in the Netherlands and in 1967 the importing organisation, Fair Trade Organisatie, was established. At the same time, Dutch-third world groups began to sell cane sugar with the message: "by buying cane sugar you give people in poor countries a place in the sun of prosperity." These groups went on to sell handicrafts from the South.

During the 1960s and 1970s non-governmental organisations (NGOs) and socially motivated individuals in many countries in Asia, Africa and Latin America perceived the need for fair marketing organisations which would provide advice, assistance and support to disadvantaged producers. Many such Southern fair trade organisations were established, and links were made with the new organisations in the North. These relationships were based on partnership, dialogue, transparency and respect. The goal was greater equity in international trade.

Fair trade (or alternative trade as it was called in the early days) grew as a response to poverty in the South and originally focused on the marketing of craft products. Its founders were often the large development and sometimes religious agencies in European countries.

In 1973, Fair Trade Organisatie in the Netherlands , imported the first "fairly traded" coffee from co-operatives of small farmers in Guatemala. Hundreds of thousands of coffee farmers have since benefited from Fairtrade-certified coffee. After coffee, the food range soon expanded to include products like tea, cocoa, sugar, tea, fruit juices and spices.

In the 1980s, a new way of reaching the broad public was developed. A priest working with smallholder coffee farmers in Mexico and a collaborator of a Dutch church-based NGO conceived the idea of a fair trade label. Products bought, traded and sold in ways that respected fair trade conditions would qualify for a label that would make them stand out among ordinary products on store shelves, and would allow any company to get involved in fair trade. In 1988, the "Max Havelaar" label was established in the Netherlands. The concept caught on: within a year, coffee with the label had a market share of almost 3 per cent.

In the ensuing years, similar non-profit fair trade labelling organisations were set up in other European countries and in North America. From the beginning, the fair trade movement aimed at raising awareness of consumers about the problems caused by conventional trade, and at introducing changes to its rules. The sale of products went alongside information on the production, producers and their conditions of living.

FAIR TRADE SHOPS AND NETWORKS

World shops and fair trade shops continue to mobilise consumers to participate in campaigning activities for more global justice.

The first European World Shops conference took place in 1984 and marked the beginning of close co-operation between volunteers working in World Shops from all over Europe . The Network of European World Shops (NEWS!) was formally established in 1994 and represents approximately 3,000 World Shops in 15 European countries. NEWS! co-ordinates European campaigning activities and stimulates the exchange of information and experiences about development of sales and awareness raising work. In 1996, NEWS! established the European World Shops Day as a Europe-wide day of campaign on a particular issue, often with a goal at the European level. To further co-operation, the European Fair Trade Association (EFTA) was founded in 1987. EFTA is an association of the eleven largest importing fair trade organisations in Europe.

The first World Fair Trade Day, which involves the worldwide fair trade movement, was celebrated on 4 May 2002 (see Reason 45).

The International Fair Trade Association (IFAT) started in 1989 (it was originally set up as the International Federation for Alternative Trade). It is a global network of 270 fair trade organisations – and is still growing. Its membership covers five regions: Africa, Asia, Latin America, Europe and North America and the Pacific Rim. It also has regional chapters: the Asia Fair Trade Forum (AFTF), Cooperation for Fair Trade in Africa (COFTA), and the Associacion Latino Americana de Commercio Justo. IFAT's aim is to improve the livelihoods of disadvantaged people through trade, and providing a forum for the exchange of information and ideas. The British Association of Fair Trade Shops, (BAFTS) promotes fair trade retailing in the UK.

Other fair trade networks have been established, including the Ecota Fair Trade Forum in Bangladesh, Fair Trade Group Nepal,

Associated Partners for Fairer Trade Philippines, Fair Trade Forum India and Kenya Federation for Alternative Trade.

IFAT launched a fair trade mark, the FTO Mark, in January 2004 at the World Social Forum in Mumbai, India. The Mark identifies registered FTOs worldwide. It is not a product label, but sets organisations apart from other commercial businesses, "making recognisable mission driven organisations whose core activity is Fair Trade". The Mark serves as a common voice for solidarity amongst FTOs in the North and South.

To increase awareness of the Mark, IFAT began a "Global Journey", a world tour, in January 2004. Setting off from one of the poorest slums in Mumbai, members of IFAT have carried a banner with the FTO Mark through countries in which IFAT has members. Hundreds of thousands of people have since celebrated and promoted fair trade, it says. Following Asia, the Global Journey travelled to Latin America, North America and Africa. It reached Europe in mid 2006.

The fair trade movement has become more professional in its awareness-raising and advocacy work. It produces well-researched documents, attractive campaign materials and public events. It has also benefited from the establishment of European structures which help to harmonise and centralise its campaigning and advocacy work.

FLO International, IFAT, NEWS! and EFTA started to meet in 1998 and, when they work together, are known by their acronym, FINE. From its advocacy office in Brussels, FINE seeks to influence European policy-makers. It enables the four networks and their members to co-operate on important areas of work, such as advocacy and campaigning, standards and monitoring.

GROWTH

Fair trade's growth has been helped since the late 1990s through the opening of new channels, notably supermarkets. The 2005 Annual Report of FLO International tells of this growth. It shows that global sales of Fairtrade-certified products reached £758 million in 2005 – an increase of 37 per cent over 2004.

All the product lines are expanding, especially Fairtrade coffee in the United States (+70.9 per cent) and the U.K. (+34 per cent), bananas in Austria (+46 per cent) and sugar in France (+125 per cent). Non-food products did well too: sales of Fairtrade flowers, newly introduced last year in Canada, Germany and Belgium surpass the most optimistic expectations.

Globally, the number of certified producer organisations has grown by 127 per cent since 2001, to 580 groups in 58 countries, and the number of registered traders has increased by 132 per cent in the same period.

Fair trade products can now be found in 55,000 supermarkets all over Europe and the market share has become significant in some countries. In Switzerland, 47 per cent of all bananas, 28 per cent of the flowers and 9 per cent of the sugar sold are fair trade labelled. In the UK, a market with eight times the population of Switzerland, labelled products have achieved a 5 per cent market share of tea, a 5.5 per cent share of bananas and a 20 per cent share of ground coffee.

All this makes fair trade one of the fastest growing markets in the world. And it represents millions of pounds returned to disadvantaged producers around the world.

Every time you buy a fair trade product, you are part of this growing global movement.

12. Say "Nuts!" to unfair trade

It's hard to make a living from nuts whether you grow or gather them. As with most developing country crops, the terms of trade are simply unfair. Fair trade nuts offer producers a better deal.

Processed nuts are high-value foods in great demand in North America and Europe. As with other food and drink commodities, the international trade is dominated by a few large companies that make sky-high profits. World prices fluctuate depending on the size of each year's crop, weather patterns, and market conditions. But whatever the price, only a tiny fraction of the proceeds trickles down to the people at the bottom of the supply chain.

Farming, harvesting and collecting nuts provides income for millions of rural people in Africa, Asia and Latin America. Nut farmers and gatherers are among the most disadvantaged workers. They usually depend on intermediaries who buy at rock bottom prices at a time when producers are desperate for cash, and sell on the national or international market. Trickery is common. In Malawi, one of the world's poorest countries, Judith Harry recalls when she began to farm peanuts (groundnuts):

> The vendors who bought them used to bring tampered scales in order to steal. They used to buy unshelled groundnuts using a 50 kg sack for measurement, but they used to boil it first in order to enlarge it so that it carried more groundnuts than the 50 kg it was meant to hold. They always paid low prices.

Besides peanuts, Africa also produces a third of the world's cashew crop. But with most of the raw cashews exported to India and Viet Nam for roasting and peeling, small-scale African growers remain poor. Farm-gate cashew prices reached a 30-year low in 2002. Africa once had more of a cashew-processing industry, but it has not survived.

Across the Atlantic, just one part of the Amazon rainforest, spanning Bolivia, Brazil and Peru, produces all the world's brazil nuts. The tall brazil nut tree *Bertholletia excelsa* grows wild in the forest but not in cultivation, and only one local species of forest bee can pollinate it. Gathering wild brazils is exhausting and labour-intensive. The nuts have to be collected from the undergrowth after falling from the trees during the rainy season. Nut harvesters in Brazil earn well below the minimum wage.

Every now and again the market price for brazils rises, and big business moves in. As disputes break out over access to patches of forest, nut-gatherer families may be on the receiving end of violent attacks from hired workers.

Employment conditions are tough too for the largely female

workforce in the world's nut-processing industries. Poverty-level wages, insecure employment and hazardous working conditions are the norm.

NOT SLAVES ANY MORE

But there's hope. Brazils, cashews and peanuts have a corner of the fair trade market, with small-scale nut farmers, collectors and producers getting standard fair trade benefits (see Reason 3). Alternative trading organisations like Equal Exchange, Twin Trading and Traidcraft were among the first to import and sell fair trade nuts and nut butters as far back as the 1980s. Traidcraft buys brazils from the CAI Campesino co-operative in the Bolivian Amazon, which supports 300 nut-gathering families. Agrocel, a fair trade organisation in western India (Reason 10), supplies Traidcraft's cashews, and the 1,500 Zambian farmer-members of the Producer Owned Trading Company grow its peanuts.

In early 2006 Fairtrade-certified nuts went on sale for the first time in UK supermarkets: brazils in Tesco, peanuts at the Co-op. (The first Fairtrade-certified brazils were available from Equal Exchange through wholefood stores and mail order over a year earlier.) Bolivian and Brazilian brazil nut producer co-operatives supply Tesco under an arrangement set up and supported by Twin Trading and Equal Exchange. The co-ops store, transport and process the brazils, so members have more control over the supply chain and earn a bigger share of the profits than if they only did the gathering. Benedicto Gonzalez, a member of the Coinacapa co-op in Bolivia, comments, "It feels like we're not slaves any more. We have more income, more work and more dignity."

Crisis struck Coinacapa within weeks of its first shipment of Fairtrade brazils to the UK in March 2006. In heavy seasonal rains, the forest flooded. Rivers burst their banks, roads collapsed, villages were surrounded by flood water, and some people even died in the mudslides. Coinacapa persuaded the Bolivian government to provide a relief plane to airlift the nuts to the capital La Paz, for onward transportation by road and ship to the UK. But no fuel was available for the plane. Co-op members then searched for several days for an alternative route and, when the rains eventually eased, found a passable road to La Paz. "We think the actions of the Coinacapa members speaks volumes about their commitment to the Fairtrade market," said Duncan White of Twin Trading.

The Co-op launched the world's first fair trade peanuts in April 2006: roasted, salted peanuts from the National Smallholder Farmers' Association of Malawi. This organisation represents many local farmers' associations and more than 100,000 smallholders.

Peanut farmer Judith Harry chairs her local association. "I am very proud to have grown some of the groundnuts which have become the world's first Fairtrade salted peanuts," she says.

> In the future we will use the [Fairtrade] premium to start a clinic which will mean health facilities are nearer for families. We also need a guardian shelter at the hospital: somewhere for the sick and their carers and relations to stay and make meals while they wait for a chance to be seen to at the clinic.

Nuts and nut pieces are also available in a range of other Fairtrade-certified products including biscuits, chocolate and energy bars, muesli, nut butters and Divine's chocolate-coated brazils.

Divine sources its brazils from the Madre de Dios region of the Amazon in south-east Peru. There the local producer and export organisation, Candela, supports nut gatherers with credit, transport, and shelling and drying facilities, as well as buying their nuts at fair trade prices. Candela in turn gets support from the Shared Interest co-operative lending society in the UK (Reason 47).

It sounds like another good reason to be nuts about fair trade.

13. Enjoy real quality, produced with pride

For quality, today's fair trade products take some beating.
They are grown and made by people who have a real stake
in what they are doing.

Time for confession. When coffee that claimed to be fairly traded first appeared in Britain in the mid 1970s, you had to be a very devoted person to drink it. "It was a little bit like train-spotting but less enjoyable," was a comment of someone who tasted it. The quality left much to be desired and put some people off for years. If you were one of them remember that was 30 years ago – before the advent of Fairtrade-certified labelling. Time to leave the past behind and enjoy the present.

Today's fair trade products are in a different category altogether. For quality, they take some beating. From coffee to rugs, from tea to cotton, fair trade products are quality products. With fair trade, consumers are discovering the pleasures of distinctive origins of quality products – like organic coffee from Peru, forest honey from Zambia and mangoes from Burkina Faso.

Fair trade food products are grown by small farmers or plantation workers who take great care with their crops. They know the difference that fair trade is making to them. They know that quality sells – that the higher the quality, the more chance there is that buyers will stay buyers and will recommend the products to others. A rising fair trade market can mean a declining poverty rate, so fair trade growers feel passionately about the quality of their produce, their way of life, and the future of their families.

Take Fairtrade-certified bananas. All of them are quality-tested at least twice – at the farm and at the ripening depot. Growers are committed to reducing the use of pesticides and herbicides.

Luis is an example. He is the president of a small group of workers in Ecuador who inspect the quality of bananas supplied by fair trade farmers. Fairtrade certification requires that all workers have the right to represent themselves collectively. So the fair trade banana farmers helped the quality controllers organise themselves into a proper worker's association. Luis is proud to be part of a legally recognised group. He wants the association to evolve so that it can provide health care for members who are sick. He doesn't have any great dreams of wealth: "I just want to do all I can to help prepare my children for what tomorrow may bring."

Once a week, at the farms of each small grower, the week's crop of bananas have to be washed, trimmed, checked and packed. So, for one or two days a week, Luis and his colleagues travel to the farms and carry out spot checks on the boxes to ensure that the bananas are free of blemishes and are exactly the right size. Another group of workers double-checks the quality of the bananas at the port. Luis also has two other jobs. He is a night watchman, and works one day a week as the president of the workers' association.

And back to coffee. Few who have tasted today's Fairtrade-certified coffee have any doubts about its quality.

A WIDE RANGE

There is now a wide range of premium-quality Fairtrade-certified coffees. These include freshly roasted filter, espresso and cappucino, single origin, blends and organic.

Some fair trade coffee may cost a little more than other coffees, but prices are generally competitive and you might find bargains. Some may be on offer in your supermarket at prices which are lower than well-known brands. "Paying a higher Fairtrade price", says the Fairtrade Foundation, "gives farmers options – to invest in quality improvements and gain access to speciality markets or diversify into other crops to reduce their dependence on coffee."

"Consumers are increasingly choosing Fairtrade products because they're good in quality and help some of the poorest people in the world earn their own living," says Clare Short, the UK's former international development secretary.

Quality was very much on the mind of Silver Kasoro-Atwoki from the Mabale Growers Tea Factory Ltd in Uganda when he spoke in London at the launch of Fairtrade Fortnight 2006. He explained what Fairtrade means to tea growers in his country: "Through Fairtrade, we have been able to change our agricultural techniques to improve the quality and quantity of our teas," he said. Fair trade products are grown and made by people who have a real stake in what they are doing. Doing this connects with the people who produce with those who buy. So consumers can enjoy fair trade products – and feel good about them.

Chocaholics can especially enjoy Fairtrade chocolate (see Reason 44). Ghanaian cocoa farmers jointly own the company that makes Divine chocolate, Britain's first mass market Fairtrade bar. Whereas cocoa farmers generally are suffering because of the collapse in world prices, the farmers of Ghana's Kuapa Kokoo collective, on whom more than 100,000 people depend, are prospering from Fairtrade, with a stake in their product and directors on the board. "We're not asking for help," says Ohemeng Tinyase, Kuapa Kokoo's managing director. "We want people to feel good about our chocolate. We're the very best. That's what is important."

People are buying fair trade products in increasing quantities because they are quality products. And yes, because buyers can feel happy about their choices. When we buy fair trade we not only buy quality, we get the well-being that comes from giving practical help to people who need it.

Says Tadesse Meskela – the general manager of the Oromia Coffee Farmers Co-operative Union in Ethiopia, with members that produce Fairtrade-certified coffee – "Fair trade is not just a buying and selling process. It is creating a global family." It's a family united in benefiting from quality.

14. Send a child to school

Time and again, producers and plantation workers say how important fair trade is in helping their children get a good education.

Of the world's 2 billion children, more than 120 million girls and boys (more girls than boys) of primary-school age don't go to school. Almost half the girls in the world's poorest countries get no primary education at all, and in 19 African countries fewer than half the children complete primary school. Youngsters with a primary education are far less likely to contract HIV than those without.

Rural poverty is the biggest obstacle to children's schooling, and rural children are the most affected. Primary education is usually free in the South, but parents need money for uniforms, books, pencils, daily travel and food at school. In Ethiopia the nearest primary school can be up to 20 kilometres away. Secondary schools in developing countries are more likely to charge fees. Not surprisingly, a third of the world's children never get that far.

When the world market price of coffee, tea, cocoa, sugar or bananas drops, what we pay in the shops usually stays the same. But farmers' earnings and plantation workers' wages fall. This often leads them to withdraw their children from school, either to save the expense, or to raise family income through having the children work, or both. Hundreds of thousands of children work on West African cocoa farms instead of going to school, for example.

"We have to pay for schooling. Earlier we could cover expenses, now we can't. ... Three of the children can't go to school because I can't afford the uniform," says Ethiopian coffee farmer Mohammed Ali Indris.

In rural Uganda, teenage brothers Bruno and Michael Selugo had to leave secondary school because of the fees. "I have been sent home again and again," Bruno reveals. "They just send you away if you don't have the fees. ... Everyone used to go back to school with the money from coffee, but now ... the price is so low people are not even picking coffee." Patrick Kayanja, headteacher at Bruno's school, comments: "Much as we try to reduce the fees, the parents cannot pay."

Falling farm-gate prices also mean that many rural men in developing countries have to seek work away from home (see Reason 48). When women and children are left to tend the family farm without them, the children often have to give up school to help their mother.

EDUCATION IS TOP PRIORITY

Southern farmers, rural workers, craftspeople and their organisations say it loud and clear: children's education is top priority. Fair trade means they can put their money where their mouth is. When Igara Growers in Uganda began selling to Traidcraft and Teadirect, recalls Juliet Ntwirenabo, chair of the premium committee, "Our first priority was education. We bought exercise books, pens and pencils for four children in each family." For José Rivera Campoverde, a Peruvian fair trade coffee grower, "The higher price we get when we sell coffee on fair trade terms means that I can afford more food for my family and send my children to school properly equipped with pens and notebooks for the first time."

Farmers' organisations often use the "social premium" (Reason 4) to finance educational scholarships. Costa Rican coffee co-operative Coocafé has supported hundreds of youngsters at school and university this way. The premium pays to build and equip schools too. There are plenty of inspiring examples, and producer organisations take pride in investing to benefit the wider community, not just the producer group.

Kuapa Kokoo, a thriving Ghanaian fair trade cocoa co-operative with 45,000 farmer members, has set up schools and nurseries for non-members as well as members. Pupil attendance and education quality have improved significantly. Kuapa is reckoned to have earned about US$1 million in extra income through fair trade over eight years – equivalent to annual primary schooling costs for 245,000 children in Ghana. Apaco, an orange growers' co-operative in southern Brazil, supports a boarding school for girls from difficult family backgrounds, where the girls receive psychological support and therapy as well as a regular education. The workers' and management "joint body" on the Nilgiris tea estate in southern India has bought computers for local schools and a school bus.

"We built five primary schools," says Cecilia Mwambebule, a Tanzanian grower for Teadirect. "We ... build the schools and the government will then send teachers." Cecilia adds: "Everyone can send their children here, not just the tea farmers. The tea farmers want everyone to get education ... so everyone can benefit."

Ethiopia's Oromia coffee co-operative is building four primary schools, while the Union de Comunidades Indigenas de la Region del Istmo coffee co-op in Oaxaca, Mexico (Reason 49), has set up the region's only secondary school. Nicaraguan fair trade coffee co-operative SOPPEXCCA has constructed and fitted out several primary schools and provides secondary school scholarships, contributing to students' food, books and uniforms. One of its programmes gets parents planting trees – important in a region badly hit by Hurricane Mitch in 1998 – in return for supporting their youngsters through school.

Tea pickers interviewed on the Stockholm estate in Sri Lanka told how fair trade had benefited their children's education. One had borrowed from a small loans scheme to build a shop extension to his home and sell biscuits and sweets, and the extra income helped him keep his children in school. Other households were using the higher wages from working on a fair trade estate to keep one or more children at school up to A level, with the aim of a better job in the future.

High-street retailers Marks & Spencer proudly report that sales of Fairtrade-only tea and coffee in their Café Revive coffee shops are helping pay for 68 new schools in Ethiopia, Honduras, Peru and Sumatra. One of these, the new Ngelle Gorbitu School in rural Ethiopia, enables almost 600 children from the local community to attend school, as opposed to just 50 before.

15. Keep on making poverty history

Buying fair trade helps producers to build more sustainable businesses and overcome poverty.

I didn't have any breakfast and walked around half dizzy. The daze of hunger is worse than that of alcohol. The daze of alcohol makes us sing but the one of hunger makes us shake. I know how horrible it is to have only air in the stomach. ... I think that when I was born I was marked by fate to go hungry.

Brazilian slum dweller

Poverty is a dreadful disease and a quarter of humanity suffers from it, surviving on the equivalent of a dollar a day or less. Poverty means that people cannot afford to eat, to work, to live in dignity. It means they die young. Poverty kills an average of 30,000 children a day, ten times more than died on 9/11. Every day. One every three seconds. Poverty can and should be made history.

The Make Poverty History campaign in 2005 was one of the biggest campaigns the UK has ever seen. It brought a together a wide cross section of over 500 organisations – aid and development agencies, charities of many kinds, trade unions and faith groups among many others. And a number of fair trade organisations were members of the campaign, including the Fairtrade Foundation, People Tree, Shared Interest and Traidcraft. The aim was just what the campaign's name declared – to consign poverty to the scrap heap.

The campaign was launched in late December 2004 to press the UK government for action in three areas: on trade justice, more and better aid, and debt relief. Especially as Britain held the presidency of the G8 in the last six months of 2005, the year offered a good opportunity for the UK government to take the steps that were necessary to end poverty.

Make Poverty History campaigners pressed for trade rules to be rewritten in favour of developing countries so they can develop and build their own industries (see Reason 43). They urged that the debts of the poorest countries be cancelled in full. That debt cancellation should come without economic policy conditions such as liberalising or privatising economies. And all funding for debt relief should be additional to the existing and proposed increases in aid budgets. They pointed out that most of the funding for the debt relief delivered had so far come from donor country aid budgets, rather than being genuinely new money (Reason 29).

Pressing for more and better aid, the campaign said that without proper funding, "30,000 children will continue to die needlessly every day from causes associated with extreme poverty. ... Eight million lives could be saved every year if minimal healthcare was available in developing countries."

And again, aid should be given without economic policy conditions: "Many donors, including the UK, critically undermine the effectiveness of their aid by attaching economic policy conditions." Aid must be made to work more effectively for people in poverty. It must also be given in ways that help poor people, not donor country firms and citizens. At the moment, too much aid goes to politically important middle-income countries, rather than the poorest.

The Make Poverty History campaign generated a huge amount of public interest. Some 10 million people bought Make Poverty History wristbands. Around a quarter of a million people marched through Edinburgh in July 2005 to ask world leaders to take action to make poverty history. But leaders meeting in nearby Gleneagles responded with "a whisper to the roar of the people", as a South African campaigner said. They failed to rise to the occasion.

There was some progress on aid and debt in 2005 but not nearly enough. Aid is due to increase from $79 billion in 2004 to $130 billion by 2010. Grand pronouncements were made on debt, but it is by no means clear whether the debt cancelled will be new money, or whether it will come from aid budgets. And there were no measures for trade justice.

The campaigning must go on. While the national Make Poverty

History campaign was limited to 2005, communities around the UK are continuing to campaign locally. One example is the "Reading Campaign to Make Poverty History". Since February 2006 this has been campaigning to "end the poverty that affects 800 million people worldwide ... [and] on matters directly related to poverty, such as aid, debt relief, trade justice, armaments control and climate change".

Many of the organisations that supported Make Poverty History now have campaigns which focus on ending poverty. Continued campaigning is vital, not least to release the energies and potential of people in developing countries. For many could be making poverty history for themselves if the international economic system, especially the trade system, was not so stacked against them. Some are already doing so by supplying the fair trade market. Fair trade has proved that it can reduce poverty and promote sustainable development.

> Leaders ... would do well to take note of the success of Fairtrade as an economic model that works. It is commercially successful not despite the priorities and regulations which create a bias in favour of development goals, but rather precisely because of them.
>
> Harriet Lamb, executive director, the Fairtrade Foundation

AFRICA AND FAIR TRADE

Africa, the poorest continent, is the fastest growing region within the Fairtrade network, says the Fairtrade Foundation, with approximately 124 producers' organisations in 20 countries currently certified to Fairtrade standards. The range of products African producers are bringing to UK markets includes tea, coffee, wine, cocoa, honey, nuts and fruits.

Raymond Kimaro works for Tanzania's KNCU coffee co-operative, which supplies 20 per cent of its coffee to the Fairtrade market. He says:

> By strengthening their organisation and marketing skills, by improving health, water and education facilities, by

diversifying into new economic activity, and by improving environmental protection programmes, farmers and farm workers in Africa who supply the Fairtrade market are already working towards making poverty history for themselves. Being able to make a living from the sweat of one's labour should be a basic human right, safeguarded by governments, for all people in Africa and elsewhere.

Fair trade provides an "inspiring example" of a new partnership between developing countries and the developed world, agrees Tony Blair. Visiting cocoa farmers in Ghana, he says he had the privilege of seeing for himself "how Fairtrade in cocoa is increasing incomes and empowering local producers operating in global markets".

Fair trade is an inspiring and vital component of the ongoing and urgent task of making poverty history.

16. Make your town a Fairtrade Town

Fairtrade towns, cities, boroughs, villages, counties, universities, colleges, schools and places of worship are breaking out all over the UK and Ireland. Organise your own local initiative and spread the word.

In May 2000 Garstang Parish Council, Lancashire, voted itself the world's first Fairtrade Town, promising to use and promote fair trade products as much as possible. Local vet Bruce Crowther and the Garstang Oxfam group led the campaign, which involved the mayor, churches, headteachers and traders, as well as local dairy farmers who were protesting at the time against falling milk prices. Working with Garstang's schools, the group explored links between the slave trade, racism and fair trade.

MP Hilton Dawson tabled an Early Day Motion in the House of Commons congratulating Garstang. George Foulkes, then a minister at the Department for International Development, visited the town and gave his backing: "It is a great initiative. ... I want to try to ensure that the initiative is followed in many other towns and cities."

The first ten Fairtrade Towns were Aberfeldy, Ammanford, Chester, Garstang, Haworth, Leicester, Nailsworth, Strathaven, Stroud and Wells, and the movement has taken root across the UK. In January 2004 Fair Isle, between Orkney and Shetland off Scotland's northeast coast, became the first Fairtrade Island – followed by Jersey, Shetland and the Isle of Wight. March 2004 saw ten simultaneous Fairtrade Town declarations: Dundee, Aberdeen, Lancaster, York, Oxford, Cambridge, Portsmouth, Southampton, Leeds and Liverpool. In 2005 Manchester and Salford became joint 100th Fairtrade Towns. By mid 2006 there were 200 declared Fairtrade Towns, Cities, Boroughs, Villages, Zones, Islands and Counties around the country. Edinburgh and Cardiff are both Fairtrade Capitals. Fairtrade Fortnight 2006 saw 25 towns, boroughs, villages and zones declared Fairtrade, plus Cumbria as a Fairtrade County.

Garstang's Bruce Crowther has become national Fairtrade Towns co-ordinator for the Fairtrade Foundation and is still full of enthusiasm:

> The network of Fairtrade Towns has become a wonderful way of involving people throughout the community. ... The Towns raise awareness and sales of fair trade which both contribute to tackling poverty and improving the lot of marginalised and disadvantaged farmers.

"One of the biggest achievements," Bruce adds, "has been to crack the complex world of catering and procurement and getting Fair trade into local authorities, workplaces, schools and primary healthcare trusts."

To achieve Fairtrade status, a local council must pass a resolution supporting fair trade and agree to serve Fairtrade-certified coffee and tea in its meetings, offices and canteens. Fair trade products must be available in the area's shops, cafés and catering establishments, and used by local workplaces and community organisations. A steering group needs to be set up to ensure continuing commitment.

Well over 200 more places in the UK are working towards Fairtrade status, including (at the time of writing) Anglesey, Chesterfield, Chichester, Durham, East Sussex, Gateshead, the Isle of Man, Knutsford, Llandrindod and Builth Wells, London, Nottinghamshire, Powys, Shropshire, Welwyn Garden City, Wigan and Yeovil. The Fairtrade London Campaign, supported by Mayor Ken Livingstone, aims to increase awareness and availability of fair trade products across the capital. London boroughs of Camden, Croydon, Greenwich, Hammersmith & Fulham, Islington, Kingston, Lambeth, Lewisham and Richmond had declared Fairtrade status by mid 2006, and many others were working on it. The Welsh Assembly plans to make Wales the world's first Fair Trade Nation.

The idea has spread to Ireland too. By 2006 the Republic had eight Fairtrade Cities and Towns: Clonakilty, Cork, Kilkenny, Kinsale, Waterford, Limerick, Galway and Thurles.

UNIVERSITIES, COLLEGES AND SCHOOLS

Oxford Brookes became the first Fairtrade University in October 2003 after a campaign led by graduate students in the School of Built Environment inspired by course chair Hugo Slim. After 16 months of Fairtrade status, Oxford Brookes students and staff reckoned to have consumed 750,000 Fairtrade drinks – 11,600 packs of medium-roast coffee, 390 packs of vending coffee, 115 kg of cocoa powder, 48,000 teabags, 130 kg of espresso beans and 2,500 orange juices. They had munched their way through many thousands of fair trade cereal and chocolate bars, cookies and flapjacks.

Today the 30-plus Fairtrade Universities and Colleges include Birmingham, Bristol, Derby, Edinburgh, Glasgow, Hertfordshire, King's College London, Leeds, Leeds Metropolitan, the London School of Economics, Manchester, Nottingham, Portsmouth, Queen's University Belfast, Royal Holloway, Sheffield, City of Sunderland College,

Swansea, Warwick, Worcester College of Technology, York and the University of Wales. More are working towards the award.

Warwick University, with an active People & Planet student group, has gone further than many. Once it had achieved Fairtrade status, its students' union adopted a 100 per cent Fairtrade policy for tea, coffee, hot chocolate, sugar, fruit, fruit juice and vending machines. And more: "Staff and union officers' uniforms will now be made from Fairtrade cotton, as well as being made in factories guaranteeing International Labour Organization standards," said a university campaigner. "We can be very proud of what we have achieved. This policy will make a real difference to real people's lives."

Plenty is going on among school students and teachers too. Secondary school students in Hartlepool got the ball rolling in 2001 with co-operative-run fair trade tuck shops (see Reason 40). Shaftesbury School declared itself a Fairtrade School on Red Nose Day (11 March) 2005, as did King Edward VI High School for Girls in Birmingham, Tiffin Girls School in Kingston and 13 Liverpool schools that year.

Formal Fairtrade Schools criteria have recently been agreed, and plenty of schools get involved during Fairtrade Fortnight each March. In early 2007 the Fairtrade Foundation plans to launch its Fairtrade Schools initiative with support from the Department for International Development.

Good support also comes from many city, town and borough councils, and organisations like People & Planet, Comic Relief, the Co-op Movement, and SCIAF (the Scottish Catholic International Aid Fund). Oxfam and Leeds Development Education Centre have both produced Fairtrade handbooks for schools. Telford MP David Wright has written to every school in his constituency asking them to consider making their tuck shop or canteen fair trade. An Early Day Motion in Parliament has congratulated schools that have done this and called on the Department for Education and Skills to encourage more fair trade in schools. Ethical clothing company CleanSlate recently launched the UK's first fair trade and organic school uniform range.

PLACES OF WORSHIP

Christ Church & St Mark's in Watford, Herts, became the first Fairtrade Church in 2004, and the idea took off. By mid 2006 there were more than 2,800 Fairtrade Churches. Fairtrade Cathedrals include Coventry, St John's Portsmouth, and St Mary's Edinburgh. Both the Church of England and the Roman Catholic dioceses of Portsmouth are Fairtrade Dioceses.

Fairtrade status means a church serves fair trade tea and coffee at all meetings, commits to using other fair trade products such as sugar, biscuits and fruit, and participates actively in Fairtrade Fortnight.

The Fairtrade Foundation offers churches a range of ideas for worship, bible study and reflection and publishes criteria for becoming a Fairtrade diocese, district, synod, presbytery, association or other denominational area. Guidelines for churches are also available from Traidcraft, along with poems, prayers, studies, service ideas and other resources. Faith-based NGOs like Tearfund and the Methodist Relief and Development Fund have also help promote fair trade in churches.

During Fairtrade Fortnight 2005 the Shah Jehan Mosque in Woking, Surrey, became the first Fairtrade Mosque. The *mufti*, Liaquat Ali Amod, said: "Many here come from countries such as Pakistan. They know how difficult life can be for workers there and so they realise the importance of a fair deal."

A year later Birmingham Central Synagogue became the first Fairtrade Synagogue, and a dozen more have since achieved Fairtrade status.

17. Build confidence, reduce risk

Here's how fair trade's guaranteed minimum price reduces risk for producers.

Falling prices. Erratic prices. Both cause havoc for millions of small-scale farmers who grow crops for export. Farmers in developing countries can watch helplessly as the price of their crop swerves all over the place and, even worse, drops like a stone. As if growing crops for export wasn't risky enough anyway.

All this matters a great deal. The first and possibly only connection that millions of the poor have with the world trading system is through the crops they grow for the export market. But they have no idea how much their crops will fetch.

Take world coffee prices. The figures speak for themselves. The average price of coffee on world markets over the last 30 years has followed this pattern:

January	1976	95	US cents/lb	
"	1977	218	"	"
"	1978	192	"	"
"	1990	64	"	"
"	1995	152	"	"
"	2002	43	"	"
end-July	2006	89	"	"

These figures, from the International Coffee Organization, illustrate the astonishing variation in price. They show that the coffee price in January 2002 was only one-fifth of its price 25 years earlier.

When prices vary so much, the lives of growers are made so much harder. They cannot plan. Do they have enough money to send their children to school, to pay for healthcare? It all depends on a "free-trade" world market which is outside their control. The price is decided by the laws of supply and demand – which also decide their poverty.

The really bizarre thing about coffee prices is that the world price in July 2006 was lower than in January 1976. Inflation over those 30 years has considerably reduced the value of money. A pound in 1976 could buy what £4 or £5 can buy us today. Had it kept pace with inflation, the world price of coffee would be four to five times higher in 2006 than it was in 1976. The real price of coffee – what it can buy the grower – is only a fifth what it was 30 years ago. Growers are therefore earning massively less for their crop.

Millions of farmers continue to grow coffee, however, despite prices so low they may be less than the cost of producing the crop. But then the crop may be their only source of a cash income. Instead of reducing production when prices fall, some farmers increase their output – to try to sustain their incomes by squeezing more from their land, sometimes at the expense of quality.

Among mainstream export crops, coffee has fluctuated and fallen the most. But the prices of other important crops for growers in developing countries – including tea, cocoa and bananas – have also fluctuated and fallen drastically in the last 30 years.

It is countries as well as growers who are affected. Many developing countries depend on a small number of crops for their export earnings, and some on only one. Uganda, for example, depends on coffee for around two-thirds of its export earnings. In 1998 it was one of the first countries to have some of its debt cancelled. But the collapse in the world price of coffee more than wiped out the benefit of debt relief.

FAIRTRADE PRICE

The fair trade system is very different. Growers are guaranteed a minimum price for their crop. This is achieved by payment of a guaranteed fair price, and by reducing the number of intermediaries in the supply chain so that the growers get a larger share of the export price (see Reasons 2 and 21). The Fairtrade minimum price is calculated to cover the costs of sustainable production and a sustainable livelihood. All stakeholders, including producers and traders, are consulted in the price-setting process. There is an additional premium for investment in social, commercial or environmental development projects (Reason 4).

Take coffee. The price for Fairtrade-certified arabica coffee is 126 cents a pound. This comprises a minimum price of 121 cents a pound plus the premium of 5 cents a pound. If the international price is higher than the fair trade price then the price comprises the world price plus the Fairtrade premium, says the Fairtrade Foundation. So under the fair trade system the price paid to growers rises when world prices rise, but does not fall below the minimum price when world market prices fall. Fairtrade Labelling Organisations International (FLO) audits each transaction to ensure the price and premium for Fairtrade-certified products are paid to the producer organisation.

The producer organisation and trader sign contracts that allow for long-term planning and sustainable production practices. Producers can, in addition, request pre-financing of up to 60 per cent of the contract. This is important. Without access to this capital, co-operatives might have to take out costly loans to purchase members' coffee. And loans are frequently unavailable from local banks as many do not consider farmers' organisations to be creditworthy.

Fairtrade-certified coffee is produced by farmers who are members of village-level co-operatives, which are usually affiliated to regional co-operative societies and/or national co-operative unions. These organisations buy, collect, process, market and export coffee on behalf of hundreds or even thousands of farmers. Such services are mainly financed by a percentage taken from the selling price (Reason 40).

The Fairtrade premium is paid into the bank account of an elected committee set up specifically to administer the premium fund. The fund is reserved for investment in projects that are decided on with the agreement of co-op members (or following consultation with the workforce in the case of plantations). The committee must produce an annual premium plan and budget which is available for scrutiny by the beneficiaries and FLO.

The Fairtrade price does more than provide a higher income. It helps to give growers the encouragement to branch out. Many fair trade producer organisations have the capacity, for example, to process their commodity and so add value to it.

The great thing about fair trade is that growers can plan ahead with confidence.

18. Give someone's health a boost

Workplace health and safety, and free or affordable health-care, are things we in the West mostly take for granted. Both can be hard to come by in the global South, but not so hard for people linked up with the fair trade system.

In developing countries, poverty and ill-health often go hand in hand – including in the workplace. For low-paid people, going to work can be hazardous.

Take the banana industry. Many commercial plantations try to cut costs by using heavy doses of the most dangerous agrochemicals. The food and drinking water of many banana workers living close to plantations contain poisons from daily aerial spraying. A study in Costa Rica found 20 per cent of male banana workers sterile after handling such chemicals, and women banana packers had twice the average rates of leukaemia and birth defects. Maria, wife of a Costa Rican banana worker, gave birth to a baby with a head four times bigger than his body. "I couldn't even hold him," she said. "It's the worst thing that can happen to anyone."

Too many plantations, factories and workshops across the developing world neglect employee health and safety. For instance, scores of Bangladeshi garment workers have been killed by fires in textile factories in recent years. And overwork takes its toll as poorly paid employees, scared of losing their jobs, sacrifice their health or fall victim to accidents through tiredness.

Away from the world of work, the picture is also desperate. Ten million children die each year before their fifth birthday, many from easily preventable diarrhoea. One in 50 women in the South dies during or after pregnancy. Hundreds of millions lack access to safe drinking water, decent toilets, basic medicines or healthcare. Millions more suffer life-threatening yet treatable diseases like HIV/AIDS, malaria and tuberculosis.

Despite a host of good intentions and brave initiatives, many developing country governments have become less – not more – able to meet their citizens' health needs. Cuts in state budgets have reduced official spending on water, sanitation and health. Many services are part-privatised, their user charges beyond the means of poor people. Nicaraguan health union leader Evile Umaña described during a recent visit to the UK what happened when a local man, Cristobal Chavarria, aged 86, suffered a sudden heart collapse:

> There was no ambulance, his family had to pay a taxi. Once in the hospital, they had to provide sheets, pillows, toilet paper, soap, food ... on top of any medical requirements. The person in the next bed was already dead. ... His family brought him home after two nights [because] they could no longer bear the costs.

Evile went on:

> Hospitals are short of even basic medicines, medical supplies and the most fundamental tools. ... Many health-care professionals have to work double shifts or find other work outside their regular hours. Some take in washing and ironing, some drive taxis. ... Nicaragua is confronting rising rates of potential epidemic diseases, such as TB, AIDS, malaria and dengue.

PROMOTING BETTER HEALTH

"Fairtrade is about much more than just another packing case," says Dominican banana grower Amos Wiltshire. "It's not just that we want a healthy banana, it's that we also want a healthy banana farmer."

By buying fair trade we can support better health and safety conditions for workers, as well as a trading system that fills some of the gaps in health provision in developing countries.

One of the five basic guarantees of Fairtrade-certified farm produce is "greater respect for the environment". Fair trade growers observe legal limits on agrochemicals and have to work to reduce their use (see Reasons 25 and 27). Special standards are applied to industries like bananas, where buffer zones prevent pollution of rivers, forests, roads and water sources. On plantations and farms, in factories and workshops, the world's network of Fairtrade certification bodies (Reason 3) ensures that health and safety standards are continuously improved. And fair trade producers really do look after their workers better, providing workplace healthcare, medical checks, health and safety equipment, improved ventilation and sanitation, and sickness benefit more often than non-fair-trade competitors.

In the textiles industry, for example, the European Fair Trade Association (EFTA) has helped fair trade producers in Bangladesh, Bolivia, Guatemala, India, Indonesia, Tanzania, Thailand and Zimbabwe eliminate use of cancer-causing azo dyes. In farming, fair trade crop production in South Africa has benefited the health of women farmworkers through reduced chemicals use. Because fair trade producer and worker households are often better off than their neighbours, they look after their own health better too.

There are wider benefits at community level. Health, like education (Reason 14), is a high priority when it comes to investing the "social premium". Kuapa Kokoo, Ghana's large cocoa farmers' co-operative, has set up a trust fund to provide and equip health centres and water boreholes for local communities. By 2003, 100,000 people – members and non-members – had benefited from free medical attention under the co-op's healthcare programme. In Ethiopia the Oromia Coffee Farmers Cooperative Union invests in community health clinics and water pumps, while Mabale Growers Tea Factory, Uganda, is building and equipping clinics and supplying medicines. Mabale also builds public toilets at roadside tea-collection points.

On Sri Lanka's Stockholm tea estate, the premium has paid for an ambulance. Before, plantation workers and their families living on the estate who needed medical attention had to walk seven kilometres to the nearest surgery. The ambulance is seen as especially important for getting pregnant women to hospital in time to give birth.

In Bahia, one of Brazil's poorest regions, members of Cealnor, a federation of fair trade fruit producers, have invested in equipment to make a nutritious juice mixture for malnourished children. Their infant health drink is now sold in local supermarkets. Nicaragua's SOPPEXCCA coffee producers' co-operative has used fair trade income to run a cervical smear test programme, a service usually too costly for rural women. It has set up voluntary primary health brigades and pharmacies providing low-cost medicines, as well as supporting a women's health organisation that is independent of the co-op.

There was no sanitation in Dolora Castillo's community in the Dominican Republic until fair trade banana farmers covered the cost of building toilets next to people's homes. The farmers are also constructing a community clinic. The Fairtrade premium has paid for women's reproductive health programmes in Bolivia, Ecuador, Guatemala, Honduras, India, Mexico, Nicaragua, Papua New Guinea and Peru. In East Timor 18,000 people have used free health clinic services paid for by fair trade. Family health insurance, largely unknown in the global South, is now provided by the Bagua Grande coffee co-operative in northern Peru with the premium. Farmer Martias Huaman comments:

> About five years ago I suffered with arthritis. I was insured by the co-operative through their health insurance and I was able to improve my health. ... Without the insurance I would be below the ground – I would be organic fertiliser!

19. Promote human rights

The United Nations says that every person is entitled to enjoy development in which all human rights are fully realised. Fair trade promotes human dignity, rights and freedom.

Agreed almost 60 years ago as one of the most significant documents of its time, the Universal Declaration of Human Rights remains a document of vital importance today. It was in December 1948 that the

General Assembly of the United Nations adopted and proclaimed the Declaration, which lays down five key areas of rights – political, social, economic, civil and cultural.

There is a tendency for some regions to promote certain rights over others. In the Western world the emphasis tends to be on political and civil rights. In developing countries there is more emphasis on cultural, economic and social rights, especially on enough food to eat. When you are hungry, human rights may not end with breakfast, but that is where your concern is likely to begin. If a person is dying from lack of food, other rights are academic.

The preamble of the Universal Declaration includes these words:

> recognition of the inherent dignity and of the equal and inalienable rights of all members of the human family is the foundation of freedom, justice and peace in the world ....
>
> ... the peoples of the United Nations have in the Charter reaffirmed their faith in fundamental human rights, in the dignity and worth of the human person and in the equal rights of men and women and have determined to promote social progress and better standards of life in larger freedom ...

The Declaration then goes on to say that "every individual and every organ of society ... shall strive by teaching and education to promote respect for these rights and freedoms." Article 23 of the Declaration states:

- Everyone has the right to work, to free choice of employment, to just and favourable conditions of work and to protection against unemployment.
- Everyone, without any discrimination, has the right to equal pay for equal work.
- Everyone who works has the right to just and favourable remuneration ensuring for himself and his family an existence worthy of human dignity, and supplemented, if necessary, by other means of social protection.

"Just and favourable remuneration" is precisely what fair trade is about.

Article 25 says that "Everyone has the right to a standard of living adequate for the health and well-being of himself and of his family, including food, clothing, housing and medical care and necessary social services." Again, this is totally consistent with fair trade.

Also Article 27: "Everyone has the right freely to participate in the cultural life of the community, to enjoy the arts and to share in scientific advancement and its benefits."

Fair trade makes it more likely that people will be able to participate in the cultural life of their community and also to promote its advancement.

FAIR TRADE AND HUMAN RIGHTS

Article 28 says that "Everyone is entitled to a social and international order in which the rights and freedoms set forth in this Declaration can be fully realised." An improved world trading order is again what fair trade is about. Fair trade promotes human dignity, rights and freedom. It seeks greater equity in international trade by offering better trading conditions to, and securing the rights of, marginalised farmers and workers in developing countries.

However, although the Universal Declaration of Human Rights was agreed over half a century ago, there are problems with compliance, especially among business corporations. "There is still no mechanism to ensure that non-state actors comply with these and other international standards," says Traidcraft. It points out that failure to recognise the importance of rights "in every context means that large companies who operate internationally are often in breach of basic human rights through their actions".

A significant step was taken in August 2003 by the UN Sub-Commission on the Promotion and Protection of Human Rights when it approved the UN Norms on the Responsibilities of Transnational Corporations and Other Business Enterprises with Regard to Human Rights (also known as UN Norms for Business or UN Norms). The Norms restate existing internationally recognised standards of human rights. They set out in a comprehensive way the key human-rights responsibilities of companies. They do not create new legal obligations, but codify and distil existing obligations under international law as they apply to companies. They are a credible international mechanism setting out the Universal Declaration of Human Rights for businesses. "They give clarity for companies and create a global level playing field for company behaviour," says Traidcraft.

In 2004, the UN Commission on Human Rights requested the UN Secretary General to appoint a Special Representative on the human rights responsibilities of transnational corporations and other business enterprises. The mandate of the Special Representative includes working to identify and clarify standards of corporate responsibility and accountability with regard to human rights.

Business groups are trying to get the Norms sidelined. It may be regulation rather than Norms that's needed if transnational corporations are to help not hinder the human rights of the poor. Rights for the poor can only be realised if governments and companies uphold the Universal Declaration. Fair trade both upholds and promotes human rights and is delivering "breakfast" for tens of thousands of disadvantaged people. Arturo Gomez, a founding member of a fair trade banana co-operative in Costa Rica, sums it up when he says that it has given him and others a sense of worth and confidence in the future:

> I thank God for the new system, because it has resolved our problems. But I look around me and I see my neighbours with great problems, without water, without a house, without food. Our dream is to be free, to be looked on as human beings, as people, not objects.

And this is what the Universal Declaration is all about.

20. Free child carpet workers

South Asian children are exploited every day in appalling conditions, making oriental-style rugs and carpets for export. But when you buy under the Rugmark label you can be sure no illegal under-age child labour has been used.

In factories and loom-sheds in India, Nepal and Pakistan, hundreds of thousands of children as young as five are reported as working in near-slave conditions. They are put to work weaving and hand-knotting oriental rugs and carpets for export. Labouring up to 20 hours a day, seven days a week, they are often forced to eat and sleep where they work. Sometimes they are locked in at night. Children who make mistakes or try to run away risk being beaten, deprived of food or even tortured. These child workers are usually from the poorest families, toiling to pay off their parents' debt to a money broker. Needless to say, they don't get to go to school.

Evidence of the scandal first broke in India in the 1980s. An activist campaign led by Kailash Satyarthi, who went on to front the Global March Against Child Labour, began to free the children by raiding factories to rescue them. But the freed children were soon replaced by others. Broader action was needed.

RUGMARK'S ORIGINS

A consumer awareness drive began in Germany – the biggest importer of oriental floor coverings – in 1990. Trade unions, faith groups, and human rights and consumer organisations got involved. The campaign spread to other European countries and to North America. A coalition of NGOs, Indian exporters, the Indo-German Export Promotion Council and UNICEF began to develop a consumer label certifying carpets that were made in India without exploiting child labour. The Rugmark Foundation was set up in 1994 to supervise this label.

Carpet makers who want a licence to use the Rugmark label must sign a legally binding contract committing them not to employ children under 14, to pay fair adult wages, to allow unannounced Rugmark inspections and to notify Rugmark of all sales of labelled carpets and rugs. Rugmark will certify rugs and carpets woven on family looms, where children may help their parents for an hour or two at home after school, provided such children also attend school regularly.

Rugmark trains and supervises its own inspectors and allows monitoring of certified factories and loom-sheds by independent child welfare organisations. Inspectors work in teams of two, and since 1999 those based at Gopiganj have used motorbikes for visiting up to eight village workshops a day. "The monsoon period is the worst," comments Santosh Nair. "Sometimes, the tyres spin around in the mud forcing you to go very slowly." Rashid Raza, who co-ordinates inspections in northern India from Rugmark's office in Gopiganj, points out that: "It is impossible for a Rugmark inspector to warn the weavers of a village beforehand, because he himself doesn't know when inspections will be done in that village."

The first Rugmark-certified rugs and carpets were exported from India, mainly to Germany, in 1995. By 1999 the scheme was also working in Nepal and Pakistan. There are now Rugmark offices in Germany (also covering Belgium, Luxembourg and the Netherlands), the UK, the USA (also covering Canada), India, Nepal and Pakistan. So far more than 4 million certified rugs and carpets have reached Europe and North America. Every Rugmark-labelled product carries a unique serial number so that the product's place of manufacture is traceable via a central database. This helps protect against counterfeiting.

Rugmark's licensed exporters and importers fund much of its work, paying a small tariff on the price of each certified item. Most of this money returns to the producer countries to cover rehabilitation and education costs.

REHABILITATION AND EDUCATION

Where Rugmark finds children working illegally, it takes them into rehabilitation and education centres and seeks ways to reunite them with their families. It also addresses problems that lead families to send away their children in the first place. For example, adult literacy programmes and self-help classes assist parents of former child weavers in finding new ways to earn a living.

Rugmark builds and runs its own schools and works with the state education system. Thousands of former child workers, and other children from weaving communities, have now had educational opportunities and health and nutritional care as a result of its programmes. Rugmark provides intensive non-formal literacy and numeracy training to prepare children for formal education. In Nepal the programmes are designed to take two years, but many children are said to be so motivated that they complete within eight months. Classes include mother-tongue language, maths, science, English, physical education, music and other extra-curricular activities.

Children who go back to live with their families receive different levels of support depending on need, such as help with school fees and payments for books, uniforms and other materials. Children aged over 14 get vocational training in occupations like electrical and vehicle repair, tailoring, textiles and masonry.

Unlike Fairtrade labelling, Rugmark does not guarantee minimum prices. Nor does it cover health and safety or environmental standards, partly because most carpet making in India takes place in small workshops rather than large factories. But it does certify that children have not been exploited, under-age children have not been employed, and adult workers have been paid the producer country's official minimum wage. Workers' rights organisations see this as a key step in ensuring that all such jobs go to adults who can bargain for better wages.

There has been real impact. In Nepal, the number of children in the country's carpet industry had fallen from 11 per cent of the workforce to less than 2 per cent by 2001.

As nine-year-old Maya replied when asked what it meant to her to move from a 50-hour working week in a carpet factory to the warm friendly atmosphere of Rugmark's centre in Nepal: "Now I can be free."

21. Bypass the intermediaries

Fair trade coffee is more likely to be traded directly from co-operatives to roasters such as Cafédirect.

How much of the money that we pay for coffee, bananas, sugar and similar commodities goes to the intermediaries, the people in between the grower and the consumer? It can be a sizeable proportion. While intermediaries can play a useful role, they can also exploit farmers, especially farmers who lack knowledge of prices. And there are often too many people "in the middle". Non-fair-trade coffee, for example, can change hands up to 150 times before it reaches your cup.

Fair trade goods, by contrast, are usually sold direct from co-operatives to manufacturers. Fair trade cuts down, and may even cut out, the intermediaries. The following three farmers speak of the effects of intermediaries.

SUGAR

Juan Valverde Sánchez is a sugar cane farmer in Costa Rica. Thirty-five years old, he is married, with five children.

"I guess my passion is my work. I'm always thinking about my work," he says. "In the evening, I'm thinking of what I have to do in the morning. I love farming sugar-cane. It's hard, because the sun is very hot. But you get used to it." Juan's working week consists of three days cutting cane, one day transporting the cane (by ox and pick-up), and one day processing the cane to convert it into sugar.

On processing days, Juan gets up at 2 a.m., never needing an alarm-clock. Like many of his neighbouring small farmers, he has a *trapiche* next to his house, a plant where the juice is extracted from the cane, purified and then boiled to turn it into sugar. It's a cottage industry in which all the family gets involved. The plant's furnace has to be fed with firewood and cane pulp. To conserve energy Juan processes all his cane on one long, hot day. He relaxes in the evening by watching television.

Juan sells his sugar to Asoprodulce, a local farmer's association that his father helped found. Asoprodulce in turn sells 60 per cent of its produce to the organic fair trade market. He says:

> I know that if I bring my sugar to the association they'll buy from me at a fixed price. I've got security. Whereas in the old days, selling was more difficult. Sometimes the middle-men bought sugar from one person, sometimes from another. You never knew. There were always fluctuations in the national price. There were very bad months.

Thanks to this new security, Juan has been able to buy his sugar-processing mill from his father and improve his house.

BANANAS

Renson is proud of the new home he been able to build in Ecuador for his wife and his two young children since he began selling his bananas to the fair trade market. His father now has a place of his own, in the old wooden house next door. Renson's ambition is simply to be able to carry on selling bananas in the market that gives him a fair price. "We're proud of being in Fairtrade. We can help each other and we can help our workers." He hopes to give his children the education he missed out on.

By 7.30 each morning Renson is at work on his three-hectare farm alongside his father and uncle. He and his family work at irrigating, keeping down weeds, and wrapping the growing bananas in plastic bags for protection. With a break for lunch at eleven, Renson works till four in the afternoon. Once a week, with the help of a team of local workers, boxes of bananas are scrupulously checked for size and defects, then packed into boxes for despatch to the local port.

Outside work, Renson relaxes with his family, plays for the co-operative's football team, and enjoys the social side of being in a Fairtrade registered co-operative. As well as holding weekly meetings, the farmers organise parties.

Renson is a member of the El Guabo banana co-operative, the only group of small farmers in Ecuador who, with the help of the fair trade system, manage to avoid the intermediaries and export their own bananas. For Renson, the benefits of fair trade include a stable, higher price for his crop, and the encouragement to stop using chemicals on his farm.

"The bananas are sweeter," he says. "They have a better scent. Other companies don't care how many chemicals you put on the crop." The co-operative gave Renson a loan to irrigate his land and install tanks for washing the bananas. The members of the co-operative also help each other, loaning small sums of money in times of need.

COFFEE

Guillermo Vargas Leiton is a coffee farmer and also the manager of his local farmer's co-operative in Costa Rica, which sells 100 per cent of its crops to the Fairtrade market. He is 41, married, with two daughters, aged eight and two. The older one likes to read every day and is currently working her way through the Harry Potter books.

"We want our children to continue growing coffee, to retain the love and passion for working the land and being part of nature. We don't want them to leave the land and be dependent on other people for their food," he says.

On a typical day, Guillermo wakes up at 5.30 a.m. In his job as general manager of the co-operative he has to work long hours, from about 8.30 a.m. to 7 at night. He'll start the day checking how things are going at the coffee-roasting plant, and spends the rest of the day in the office. If Guillermo gets home early, he'll spend time with the family, and watch the news. If not, he goes straight to bed.

As manager and a long-term member of Co-op Santa Elena, Guillermo is in a good position to see the benefit that Fairtrade has had for the coffee farmers "If we didn't have fair trade sales, most of the farmers would be cutting down their trees. The current price of coffee in the conventional market doesn't cover the cost of producing the coffee." He goes on:

> When I think of fair trade, I think: fair for the producer and fair for the consumer. To my mind, the two main players involved in trade are the producer and the consumer. The people in between – the middlemen – should be the bridge, facilitating the trade. They shouldn't secure all the benefits for themselves.

22. Drink to a better world

Enjoying a glass of Merlot or Sauvignon Blanc is not the most obvious way to help a poor family build a home or get their children to school. But opening a bottle of fair trade wine means doing something practical to make the world a better place.

There's a growing range of enjoyable Fairtrade-certified New World wines on the market. If you've ever wondered what makes these brands different, the award-winning Los Robles ("The Oaks") label is as good a place as any to start. Vinos Los Robles is a wine co-operative in Chile's Curicó valley, a few hours by bus south of the capital Santiago. Owned by its 67 members – small-scale and medium-size wine growers – it employs around 90 people full time and up to 250 during harvest time.

There are not many wine co-ops left in Chile. The Pinochet dicta-torship disbanded most of them in the 1970s. Los Robles, established in 1943 in the aftermath of a devastating earthquake in the valley that killed thousands, is one that survived.

Los Robles's fair trade connection began in 1990 in association with Oxfam Belgium and Max Havelaar Netherlands. Fair trade links with the UK (Traidcraft), Germany (Gepa) and Switzerland (Claro) followed. Nowadays independent retailers and supermarkets are in on the act. Today, 15 to 20 per cent of Los Robles wine is Fairtrade certified and exported to Western Europe, and it's aiming for 100 per cent certification.

ECOLOGICAL AND SOCIAL FUND

The key to Los Robles's efforts to make its part of the world a better place is its Ecological and Social Fund, established in 2000 with money from the "social premium" (see Reason 4) received from fair trade importers. This fund supports an impressive range of activities that benefit not just employees of the co-operative and of its member growers but also poor farmers and their households in the surrounding towns, villages and countryside.

The fund has provided technical support and loans to enable Los Robles's members to replant and expand their vineyards with more marketable varieties, introduce drip irrigation and make other improvements. Visits are organised so that growers can exchange skills with each other.

Benefits for employees have included major pay rises for the lowest paid, help with home buying and repairs, a staff canteen, supplementary health insurance and support during personal and family emergencies. All good stuff, but nothing remarkable for any decent employer perhaps. It's when it comes to working with some of the poorest people in the surrounding communities, and the range of social partnerships that the co-op has entered into, that the approach begins to look really impressive.

In partnership with a non-governmental anti-poverty programme, Los Robles supports young graduate agronomists and social workers who live and work with local communities.

Finding that local children were often unable to get to school because private bus drivers did not want to pick them up and collect only a child's fare (lower than an adult's), the co-op drew on its Ecological and Social Fund to buy a school bus and donate it to the nearest municipality. "The school bus – that really was a fantastic gift," says Marta Aguilar Rojas, an education official with the local council:

> Having this bus has meant less absenteeism from school, and the average school attendance has gone up, because in those areas where the children had more difficulty to travel to the school, because of transport problems or poor roads, there is now no more excuse for absenteeism.

Another project involves helping groups of low-income people buy land, grow produce and build their own homes. This time the partner is a specialist housing foundation for poor rural areas. The local mayor's office and community organisations have a say in who benefits. One of the beneficiaries of the project, 29-year-old Ruth Funzalida Nuñez, who belongs to one of the housing groups, describes the benefits:

> I came to this area seven years ago. I am married, I have two children and currently live with my parents-in-law and with the hope of later getting our own little house. ... I think it is the best thing that could have happened in this area; we are a rural area, isolated, one of the lowest priority sectors, always we only got the least help, but now things are excellent. ... Two years ago we had no hope – no hope at all; with the funds we had it would have taken six years or more probably, but now we are all terribly motivated, we have done a lot of activities to raise funds and now after all this support, well, we expect to be able to start a housing development very soon. ... It is like a dream, it has been so many years; there are people who have been longer than us living with their in-laws, so it is been a great help to the area. ... Before, everything was very stressful, one almost was sick;

now it is different, we have new expectations and we can look forward to a future. ... My husband grows seasonal fruit, watermelons, melons and that sort of thing. I work with the fruit, I have a stall on the pavement and it is a big help for my family.

Los Robles also has a joint project with the University of Chile's social science faculty to support the formation of student co-operatives in local schools. The aim is to enable school students to experience democratic decision making and to address problems of low self-esteem that are common among poor rural people. One activity involves students in choosing books and materials to buy for community use.

There's plenty more. Los Robles has provided computers and printers for community IT classes for children and adults. There's a micro-credit scheme and support for local smallholders in the production and domestic marketing of chillies and olives. The co-op works with the community in lobbying for public works such as riverbank flood defences. It arranges educational outings by bus for low-income mothers and children. There's support for poorer households in paying university fees for their children too.

And the future? Plans are afoot for an English teaching programme in local schools, both as a practical skill and to raise self-esteem. The partner for this activity is the UK's University of Northumbria. Organic production is another target. And Los Robles wants to see the benefits of its social and environmental programme broadening to include all the 53,000 people who live in the surrounding municipalities. Naturally enough, the co-op – voted best Chilean winery in 2001 – wants to keep winning prizes for quality too.

UK wine lovers can choose from more than 90 different Fairtrade-certified wines from Chilean and South African producers, including a new range launched in summer 2006.

23. Transform lives

"Fair trade has transformed the lives of small farmers,"
says banana grower Regina Joseph. Here's how.

Regina Joseph grows bananas in Dominica, one of the chain of islands
in the Caribbean that make up the Windward Islands. Says Regina:

> Before the fair trade system, I was not able to sustain my
> family. Now I can help myself, my children, my community
> and my country as a whole. My life is completely changed.
> Before we could only eat what we grew. Now, in addition, I
> can buy food for the family that I could not afford before. And
> I can pay my bills and still have something in my pocket.

One of twelve children – the only girl – Regina is now the mother of
five children aged 17 to 26. Aged 43, she belongs to the Carib indigenous people's group (see Reason 49). Some 5,000 Carib people live
today on Dominica, out of the island's total population of 73,000.

Dominica was the last of the Caribbean islands to be colonised by
Europeans, due chiefly to the resistance of the native Caribs. And the
Caribs remain the only pre-Columbian population in the eastern
Caribbean. Over a hundred years ago, a 3,700 acre reserve was
earmarked for the Carib people. Regina lives in this territory, in the
east of Dominica. "We are separate, but within Dominica," says
Regina, "we don't buy land, the land belongs to us."

Regina is an active member of her community and of her Fairtrade
Group, which she previously served as treasurer. In addition, she is
their representative on the National Fair Trade Committee.

On her land, ten minutes' walk from home, Regina grows a variety
of crops planted between her banana trees for family consumption and
for sale to local and regional markets. Hot peppers are sold to two large
spice companies; traders buy her yams and tania, another root crop, and
cabbages and lettuces are sold locally. Regina has also planted a selection of fruit trees including grapefruit, oranges and coconut palms, as
well as several native tree species which fetch a good price for their

timber. Regina has never used chemicals on her farm because she believes they are a health hazard and are contrary to the Carib tradition of respecting the natural environment (see Reason 27).

Dominica's economy depends on agriculture, primarily on growing and selling bananas to the UK. While thousands of livelihoods hinge on bananas, growing them has become an increasingly precarious occupation in recent years. In the 1990s the island's banana industry was in crisis, unable to compete with lower cost, so-called "dollar" bananas grown on Latin American plantations. Many small farmers gave up. The Windward Island's share of the UK banana market has declined from 60 per cent to less than 20 per cent in the last 15 years.

Regina now sells all her bananas through the fair trade system. To qualify for inclusion in the system, the farmers organise into groups. Regina is a member of the Carib Territory Fairtrade Group, which has a chairman, vice-chairman, secretary and treasurer. Regina now serves as public relations officer.

In addition to the price per box of bananas the farmers receive, the group also receives an extra payment – the social premium – of US$1 a box.

THE COMMUNITY

Regina describes her community:

> Our group – of 50 members – discuss what to use the social premium for. But we do not see the premium as belonging to the group. Rather it's for projects that are for the good of the community as a whole. So we invite the community to have a say in how they believe the premium should be spent, what projects to go ahead with.

The first thing the community did with the social premium was to lay down roads so that they are no longer isolated and don't have to carry the bananas on their heads any longer. Transport can now reach them. They have used some of the premium to upgrade their water system, had the reservoir enlarged and water is now piped to their homes which means people have no need to go the river for water.

"In our community there are two schools and neither knew anything about computers," Regina says.

> We used some of the premium to buy each school a computer. I don't know anything about computers but my children and grandchildren will make use of them. We also used some to help towards the cost of building a hospital. And we bought a lawn mower! There's a playing field in our village and it can now be kept in good order so that people can participate in sports. There was a family whose houses were burnt. We assisted them with US$500 so that they can rebuild. We are hoping to build a resource centre, so that people in the community can go and learn different skills, like plumbing and woodwork, so that people have the skills they need to move out of poverty. So the fair trade system does not just help banana growers. It benefits the community as a whole.

Dominica has around 300 banana growers, 90 per cent of them now selling through the fair trade system. "We are inviting the remaining 10 per cent to come in," Regina goes on. "In the meantime we co-operate with them, through for example, selling them fertiliser at the lower rate that we buy it as a co-operative group." (Since this interview was conducted, all banana growers in the Windward Islands have joined the Fairtrade system.)

Infrastructure in Dominica, especially roads, is generally poor. In pre-fair trade days, Regina had to carry her 18-kilo boxes of harvested bananas on her head to the nearest road, "which, in my case, was half a mile away," she said. Regina now harvests 35 boxes of bananas every two weeks. Collection lorries can drive right up to her packhouse on harvest days, so she no longer has to carry her bananas on her head – or make the same journey to collect water for her packing operation from the roadside standpipe.

The government is constructing a new small hospital for the area, made possible by local community organisations agreeing to part-fund the project. The Fairtrade Group originally pledged Eastern Caribbean $5,000; then in February 2005 they reviewed it in the light of increased premiums earned from Fairtrade sales and took the decision to double their contribution to EC$10,000 (US$ 3,700 approx).

Regina also exports fair trade coconuts to the UK. Again she receives almost three times as much as she did before. And she is skilled in the traditional Carib handicraft of basket weaving which supplements her income. Regina has passed her skills on to her two daughters who work as self-employed artisans, selling their baskets to tourists from Carib handicrafts shops.

Her 18-year-old daughter is studying history and herbal medicine at college and is optimistic that she will be able to get a scholarship to continue her education at university.

At the end of a hectic two-week tour of the UK in 2005, ranging from visiting supermarkets to a meeting at the Treasury, Regina has a message for UK shoppers: "When you go to the supermarket, make sure you buy Fairtrade-certified bananas."

24. Give bad balls the boot

The people who sew fair trade footballs, basketballs, volley-balls and rugby balls get a living wage, decent working conditions, medical care and low-cost loans. That's a real first in the sportsball industry.

It's a little known fact that around three-quarters of the world's footballs are made in and around the city of Sialkot in Pakistan, whose sportsball industry employs approximately 30,000 people.

It takes close to 700 hand-stitches to make a 32-panel football, and an experienced stitcher will complete up to five balls a day. Wages are low for the men, women and children who sew the balls, mainly working for subcontractors. In the past, thousands of children as young as seven had to work long hours with their families to help make ends meet, often going entirely without any school education.

In 1997, under pressure from Save the Children, UNICEF, the International Labour Organization and others, major sportsball brands like Nike, Adidas, Reebok and Puma signed the "Atlanta Agreement", which committed them not to employ child stitchers younger than 14. The next year the world football governing body FIFA adopted a code of conduct prohibiting use of child labour for international soccer balls.

Despite reported violations, the Atlanta Agreement and FIFA code were steps in the right direction. But they caused new problems. Manufacturing of low-quality machine-made balls moved to China. In Sialkot, where most of the stitching had previously been done in family homes, the subcontractors set up stitching centres so that they could monitor the agreement. Many women – unable to leave the home to work, and prevented in Pakistan's Islamic society from working in the same room as men – lost their only source of income.

FAIR TRADE COMES TO SIALKOT

In 2002 three Sialkot sportsball manufacturers began making fairly traded and subsequently Fairtrade-certified balls. Initially for sale in Sweden and Italy, the balls are now also available in Australia, Canada, Germany, Japan, New Zealand, the UK, the USA and other countries.

Fair trade has made a big difference to the stitcher families. Pay has risen to about 50 per cent above the industry average. Wages are calculated to provide a decent income for a family as long as two adults sew fair trade balls eight hours a day. This works out at around 6,000 Pakistani rupees (£57.00) per month per family – a decent income by local standards that ensures children can go to school.

No children under 15 are allowed to work on fair trade balls. Over 15 they can work, but only part time so that they can continue their education. One of the supplier companies, Talon Sports, was an early winner of the International Labour Organization's "Without Child Labour" award.

The work is organised differently from before. Fairtrade-certified suppliers organise stitching in small village centres. Designated women-only units enable women to work without sharing the space with men. Acceptable standards of ventilation, lighting and safe drinking water availability have to be met. Workers receive information on fair trade conditions, wage rates and the monitoring system in their own language, Urdu.

The fair trade "social premium" on sportsballs is about 10 per cent of the price that the supplier company receives. "Joint bodies" of workers and management agree how to spend it (see Reasons 4 and 7). At Talon the premium covers free healthcare for all employees, including hospital costs for pregnant women. Other benefits include small-business credit schemes to enable workers to develop new sources of income, and funds for local irrigation projects and for buying school exercise books. Talon has set up nurseries in some of its production centres, where women can leave their children to be properly cared for and prepared for school while they go to work. A third of Talon's balls are now reported as sewn by women.

Talon's Fair Trade Workers' Welfare Society, which manages spending of the premium in partnership with the sewers and local non-governmental organisations, also supports a relief programme for refugees from Afghanistan.

PLAYING BALL

The range of fair trade balls now includes volleyballs, rugby balls, basketballs, and junior and mini-footballs, as well as FIFA international match ball standard footballs. Football kits and goalkeepers' gloves (not yet Fairtrade certified) are also available. In the UK, the main supplier, FairDeal Trading, reckons the balls are no more expensive than other good quality balls.

Fair trade sportsballs are becoming popular in the UK. Football clubs using them include Genesis FC, a Christian team from Loughborough who play in the North Leicestershire League. And when Royal Holloway, University of London, won University Fairtrade status in late 2005 (Reason 16), the college rugby club played its part by using fair trade balls.

Much has been achieved, but fair trade sportsballs are still just a small fraction of those made every year in Sialkot, and only a small percentage of the sewing families currently benefit. There's never been a better time to kick your old ball into touch.

25. Stamp out pesticide poisoning

Chemical pesticides poison 20,000 people a year and have been linked to Alzheimer's disease. Fair trade growers either use natural, organic pest control or are steadily reducing pesticide use.

"Aren't you afraid to eat chocolate?" The question was asked by a worker on a cocoa plantation in Brazil. The question was understandable, for the worker and his colleagues sprayed the cocoa plants with some of the world's most powerful and dangerous pesticides. These include paraquat and 2,4-D. And, inevitably, some residue from the pesticides may be there in that glamorous box of chocolates. A Friends of the Earth study of pesticides in our food found that "nearly all of the chocolate that was tested contained residues of the hormone-disrupting pesticide lindane, which has been linked to breast cancer".

Cocoa is by no means the only crop that is sprayed to try to keep pests and disease at bay. Bananas, coffee, cotton ... the list is lengthy. And it's producers who are in the front line. Spraying chemicals can have serious effects on the health of producers, including lungs, skin, eyes and nose. While more than 80 per cent of pesticides are applied in developed countries, 99 per cent of all poisoning cases occur in developing countries where regulatory, health and education systems are weakest, according to the UN Food and Agriculture Organization. In developing countries, an estimated 25 million agricultural workers may suffer at least one incident of chemical pesticide poisoning each year.

Many crops grown for export are sprayed with chemicals. Take bananas. Most of the world's bananas are grown on large plantations in Latin America, owned by transnational corporations. While these bananas are cheap for consumers they carry huge social and environmental costs. Heavy use of chemicals has a devastating effect on workers and the environment. In Costa Rica, sprayers on banana plantations use the equivalent of 65 kg of pesticides per worker per year, and poisonings are rife.

Male workers may be left sterile after handling toxic pesticides. Honduras banana grower Gilberto is one of them. "Many of my colleagues have suffered from the pesticides that we must spray on the bananas. Now they can have no children," he says. Yet companies refuse to stop using such dangerous practices.

The bananas that we eat in Britain may have pesticide residues. Also oranges, yams and sweet potato.

Pesticides use on coffee can be high, harming both people and the environment. Coffee may be sprayed with aldrin, dieldrin and endrin – pesticides so dangerous they are banned for use in most Western countries. Nicaraguan coffee grower Oscar Zamora describes his life when he grew the crop with chemicals:

Very often, poison from the chemicals I was using fell into my eyes. ... Of course if you read the ticket you know the dangers of this. The first thing it says is: 'Poison is highly dangerous. Avoid contact with eyes and your whole body.' This poisonous chemical was so strong that it burnt my eyes, and very often I would have to run to wash it off. After this there's your back: you see when I wore a knapsack sprayer to treat the coffee plants, poisonous liquid escaped and wet my entire back.

When I arrived home there was a burning feeling all over my back and I had to make myself wash – even though I was in so much pain and my skin was irritated. I made myself wash all the poisonous chemicals off because if you don't there's a risk that you may become terminally ill, for example in your lungs.

Oscar Zamora has now switched to using organic methods and is reaping the benefits. "I am now protecting my health; the consumer of my coffee can protect theirs too. They can consume a healthy, organic product; without any fear that that they are putting themselves at risk because too many chemicals are dangerous," he says.

Fair trade and organic often go hand in hand. Many Fairtrade-certified products are also certified organic. So the consumer gets a double benefit.

COTTON

The heaviest doses of agrochemicals are sprayed on cotton – it takes about a quarter of all the world's pesticide. Yet cotton takes up only 2.5 per cent of the world's cropped area. While it is cultivated in 70 countries, just four – China, the USA, India and Pakistan – account for two-thirds of cotton production. In eleven countries in Africa, cotton accounts for more than a quarter of export revenues.

Cotton production has severe impacts at the farm level on human and environmental health. Increasingly, the social impacts of pesticides use are becoming apparent – affecting food security for example.

Fair trade growers either use natural or organic pest control or are steadily reducing pesticide use. While the two systems are complementary – and many producers benefit from both – Fairtrade certification does not exclude producers who are unable to meet organic standards, as its priority is towards the most marginalised producers.

In cotton growing, organic cotton is proving to be a viable and beneficial option for farmers (see Reason 10). Organic production tends to lead to lower costs and give higher net incomes to producers; it thus contributes to poverty reduction. Organic cotton can also increase food security, through crop rotations, by placing less emphasis on growing as much cotton as possible to steer clear of debt, by having more wild foods available in a more diverse ecosystem, and more and healthier livestock. Organic cotton production, while sometimes leading to lower yields, allows farmers to intercrop food and livestock, helping achieve food security and more secure livelihoods.

In the organic sector, women cotton growers can gain increased independence within the community and as independent producers. They are also attracted by reduced health risks and increased food security.

There are also improvements to the environment when pesticide usage is reduced. Elia Ruth Zuñiga is a banana worker for an organisation called Coopetrabasur in Costa Rica. Ruth has noticed a number of changes since Coopetrabasur started working with fair trade:

> We use much less chemicals than other companies, and we manage the environment better. The bananas are almost organic. Before Fairtrade it was a lot dirtier here. Now it is clean. We have cleaned up the quadrant and we separate our waste to recycle plastics, and save our organic waste to be used as compost for the bananas.

Coopetrabasur has built buffer zones around the boundaries of the plantations so that chemical and other waste doesn't pollute rivers, walkways and living quarters.

26. Travel with respect

Community or ethical tourism, "people to people" tours – call it what you like – does more than pay a fair wage for the services people provide. It gives you a fuller experience without harming the local environment or exploiting local people.

Tourism is the world's largest service industry, employing one in ten of the world's workers. It's growing. People increasingly want to travel abroad, and low-cost flights make it easy. One billion of us will have travelled abroad by 2010.

But whoever first said "Tourism is whorism" had a point. Tourism exploits poor people and the environment mainly in poor countries for the benefit of richer people mainly from rich countries. It's dominated by large Western companies, which take most of the profits. Poor host countries have to provide plenty of clean water and electricity to hotels and tourist complexes while local people often do without.

Job creation? Yes, but how much of the money is left for wages when close to 90 per cent of the price of an average all-in foreign holiday goes to the home-country operator, airline, insurance company and travel agent? The local hotel gets only 3 per cent – and its service workers, peanuts. As Tricia Barnett, founder-director of Tourism Concern, puts it: "Cheap holidays for us mean people in destination countries earn a pittance."

Many of the cleaners, cooks, drivers, porters, receptionists and waiters who service the industry have to work unpaid overtime and without paid holidays, employment contracts or union rights. Tips may be the only way they can make ends meet. "We live thinking every day what we're going to eat and how to pay for the electricity," says a chambermaid from a 4-star hotel in the Dominican Republic. "We have to smile to the tourists, but it is not what we are feeling in our souls."

In the idyllic Maldives, voted Britons' most desired holiday destination in 2005, almost half the population lives close to the poverty line, and one in three children is undernourished.

Sometimes there's not even a low wage in it for local people. A breakdown of the proceeds of a wildlife holiday in Kenya finds that an average of 20p of every £1 spent goes to the travel agent, 40p to the airline, 23p to the hotel chain, 8p to the safari company and 9p to the Kenyan government (largely to pay for imports to satisfy tourist tastes). The Maasai, whose natural environment is the main attraction, often get nothing at all – in fact many Maasai communities have been thrown off their land to make way for safari parks.

Head for the mountains, and there's a similar pattern of exploitation. Trekking porters in Nepal and Peru often carry huge loads for very low pay without proper clothing or equipment. Nepalese porters, more likely to be poor farmers from lowland areas than hardy mountain sherpas, suffer four times more accidents and illnesses than Western trekkers, although a new trekking companies' code of conduct is beginning to change things.

Environmentally it's also pretty bad – and it's not just the air miles (see below). Western-style hotels use thousands of gallons of water a day, often in drought-stricken countries where rural women walk for hours each morning to fetch a few litres. One tourist may use as much water in a day as a rice farmer needs to grow rice for 100 days.

Waste water from hotels is destroying coral reefs in Barbados, and dive tourism also causes heavy damage to reefs. The Bimini Bay tourism development in the Bahamas has fenced off local people's access to most of the land and many of the beaches. Mangroves have been bulldozed, and the lagoon is silting up. A one-week Caribbean cruise may dump a million gallons of waste water and thousands of gallons of sewage and contaminated oil in the sea, much of it untreated.

Then there's human rights. Some of the worst impacts of tourism have been documented in Burma, where the military regime has built its infrastructure on the backs of near-slave labour.

And sexual abuse. With 13–19 million children working in tourism around the world, the UN estimates that more than 1 million youngsters are sexually abused by tourists.

As one Malaysian commented: "The raw material of the tourist industry is the flesh and blood of people and their cultures."

A DIFFERENT KIND OF TRAVEL

Growing public awareness and pressure from campaigners have led mainstream travel companies to develop responsible tourism policies, and the UK government has supported work on making tourism more sustainable and less exploitative. Some small independent operators go much further. They have found ways to give local people more control and benefits from tourism, to protect the environment and the dignity of local cultures, and to encourage more respectful visitor behaviour.

While there's no such thing yet as a Fairtrade-certified holiday, Tourism Concern and the fair trade movement are looking into what might be possible. In the meantime, variations on the idea of "tourism that benefits local people" are offered by many small companies in partnership with host communities.

Traidcraft, which has pioneered fair trade since 1979, has developed Meet the People Tours as a joint venture with the independent operator Saddle Skedaddle. These small-group holidays led by local guides include time with fair trade producers, visits to cultural sites, enjoyment of the countryside and wildlife, and eating locally produced foods. Visitors sleep in locally owned hotels and guest houses and travel by local means where possible. People who have gone on Traidcraft's tours have described them as "inspiring", "a privilege", "an amazing experience", "mind blowing", "unforgettable", "one of the most fulfilling and worthwhile experiences of my life" and "a trip of a lifetime".

Anther leader in the field is Tribes (Best Tour Operator in the First Choice Responsible Tourism Awards 2005), which has set up a charity to support social development and environmental protection among vulnerable communities.

Many more companies and holidays feature in Tourism Concern's book *The Ethical Travel Guide* and on the website Responsibletravel.com. Some have a strong eco-tourism element with support from the Worldwide Fund for Nature (WWF). The Rainforest Alliance is developing a similar approach for people travelling from the USA.

Even the hard-pressed Kenyan Maasai have benefited. Tricia Barnett of Tourism Concern tells of a community whose response to being forced from their land for a conservation park was to sell four cattle to buy a few tents. At first no visitors came, but when they began to market themselves as a community-based tourism destination, the project blossomed. Within a few years this community venture could accommodate 50 visitors at a time, owned its own vehicle, had built a pharmacy and provided travellers with talks on Maasai culture and guided wildlife walks. The proceeds have also funded a safe house where young women fleeing female genital mutilation can get an education and start a new life.

Similar projects are under way worldwide, such as the Nicaragua Solidarity Campaign's tours that enable travellers to live and work with an agricultural fair trade co-operative.

Air travel is best avoided wherever possible. It's set to become the number one source of greenhouse gas emissions and global warming. Go overland if you have the time, and go by train if you can. Africa and Asia can be reached overland with just a short journey by sea. It takes longer but is much kinder to the environment.

27. Be a friend of the earth

Environment friendly. That's fair trade! In the fair trade system, people are likely to use the higher returns and the premiums they receive to improve their environment.

Buying fair trade helps to promote more environmentally friendly farming methods. The so-called "free" trade system puts farmers and social and environmental concerns last, pushes prices down and monopolies up. Fair trade works in and through the market but puts farmers, their communities and the environment first.

Farmers who grow for the fair trade system are already likely to be growing their crops in an environment friendly way. Take coffee, for example. A two-cup-a-day coffee drinker consumes the annual harvest of 18 coffee trees every year. Coffee was traditionally grown by small-scale farmers in forested agro-ecosystems free of agrochemicals.

Since the 1970s, however, in an effort to raise production volumes, many coffee growers have adopted higher-yielding plant varieties. In addition to requiring massive deforestation of the shade trees that grow over traditional farms, these varieties require heavier applications of chemical fertilisers and pesticides – inputs that harm workers, wildlife and local water supplies. This has had devastating impacts on the environment and human communities.

By contrast, fair trade farms rely mainly on biological or organic fertilisers and natural pest control. There are clearly defined criteria requiring environmentally sensitive production on Fairtrade certified coffee, including promotion of integrated crop management, a farming system that combines traditional "low-input" techniques and modern technology. Fair trade farms traditionally "intercrop" coffee or cocoa with various kinds of shade and fruit trees. Such shaded farms can be as biodiverse as natural forest ecosystems, encouraging plants, insects, birds and mammals. And these shaded farms also protect topsoil from erosion by rain and wind. Belizean organic farmers supplying Green & Black's Maya Gold, for example, grow their cocoa under shade trees, helping protect the rich biodiversity of the Central American rain forest (see Reason 44). They produce their crop without chemical pesticides – which matters, because cocoa is the world's second most heavily sprayed crop after cotton.

Contrary to claims made by agro-industry, environmentally friendly farming is often as productive as, or more productive than, chemical and fossil-fuel-intensive production. TransFair USA reports that fair trade tea estates which have adopted organic cultivation have reversed long-term declines in yields that resulted from intensification and technification.

Just as important, organic and near-organic produce tastes better too.

FAIR TRADE AND ORGANIC

People sometimes assume that fair trade and organic standards are the same. This is not the case, though there is a lot of common ground. While fair trade's first priority is to benefit people in terms of income, working conditions and control over their lives, organic farming begins with production methods that help rather than harm the environment. And while organic standards can apply to farming in the industrialised North, fair trade is focused only on the South. Fair trade also recognises that not all Southern producers have the income or capacity to go fully organic, at least in the short term.

That said, the benefits almost always work both ways. Fair trade is committed to protecting farm workers from harmful agrochemicals (Reason 25), for example, while the international organic farming movement – of which the UK's Soil Association is part – has guidelines that require workers to have decent minimum employment conditions.

If the environment thrives, it's better for the people working in it. And if farmers and workers are fairly paid and have more say in decisions, they are far more likely to choose to work with, rather than against, nature.

SUSTAINABLE PRODUCTION AND LIVING

As many of the examples in this book show, fair trade almost always leads to environmental improvements. Fairtrade certification requires traders to "pay a price to producers that covers the costs of sustainable production and living". Sustainable production and living are only possible if there is care for the environment.

Fair trade producer co-operatives worldwide invest their social premium in environmental improvements and training on their farms and estates. Examples include soil and water conservation, tree planting, agroforestry (growing crops and trees together), organic production, terracing, composting and environmentally friendly post-harvest processing techniques. There are benefits for people's immediate living environment too: improved drinking water and sanitation, electric lighting, better-quality and healthier housing, cleaner and more pleasant surroundings.

Interviews with banana farmers and workers from the Juliana-Jaramillo group in the Dominican Republic show the kind of progress possible after only two years of fair trade sales to the UK – although as farmer-agronomist Felipe Rivas put it, "You need to educate people so that they understand the issues."

Felipe was leading a clean-up of the old plastic bags used to protect growing bananas. Fair trade's environmental standards ban farmers from leaving plastic lying around the countryside, a common problem in banana-growing districts. The bags are an environmental hazard, and the chemicals sometimes used in them can contaminate drinking water. The Juliana-Jaramillo banana farmers collect the plastic bags for transportation to a central site and employ a team of workers to clear away other farmers' bags from nearby roads and rivers.

Felipe, who is one of four agronomists employed by the group, also helped the farmers set up an organic compost system so that they could reduce their chemical fertiliser use. "Organic fertiliser gives to the soil what the chemical fertiliser takes away," he said.

Environmental benefits can be far-reaching. Empowered by the economic stability provided by fair trade, members of the COSURCA coffee co-operative in Colombia successfully prevented the cultivation of more than 1,600 acres of coca and poppy, used for the production of illicit drugs.

"Buying Fairtrade-certified products encourages environmentally friendly cultivation, which protects land, wildlife, and human communities," sums up TransFair USA.

28. End child exploitation

Millions of children worldwide are exploited, trafficked and enslaved by adults for money, and some are injured or die as a result. It's hard to know whether children have been exploited in producing your food, drink and other purchases – unless you buy fair trade.

Work is not always bad for children, as long as it is light, undertaken willingly, and does not interfere with their health, safety or education. Such work is allowed under international law for children aged twelve and over. But the International Labour Organization (ILO) estimates that 126 million children aged 5–14 work in hazardous and illegal conditions worldwide – 73 million of them younger than ten. Many are trapped in forced and slave labour, debt bondage and prostitution.

Poverty is the overriding reason why children are exploited. With adult wages often not enough to feed, clothe and house a family, children are sent out to work. Coffee, cocoa (chocolate), bananas, oranges and sugar are among the food industry supply chains that exploit child labour most badly. Other sectors include cotton and textiles (see Reason 10), carpets and rugs (Reason 20), jewellery and sportsballs (Reason 24).

PLANTATION SLAVERY

Cocoa is one of the worst cases. A few years ago evidence emerged about the trafficking of boys and youths as forced labourers on cocoa farms in West Africa. In Côte d'Ivoire, which produces almost half the cocoa for the world's chocolate industry, more than 200,000 children were estimated as working in dangerous conditions on cocoa plantations, many of them trafficked from Burkina Faso and Mali. There were reports of boys as young as nine working. Many were never paid. Beatings were common. Boys who tried to escape were sometimes killed. Drissa from Mali, who was enslaved as a teenager, said:

> I traveled over 300 miles from home. ... I worked on a cocoa plantation in Côte d'Ivoire ... from dawn till dusk tending and collecting the cocoa pods. I was weak from hunger. If I slowed in my work, I was beaten. When I tried to run away, I was savagely beaten.

When these stories broke, the large US and UK chocolate manufacturers denied responsibility. They could not be expected to know what happened on hundreds of thousands of cocoa farms in Côte d'Ivoire, they said.

In 2002 US chocolate companies, the World Cocoa Foundation, the ILO and campaigners agreed they would eliminate child slave labour from the cocoa plantations. Some progress has been made, but the extent of improvements is not fully known, and the agreed phase-out by July 2005 was not achieved. In 2005 the International Labor Rights Fund filed a US lawsuit against chocolate companies Nestlé, ADM and Cargill, claiming they shared responsibility in the trafficking, torture and forced labour of Côte d'Ivoire child cocoa workers. In 2006 US courts were still considering whether the case should be tried.

Children and young adults have traditionally worked on plantations in West Africa, going from poorer neighbouring countries to Côte d'Ivoire to learn farming skills and earn money for their families. But the situation deteriorated sharply as world cocoa prices plummeted from $4.89 per pound in 1977 to as low as 51 cents per pound by the early 2000s. Transnational companies drove down prices as more and more developing countries grew cocoa for export.

A fair trade activist commented, "The trade issue is exactly what is exacerbating the slavery problem."

FANCY A BANANA?

Ecuador is the world's largest banana exporter. As in many developing countries, child labour is technically illegal there. But thousands of children still work on the country's banana plantations. Human Rights Watch (HRW) found in 2002 that child banana workers as young as ten worked twelve hours a day or more, often suffering pesticide exposure and sexual harassment. HRW reported that some boys:

> had attached harnesses to themselves, hooked themselves to pulleys on cables from which banana stalks were hung and used this pulley system to drag approximately 20 banana-laden stalks, weighing between 50 and 100 pounds each, over one mile from the fields to the packing plants five or six times a day.

The ultra-modern Los Álamos plantation, Ecuador's leading exporter of Bonita brand bananas, is owned by the country's richest man and ex-presidential candidate, Álvaro Noboa. Though claiming to "love his workers", Noboa was revealed in 2002 to be employing young children.

Several of Ecuador's plantations stopped employing child workers after HRW published its report, but worker families suffered as their incomes dropped. "With my husband's salary, we did not have enough for school, not enough for food," said Patricia Céspedes, explaining why she had sent her eleven-year-old nephew to work full time.

In the unfair banana trade, wholesalers and retailers take most of the profits. Plantations get little more than 10 per cent of the retail price, and their workers just a fraction.

THE BEST GUARANTEE

The problem of child labour needs large-scale political and economic solutions. Campaigning groups such as Anti-Slavery International and Save the Children are working for change. But individual action is important too. By switching to, and staying with, fair trade produce we can help low-income households earn a decent living, so they don't have to send their children to work. We can ensure that no child has been exploited or trafficked to produce what we buy. And we put pressure on the unfair traders by showing that as consumers we are committed to, and expect, seriously ethical purchasing.

All Fairtrade-certified food, drink and other produce is guaranteed not to involve exploitative child labour. The Fairtrade Mark means that children aged under 15 are not employed at all, except in helping out on the small family farm. Older children (15–18) may only work if this does not harm their education or their social, moral or physical development, and if they are given non-hazardous tasks. International Fair Trade Association (IFAT) member organisations (Reason 3) commit to ensuring that:

> the participation of children in production processes of fairly traded articles ... does not adversely affect their well-being, security, educational requirements and need for play. Organisations working directly with informally organised producers disclose the involvement of children in production.

The Network of European Worldshops (NEWS!) permits children's work in producing goods sold as long as it is temporary, part-time, healthy and non-exploitative. NEWS! reflects the views of many who believe that an immediate and total ban on child work could force the issue underground and make child protection more difficult.

All Fairtrade-certified produce has to meet rigorous standards applied through independent inspection and monitoring of producers (Reason 3). This contrasts with claims made by big chocolate manufacturers who said it was too difficult to monitor the origins of cocoa used in their chocolate.

Buying fair trade is the best and only assurance that you are not involved – however indirectly – in exploiting children.

29. Lift the debt burden

Small-scale farmers and craftspeople are often burdened by heavy debts to moneylenders. With fair trade, they can borrow what they need at lower cost.

Small farmers and craftspeople in developing countries are often burdened by heavy debts to moneylenders. The slump in prices for their produce in the mainstream trading system, both internationally and locally, has had a catastrophic impact on the lives of millions. It has forced many small-scale producers into crippling debt, and countless others to lose their land, their homes and even their lives. For among small farmers, suicides are all too common (see Reason 10).

MOUNTING DEBTS

Thirty-two-year-old Lachi Reddy had been worried for months about the mounting debts on his three acres of potatoes in the Indian state of Andhra Pradesh. Even using all the latest pesticides and chemicals to try to increase output, Lachi struggled to make a living. Over the years, sales had not come close to covering costs.

He borrowed money, first from the banks and when they said no, from the private lenders. There were plenty of those and they rarely said no. Their yes came at a cost: 36 per cent interest on the repayments. But the situation deteriorated when the last of the surface water evaporated in the storage tanks around his village, victim of a severe drought. Without water there was no hope. So Lachi did what all his neighbours had done, and borrowed even more money – 80,000 rupees (£970) – to dig a bore well in the hope of finding water. It was a gamble but it seemed to pay off. There was water.

Only now his troubles lay elsewhere. The price of potatoes fell too low even to repay the interest on the loan for the well, let alone all his other debts which now amounted to some 170,000 rupees (£2,060).

So Lachi decided to change to another crop. Sugar cane was the answer, he thought. It seemed a more reliable cash crop than potatoes.

And he couldn't go back to traditional farming. Given his debts, just growing the crops he needed for his own family was no longer an option.

The trouble was that by then he did not have enough money to buy the sugar cane or the labour to plant the crop. The banks continued to refuse any more loans, and even the private lenders were saying no. The only option left open to this proud man was to go round to his friends and neighbours pleading with them to lend him some money. It is hard to imagine what it took for Lachi to ask this. Finally, in utter desperation, he swallowed a bottle of Endo Sulfan pesticide. He collapsed, never regained consciousness and died later that day in the local hospital.

Lachi Reddy's case has been tragically repeated thousands of times in developing countries. More than 4,000 farmers in Andhra Pradesh alone have taken their lives since 1997 "as liberalised trade policies cause havoc with the region's agriculture", says Christian Aid.

Fair trade provides farmers and others in the fair trade system with a return that enables them to pay off loans more easily. Like master craftsman Mohd Usman who specialises in making gifts:

> We were not prosperous and did not get money on time. We were in debt. It was a very hard time. When we came into contact with Tara [Trade Alternative Reform Action] Projects our lives changed. We have already paid off our debt and have saved some money for our daughters' marriages.

Tara Projects is a non-profit organisation based in Delhi, serving some 25 community-based groups of artisans from regions in North India. Tara's objective is to help craft workers to achieve self-sufficiency by providing income-generating opportunities and developing marketing skills; it is one of Traidcraft's biggest supplier of crafts.

BORROWING AT LOWER COST

If people in the fair trade system need to borrow, they can often borrow at lower cost. The Kuapa Kokoo Union cocoa farmers co-operative in Ghana, for example (Reason 44) has a credit union from which members can borrow.

The Eksteenskuill Farmers Association in South Africa produces raisins and sultanas which Traidcraft use in their muesli, cakes and snack bars. With the premium the farmers receive, they have bought equipment which the farmers can borrow, again keeping them clear of moneylenders. But many more indebted farmers remain to be covered by fair trade.

"One always lives with uncertainty, always in debt," says Vitelio Manza, a Colombian coffee farmer, expressing the insecurity which comes from relying on world market coffee prices. "It's always borrow here, borrow there; we live dependent on credit. There is no peace living with such uncertainty. It would be very good if the fair trade initiative reached as far as here."

The good news for Vitelio Manza and others in his position is that people are buying more fair trade products and helping to lift a burden that can take a heavy toll.

30. Say no to GMOs

Besides posing health and environmental risks that are poorly understood, farming based on genetically modified crops threatens the livelihoods of small-scale farmers in poor countries. Fair trade helps farmers stay independent of the biotech giants.

Commercial cultivation of genetically modified (GM) crops began in the mid 1990s with insecticide-resistant cotton and maize and weed-killer-resistant soybeans. A decade later, the debate for and against rages on.

About 8.5 million farmers in 21 countries grow GM crops. Soybean, maize, canola (rapeseed) and cotton are the main ones. Others include GM rice (in Iran) and squash and papaya (in the USA). GM coffee, tomatoes, potatoes and other foodstuffs are under development. The world's leading GM-growing country by far is the USA, followed by Argentina, Brazil, Canada and China. Other notable growers include Mexico, South Africa, India, the Philippines, Colombia, Iran and Honduras, and in the EU France, Germany, Portugal and Spain.

The main claims for GM crops are that they will help "feed the world" by increasing farmers' yields and, in future, providing foods higher in vitamins and minerals. GM crops are said to help reduce problems with pests, diseases and weed control, reduce the need for chemical applications, save fuel, help prevent soil erosion and enable crops to grow in salty or arid conditions. But the benefits claimed are largely unproven, and serious questions have been asked about the health effects of consuming GM crops and the environmental risks of growing them. Plus there's a strong political and economic dimension to the debate.

POTENTIAL TO DEVASTATE

Among small-scale farmers in developing countries – the people the biotech companies say they are trying to help – as well as development charities and the general public, there's widespread suspicion of GMOs and often strong opposition. A key objection for many is that GM farming strengthens the power of the agribusiness transnationals that develop and sell modified seeds, and weakens the ability of low-income rural communities to control their lives.

An investigation by Christian Aid concluded that GM crops offer "false promises" to farmers while giving "a handful of GM corporations ... increasing control over the global food system". The charity noted that "Too little is yet known about the possible environmental or ecological and health effects. Commercial and other interests are in danger of overriding public concern, democratic decision making and local control."

Another development charity, ActionAid, has campaigned against the development and cultivation of GM coffee on the basis that it threatens to put "millions of smallholder growers out of business" by replacing traditional, small-scale production of good quality beans on family farms with industrial-type plantations.

GM coffee, developed by a Hawaii-based company, makes all the coffee berries ripen at the same time, but only when chemically sprayed. If this coffee became commercially cultivated, farmers would need to buy the seeds and chemical sprays every year. Less manual work would be needed, suiting larger-scale mechanised coffee growing rather than small family farms. "Small farmers will be squeezed out of the market with GM coffee," says Dr Tewolde Egziabler, Ethiopia's delegate to the UN Food and Agriculture Organization. ActionAid, adds "This technology has the potential to devastate the lives of millions of growers throughout the developing world."

GM cotton is another focus of concern. According to the Fairtrade Foundation, "Research to date indicates that the benefits are negligible. Indian farmers who planted [GM] cotton reported decreased average yields compared to conventional varieties." The Foundation goes on:

> There is also no evidence that GM cotton has resulted in the promised reduction in herbicide usage. GM seeds can cost up to ten times more that conventional cotton seeds and farmers are often compelled by biotechnology companies to purchase the associated farming inputs as a package. ... This can lead them into long-term financial commitments which increase their indebtedness.

Some Indian farmers' groups have taken to pulling up and burning trial plots of GM cotton to defend their livelihoods.

As for rice – which 2.5 billion people depend on as a staple food – leading Indian journalist and food activist Devinder Sharma has joined forces with Western campaigners in warning that control over rice through genetic manipulation and patents is passing into the hands of European and US transnationals. Sharma speaks of the danger of "daylight robbery" of the genetic wealth of developing countries by Western agribusiness.

Evidence of the potential health risks associated with GM crops has at times been suppressed. One well-known case is the work of leading researcher Dr Arpad Pusztai, who was hounded out of his post at the prestigious Rowett Research Institute in Scotland by the UK's political and medical establishment after he found that rats were seriously harmed by a diet of GM potato.

In 2006 the London-based Institute of Science in Society (I-SIS) reported a trail of "dead sheep, ill workers and dead villagers" associated with severe toxicity poisoning from GM cotton grown in Andhra Pradesh, India. Similar illnesses and deaths have been found among cotton growers in Madhya Pradesh and villagers exposed to GM maize in the Philippines. According to I-SIS, local shepherds said that their sheep became "dull" and "depressed" after grazing on GM cotton crop residues, started coughing with nasal discharges, developed red lesions in the mouth, became bloated, suffered blackish diarrhoea and sometimes passed red urine. Death occurred within five to seven days of grazing. At least 1,820 sheep deaths were recorded in four villages.

There are also real risks of cross-contamination. Wind-blown pollen can transmit genetic characteristics. GM and non-GM crops cannot coexist, and there are no safe distances between them.

A DIFFERENT MODEL

There is widespread public resistance to GM crops in Europe. But the biotech giants and their supporters are unlikely to be satisfied without pushing for more control over world agriculture.

Fair trade offers a very different model. In place of high-cost, high-tech agricultural inputs developed by university scientists funded by transnationals, which then must be paid for by poor farmers with little income to spare, fair trade helps local people produce crops they know, in ways they – and we – understand. Currently all Fairtrade-certified food, drinks and cotton products are GM-free. Some fair trade organisations have committed never to buy or sell GMOs, and a few have campaigned actively against GM agriculture.

31. Do something funky with your furniture

From coffee tables to dining room suites, more and more distinctive fair trade furniture ranges are now available.

Furniture ads – you can scarcely turn on a television without seeing them. One thing you will not see advertised is fair trade furniture. But from tables to chairs, sideboards to desks, loungers to beds, sales of fair trade furniture are growing fast – without being advertised. More and more fair trade furniture ranges are becoming available. And it's making a big difference to people's lives.

"Fair trade gives us great development opportunities and can bring changes to our lives," says Dr Sharma of Tara Projects in India, which supplies fair trade crafts and furniture to Traidcraft. A non-profit organisation based in Delhi, Tara Projects serves some 25 community-based groups of artisans from all regions in North India. Several thousand people are involved (see Reason 29). Tara's objective is to help workers to achieve self-sufficiency. They have brought about major changes in groups and their communities due to fair trade sales. One of the products they make, and which Traidcraft sells, is the magnificent hand-carved "Sheesham Table", with a removable top and hinged base.

"Our fair trade furniture bring you examples of master-craftsmanship from all over the world," says Traidcraft. Also in Traidcraft's range is a handmade natural cane and wood table from Development Trading Ltd of Malawi, which works with "disadvantaged and vulnerable groups".

Based near Marlborough in Wiltshire, a small family business, New Overseas Traders (The India Shop), stocks a wide range of furniture made in India. It trades with family firms and co-operatives, aiming at long-term working relationships and continuous employment for craftspeople. Through fair trade, their aim is:

> to provide much needed employment particularly in rural areas and also to keep alive traditional craft skills. ... All

workers involved in making and packing our products are treated with respect in reasonable working conditions and are paid fair wages. No child is exploited. Our goods and production techniques are environmentally friendly. We support ideas for improving social, medical and education conditions for worker families involved in the production of our goods.

Included in its range are:

- hand-made slatted wooden sun loungers
- painted wooden bedside tables with twist legs and drawer
- white painted wooden benches
- elegant painted iron benches
- carved chairs with jute seat
- wooden tables
- coffee tables
- *bajot* tables with drawer
- occasional tables
- low tables
- Indian teak day beds
- wooden benches with ceramic tiles
- *jali* dining chair in sheesham wood and iron
- old shutter doors set into tables with glass
- traditional Takhat dining tables with hand carved side panels
- Takhat coffee tables
- grain wheel coffee tables
- *bajots* – a multi purpose piece of furniture that can be used as a footstool, plant stand or as an individual table for an oriental meal
- low long tables with carved legs
- south Indian desks
- cupboard and wardrobes
- shutter cupboards
- Himachal Pradesh chests

- old apothecary-type chests
- storage units
- lime-washed cupboards.

The India Shop is a member of the British Association of Fair Trade Shops (BAFTS).

Every toddler loves a chair of its own. Urchin specialises in fair trade products for kids. Included in its range are iron beds with raised sides that help to prevent bedding ending up on the floor. It also sells fair trade rattan chairs and stool sets, as well as Victorian-style wrought iron benches.

When you sit on your fair trade furniture to relax you can light up the room with hand-crafted candle lanterns, hanging lights and table lamps offered in the fair trade handicraft range of Bali Spirit.

Anjuna is a fair trade retail company based in County Armagh that specialises in providing furniture, gifts and handicrafts from India, Kashmir, Tibet, Nepal and Thailand. It is the first BAFTS-approved fair trade outlet in Northern Ireland. Nearly all its suppliers are BAFTS-approved importers.

For many items of fair trade furniture it's worth taking a good look in your nearest One World Shop. The One World Shop in Edinburgh, for example, stocks a wide range of fair trade furniture, including stylish Indian rosewood furniture, contemporary kitchen glassware from Bolivia, bamboo trays and vessels in citrus colours, vibrant basket ware from Ghana.

Project Feelgood Fair Trade Furniture is the name of a project mounted by students in the department of art, media and design at the London Metropolitan University. The project is using fair trade principles to design furniture such as rocking chairs, loungers, footstools/leg-rests, and drinks/reading tables. The aim is that most of the manufacturing will be done in Africa.

And why not spread fair trade furniture to the garden? Jute Works of Bangladesh supplies a hand-braided hammock, providing work that helps rural women in Bangladesh to improve their standing in society. The hammock, which is sold by Traidcraft, comes in a drawstring jute bag for storage.

Every item of fair trade furniture is unique and not mass produced. It is above all unique in the opportunities it gives the women and men who produce it. And when you invite guests to your home, your fair trade furniture makes a great talking point!

32. Rebuild lives and livelihoods

Fair trade has helped communities in the South recover from disasters like the 2004 tsunami and hurricanes Mitch and Stan. It's not just the money. Long-term relationships prove their worth in times of trouble.

Natural disasters often have a far more lasting impact in developing than in developed countries. And some human-made disasters hit the global South that would never be allowed to happen in the North. Either way, fair trade has offered a helping hand for over 30 years.

As early as the 1970s, People Tree's partner Action Bag, based in Saidpur, Bangladesh, was set up after the war of independence with Pakistan in 1971 to help Bangladesh's Urdu-speaking Bihari refugee community at a time of famine. The project initially trained 50 women, and their first orders came from Gepa, the leading German fair trade company. People Tree has worked with Action Bag for a decade.

Fair trade has played a part in Bhopal's recovery too. One night in December 1984, a maintenance error at the Union Carbide pesticide factory in the central Indian city released 40 tons of deadly gas. Half a million people were affected immediately, and 20,000 have since died. The toll continues, with blindness, breathing problems, gynae-cological disorders, cancer and birth defects. Affected communities still seek justice. In 1985 the Bhopal Rehabilitation Centre was set up to support victims of the tragedy with training in crafts production, self-employment and marketing. Leather wash bags made there are now marketed by Traidcraft.

Twenty years on, and Robert Mugabe inflicted Operation Murambatsvina ("Drive out rubbish") on Zimbabwe's urban poor, destroying the homes and businesses of 250,000 citizens. Most of the workers at Dezign Inc – a screen-printing company supplying Traidcraft – were evicted. Traidcraft quickly developed a new item for Dezign to make, providing much-needed work, and asked supporters for donations. By early 2006 sales and donations were enough to pay for land preparation, installation of water, drainage and electricity, and building foundations for new homes for 95 families.

AFTER THE TSUNAMI

When the tsunami hit South and Southeast Asia on Boxing Day 2004, an estimated 130,000 people died; 37,000 more are still missing. Half a million lost their homes. The fair trade movement was quick to respond. Traidcraft had links with producer groups in six affected countries, and some of these groups immediately helped with emergency relief.

In Sri Lanka, one of the worst affected countries, Traidcraft partner Gospel House helped deliver fresh water, food and clothing to badly hit communities and set up a medical centre. Other partners in Thailand, Indonesia and India assisted people who had lost their livelihoods, and Traidcraft made a donation towards rebuilding affected communities.

ForesTrade – importers of fair trade organic spices, vanilla beans, essential oils and coffee into the UK, USA and EU from small-scale farmers in Indonesia, India and Sri Lanka – set up a tsunami relief fund. It sent money to a partner, the Gayo Organic Coffee Farmers Association, in Aceh province, Indonesia, where the death toll was high and conditions were desperate. Gayo used its coffee warehouse as an emergency shelter and distributed blankets, clothing and food. "We're well rehearsed in disaster relief," said ForesTrade co-founder Thomas Fricke. "We were primed for immediate response. ... We have warehouses and trucks and a lot of people working, we were able to ... channel the resources where they're most urgently needed."

Many Asian members of the International Fair Trade Association (IFAT) provided post-tsunami aid and longer-term community support. In Sri Lanka the national Fair Trade Forum provided food, shelter, clothing and cooking utensils. Two Indonesian organisations, Pekerti and Yayasan Puspa Indah, set up rehabilitation programmes involving handicraft trading, home-based industry, start-up loans and business development.

India's Fair Trade Forum launched an emergency fund, while fair trade organisations provided relief and longer-term support to tsunami-affected coastal communities in southern India. Asha Handicrafts of Mumbai and the Indian Association for Fair Trade ran a rehabilitation programme for tsunami-devastated fishing communities in Tamil Nadu. Organising households into self-help groups, they distributed fishing nets, sewing machines, utensils, clothes, cooking oil and a telephone booth. Overseas support came from Tonbridge Baptist Church in the UK.

Help for Asian tsunami victims came from fair traders as far away as Peru. Café Femenino Foundation, founded by women coffee growers, sent relief funds to tsunami-affected growers in Sumatra, Indonesia.

MITCH AND STAN

Hurricane Mitch, one of the strongest, deadliest Atlantic hurricanes ever, battered Central America in October 1998. Close to 11,000 people died, mainly from flooding and mudslides. Thousands of people have never been accounted for. Honduras, Nicaragua and Guatemala were the worst-hit countries.

Fair trade importers responded wholeheartedly. Cafédirect donated £67,500 to the regional relief effort. In Nicaragua, Cafédirect partner PRODECOOP became a channel for outside aid, rebuilding homes and roads, and repairing coffee processing equipment. In Guatemala, the Fedecocagua co-operative, which supplies Fairtrade coffee to the UK Co-op, used international donations to rebuild damaged farms, processing plants, roads, bridges and a school.

Hurricane Stan, following seven years to the month after Mitch, was less severe and caused fewer deaths but still left a trail of destruction across southern Mexico and Central America. Coffee harvest losses in Guatemala were estimated at between 30 and 80 per cent.

Cafédirect took action again, setting up an online shop to assist grower communities in Chiapas, southern Mexico, and making an extra donation for every pack of Palenque-brand Fairtrade coffee sold. In February 2006 the president of the Cesmach coffee co-op, growers of Palenque, visited the UK and thanked people who had bought the coffee to help the relief effort.

Many US fair trade coffee importers raised donations and sent money to hurricane-affected farmer co-ops in southern Mexico and Guatemala too. In-country, the funds were used to reach out to remote communities where aid was most urgently needed, providing food, medicines and other essentials, and undertaking reconstruction efforts like repairing processing plants and reconditioning damaged coffee fields.

Several fair trade websites carried updates about the relief effort. "Practically all the roadways between the main cities and the communities are cut off," reported one. "Our biggest concern is for the communities that are further away and are in even steeper areas which tend to suffer landslides; these are the poorest communities."

"The major problem at the moment is disease and the associated risk of epidemics," said another. "Many people are suffering from intestinal infections, the flu, pneumonia and dermatologic diseases." A third explained:

> The harvest is about to begin, which means we will have to attend to many different situations: first, of course is providing relief where needed and then assisting with the reconstruction of the infrastructure of the production areas, and finally, the work of the harvest and export, to generate income for the producer families.

In raising funds for relief and reconstruction, US fair traders Equal Exchange said:

> Fair trade means having direct and long-term relationships with our trading partners. In addition to buying the farmers'

products at fair prices, we also try to accompany the co-operatives through whatever successes and challenges they face. ... Right now accompaniment means supporting those co-operatives whose members have been devastated by Hurricane Stan.

Others agreed: "Our commitment does not end with the purchase of the fair trade coffee bean. The families ... need our help now more then ever."

33. Make transnationals trade more fairly

Fair trade is a model of how international trade can and should be. There are signs that it's starting to put pressure on the big corporations to clean up their act.

Revolution is not too strong a word to explain the change in Britain's supermarkets when shoppers started buying fair trade goods.

At the end of the 1990s, shoppers would have found it difficult to buy a single Fairtrade-certified product from the supermarkets. Fair trade goods were largely purchased in specialist shops or by mail-order. But fair trade has proved too good for large companies to pass by. Supermarkets know that not to stock Fairtrade-certified goods would be to lose sales. They hope that the success enjoyed by these products will come to them. Sainsbury's, the Co-op, Waitrose, Tesco, Asda, Budgens, Spar, Somerfield, Booths and Morrisons – all the UK's major supermarkets – stock a growing range of Fairtrade-certified products. And it is not just food. In March 2006, Marks & Spencer became the first high-street retailer to offer a range of own-brand items made with Fairtrade-certified cotton, including T-shirts and socks.

The revolution has spread beyond the high street. Train travellers are increasingly enjoying Fairtrade-certified goods. Virgin Trains has switched all the tea, coffee, hot chocolate, sugar and chocolate sprinkles on board its trains to Fairtrade. And it has introduced Fairtrade into its executive lounges in several rail stations. The AMT Coffee takeaway coffee company – which has coffee kiosks in around 100 UK railway stations – serves only Fairtrade-certified coffee in its kiosks. Customer feedback had shown that their coffee drinkers wanted Fairtrade. Starbucks, Costa Coffee and Pret a Manger have responded to the demand.

The legal obligation of limited liability corporations is to make a profit for the people who own them – their shareholders. And selling more fair trade products helps them to fulfil that obligation. Not to respond to consumer demand would be fail shareholders. The opportunity for fair trade to scale up and influence large companies is therefore considerable.

But not all is sweetness and light. Limited liability companies can abuse their power and pursue profits in a unconstrained manner, regarding people and environment as resources to exploit. The big supermarkets have been accused of using their power to drive down prices to producers in developing countries. And while they embrace fair trade, supermarkets also engage in "price wars" that hit producers. In March 2006, for example, Asda started "a potentially savage price war" over bananas. It cut its banana prices by a quarter from an already low price "in a desperate bid to wean customers away from its rivals", say campaigners at Banana Link. They point out that:

This is a war which spells major collateral damage for people and the environment in banana exporting communities in West Africa and Latin America. Serious damage. It could mean that banana workers will be forced to stop sending their children to school.

By insisting on fair trade bananas, shoppers are making their views known to the supermarkets and can help to discourage such ruinous price wars.

THE NESTLÉ CONTROVERSY

Controversies can arise when major transnational corporations get involved with fair trade. This was brought into sharp focus when in 2005 a Nestlé product, Partners Blend, received certification from the Fairtrade Foundation.

Nestlé is Britain's most boycotted company. Campaigners have pointed to its "aggressive marketing of baby foods", "trade union busting activities, involvement in child labour, environmental destruction of its water bottling business, use of GM technology ..."

The coffee in Partners Blend comes from co-operatives of small farmers in El Salvador and Ethiopia and meets Fairtrade certification standards. "This is a turning point for us and for the coffee growers," said Harriet Lamb, director of the Fairtrade Foundation. "It's also a turning point for the many people who support Fairtrade and have been pressing the major companies to offer Fairtrade coffees. This just shows what we, the public, can achieve. Here is a major multinational listening to people and giving them what they want – a Fairtrade product."

Nestlé is the world's largest food company, with 8,500 products. Apart from Partners Blend, these continue to be traded as before. It had previously criticised fair trade but now said that market forces had changed its mind. "We found that there are consumers out there who are very interested in development issues that are probably not currently buying a Fairtrade product, and they would be attracted into this market by the strength of the Nescafe brand," said Hilary Parsons, head of Partners Blend.

Fairtrade Foundation member organisations Oxfam, the Women's Institute (WI) and People and Planet welcomed the move but with caution. Oxfam said Partners Blend was a "small first step" and that it was "pleased to see Nestlé responding to pressure from campaigners", although Nestlé and other major coffee roasters still had "a long way to go to address the coffee crisis".

The WI was "pleased that the Fairtrade certification granted to Nestlé will bring benefits to ... disadvantaged producers in Ethiopia and El Salvador. We hope the product is successful and that it will introduce the Fairtrade concept to a new audience." But it also said that it remained "seriously concerned about Nestlé's wider practices".

The student group People and Planet commented: "Whilst recognising that the introduction of a Fairtrade product is a step forward, we see no reason to review our support for the boycott of Nestlé"

Many campaigners, however, are strongly critical of this certification of a Nestlé product. According to a researcher with the Colombian Food Workers' Union, 150,000 coffee-farming families have lost their livelihoods due to Nestlé's policies. He labelled the Fairtrade product "a big joke".

According to Benedict Southworth, director of the World Development Movement, (a founder member of the Fairtrade Foundation):

> The launch of Nestlé Partner's Blend coffee is more likely to be an attempt to cash in a growing market or a cynical marketing exercise than represent the beginning of a fundamental shift in Nestlé's business model. If Nestlé really believes in Fairtrade coffee it will ... radically overhaul its business to ensure that all coffee farmers get a fair return for their efforts. Until then Nestlé will remain part of the problem not the solution.

"Anything that leads to companies such as Nestlé having a fairer relationship with suppliers is good," says Julian Oram of ActionAid. "But the FT mark could be used as a fig leaf to deflect attention away from some of the other issues that it has not resolved."

KRAFT

Problems may also arise when large companies launch products that appear to be fair trade but in reality fall short. Kraft, for example – the world's second largest food company, owning Kenco and Maxwell House – has launched a coffee brand called Kenco Sustainable Development.

Kraft says the coffee is made entirely from beans from certified sustainable farming sources and is independently certified by the

Rainforest Alliance, a not-for-profit organisation. It claims that on farms certified by the Alliance, forests and wildlife are preserved, and farm workers are treated with respect and have access to clean water, medical care and education for their children.

Kraft pays farmers who adhere to its ethical criteria a 20 per cent premium on the price of green coffee beans on the open market. When the world price is below 100 cents a pound – as it normally was between 2000 and August 2006 – farmers receive less than the 126 cents paid to them under the Fairtrade system.

The Fairtrade Foundation believes a proliferation of rival certifications "is bound to confuse people". "When people suggest these initiatives are 'like Fairtrade'," says deputy director Ian Bretman, "we have to point out they are, in fact, not Fairtrade."

Buying fair trade could help to establish improved practice among large companies. But entry into the fair trade system needs to be earned.

Paul Chandler, chief executive of Traidcraft, foresees the involvement of "mainstream" commercial companies accounting for "much of the growth in fair trade products". But more dedicated fair trade consumers will, he believes, "continue to give preference to buying from those organisations which are committed to the full fair trade vision".

Transnational companies talk much about "corporate responsibility", but need to turn the rhetoric into reality. By buying fair trade products, consumers are pressing transnational companies to trade more ethically and helping to raise standards.

The need for socially responsible behaviour by corporations is described by Paul Chandler as "more compelling than ever". Awareness of this is, he says, "in part attributable to the increased consumer support for fairer ways of doing trade".

34. Put paid to sweatshops

Worker exploitation is still all too common in the world's textile and clothing industries. Buying fair trade supports a genuine alternative that guarantees decent working conditions for all.

The world spends hundreds of billions of dollars a year on clothes. Western Europe accounts for about a third of the market. Most clothes we buy are imported from developing countries, where labour costs are lowest, and often from poorly regulated "free trade zones". In 2004 more than half the European Union's garment imports came from China, Turkey, Romania, Bangladesh and Tunisia.

Clothes are a labour-intensive, low-technology product. Labour costs are often less than 5 per cent – sometimes under 1 per cent – of the retail price. The industry is notorious for "sweatshops", defined by the US Labor Department as manufacturing workplaces that violate at least two basic labour laws such as apply to minimum wages, child labour and fire safety. Poverty pay, forced overtime, unsafe and unhealthy conditions, and lack of maternity and union rights are behind many of the high-street brand-name clothes we buy and wear. "Workers work in sweatshops because the alternatives are even worse," say UK campaigners No Sweat. "Indonesia's sweatshop workers take $60 per month ... the alternative is to join the tens of millions with no work at all in a country where there is not even a basic welfare state."

The vast majority of workers in this industry are women, often young unmarried rural migrants. Women comprise 85 per cent of garment workers in Bangladesh, 90 per cent in Cambodia. Unskilled female labour is seen as low cost and disposable. According to Oxfam's estimates, fewer than half the women in Bangladesh's textile and garment export industries have a contract; most have no maternity or health cover; they work on average 80 hours' overtime a month and receive on average only 60–80 per cent of earnings due. Sexual harassment is common. Those who complain are dismissed.

Women workers also often have to live in overcrowded, unsanitary dormitories. Severe ill health is common. Few last more than a few years in the industry.

Factory accidents happen frequently. In April 2005 the nine-floor Spectrum Sweater factory in Bangladesh – built without planning permission – collapsed at night, killing 64 shift workers. Survivors said their concerns about dangerous conditions were ignored by management.

Those who defend their rights are intimidated. After garment workers on an industrial estate near Dhaka, Bangladesh, demanded overdue wages in November 2003, a battle with police left one dead, five missing presumed dead, and 200 injured. A pay strike in May 2006 led to another clash in which one person was killed and 80 were injured as police opened fire.

Problems are not confined to developing countries. The US Labor Department found 67 per cent of garment factories in Los Angeles and 63 per cent in New York violating minimum wage and overtime laws.

Exploitation in this industry results from fierce competition between suppliers for orders. Big buyers, brands and retailers play off contractors against each other. "Reverse auctions" drive down prices. Orders are unpredictable, with short lead times. Factories cannot plan or maintain steady workloads. Workers have to stay overnight to meet deadlines. Cost-cutting suppliers use subcontractors and temporary and home workers, which means more insecurity and fewer rights.

Research since the 1990s has found oppressive and abusive working conditions behind many of the best-known brands. The UK's Arcadia Group (Topshop, Dorothy Perkins, Burton, Miss Selfridge), supermarket chain Tesco and global sportswear brands like Nike and Adidas have all been heavily criticised for worker exploitation in their supply chains.

In response, many leading brands and retailers have adopted codes of conduct, claiming this improves wages and working conditions. The UK government-backed Ethical Trading Initiative has strongly supported such schemes. Yet despite improvements little has changed for millions of the world's textile and garment workers. Codes of conduct are often poorly audited. Clothing supply chains for supermarkets, discount stores, mail order companies and sportswear are thought to perform particularly badly.

Oxfam's 2006 report *Offside! Labour rights and sportswear production in Asia* exposed the exploitation and sometimes violent oppression of Asian workers in the production of football boots and sports kits for global brands. Fila was found to be one of the worst offenders. During the 2006 World Cup, Oxfam criticised Adidas for failing to have an Indonesian supplier reinstate 33 workers whose sacking for a one-day strike was ruled illegal by the Indonesian Human Rights Commission.

SO WHAT'S THE ALTERNATIVE?

Buying clothes made from Fairtrade-certified cotton helps, because this ensures cotton growers earn a fair wage and that excessive agrochemicals use is avoided (see Reason 10). But cotton production is only the first stage in the supply chain. While major UK clothes retailers like Marks & Spencer have begun to sell some Fairtrade-certified cotton garments, the Fairtrade minimum price and social premium do not apply to other groups in the supply chain such as spinners or weavers.

This is why the fair trade movement is working on new industry-wide standards so that it can guarantee a better deal to other garment workers, but these have yet to be agreed. In the meantime, the best bet is to buy from smaller, dedicated fair trade and alternative trading companies that have signed up to the International Fair Trade Association (IFAT) code of practice (Reason 3). UK suppliers of 100 per cent fair trade clothing include Bishopston Trading, Chandni Chowk, Epona, Ethical Threads, Ganesha, Gossypium, Howies, Hug, Natural Collection, Pachacuti, People Tree and Traidcraft. These companies know which workshop produces what they sell and take a much closer interest in wage levels, working conditions and local communities' welfare than the big companies usually do.

People Tree, for example, aims to "set an example ... of Fair Trade as a form of business ... based on mutual respect between producer, trader and consumer". Its policies commit it to paying a fair price to producers; prompt payment; equal pay for women and men; safe and healthy working conditions; no exploitative child labour; giving opportunities to disadvantaged people; preserving traditional skills; environmentally careful production, packaging and transportation; and working with movements like the Clean Clothes Campaign for industry-wide change. People Tree's suppliers include small-scale producers and co-ops in Bangladesh, India, Kenya, Nepal and Peru that employ people with disabilities (Reason 49), low-income women, members of rural communities, and traditional craftspeople.

Ganesha, another leading UK ethical clothes company, works with geographically isolated and socially marginalised low-caste groups and religious minorities in India. Most dedicated fair trade clothing suppliers have a similar approach.

For people seeking sports kits, Fair Deal Trading currently seems to be the only UK supplier.

Though still tiny compared with the mainly exploitative global garment industry, the fair trade clothing business is growing steadily as a genuine alternative, offering an ever-widening range of "sweatshop-free" clothes to choose from.

35. Buy into a longer–term relationship

Fair trade importers sign long-term agreements with suppliers, sharing knowledge and commitment to help farmers succeed.

Mainstream international trade is a cut and thrust business, where loyalty counts for little. A company may think it has a good outlet for its product, customers it can rely on. But a competitor comes along, shaves a little off the price – and it's all change. Its business may collapse. There is no stability, no guarantee of a long-term business relationship.

Poorer producers especially need stability if they are to venture into exporting their goods. Fair trade encourages importers to place long-term contracts with co-operatives, and to place orders well in advance so that producers can plan their business with some security. Fair trade importers sign long-term agreements with suppliers. This enables even the poorest producers to have access to markets in developed countries for their products.

The trading standards of the "International Fairtrade Labelling Organisations" stipulate that traders must "sign contracts that allow for long-term planning and sustainable production practices", and "make partial advance payments when requested by producers".

The YMCA (Y Development Co-operative Co Ltd) in Chiang Mai, northern Thailand, has been exporting crafts to fair trade organisations since 1982, as well as selling locally. It works with more than 50 producer groups in northern, north-eastern and southern Thailand.

Many of the producers are women, who earn supplementary income through craftwork. It is also keen to encourage traditional skills, which are in danger of dying out, and to promote environmental awareness. Fair trade provides a significant market for some of the producers linked to the YMCA – ceramic and jewellery makers for example. Benefits include advance payments and design advice.

Some small-scale producers find it difficult to obtain finance to make their products available for export and often have to pay very high interest rates. Under the fair trade system, producers may request part-payment of orders in advance of delivery, for which a fair commercial cost should be passed on by the importer.

"The long-term relationship with fair trade organisations is important," says Nalinee Pussateva, the YMCA's export manager. Traidcraft point out that the stability that comes from a long-term trading relationship can encourage producers to "find wider groups of customers in a range of markets". One of Traidcraft's five key aims is to "build up long-term relationships, rather than looking for short-term commercial advantage".

The value of long-term trading relationships is stressed by all fair trade enterprises, and with different emphases. Gossypium, which specialises in fair trade and organic cotton products, highlights trust and understanding:

> We aim to work respectfully with our suppliers through a process of mutual respect and review. We believe in building up long-term trading relationships with our suppliers which enables all parties to develop the highest level of understanding about each others needs and constraints ... to foster trust and enable the development of quality products and the continuous assessment of ethical and environmental techniques ... leading to the development of reasonable and positive working conditions.

A long-term relationship allows more scope for buyers to share information with producers that will help them succeed in the marketplace. And the knowledge that funds are assured for a certain period makes producers more willing and able to invest in their enterprise. According to a report on the development of Max Havelaar coffee:

> Insecurity about income makes farmers and their organisations become hesitant to invest in, for instance, soil conservation or the best maintenance for their coffee plants. For this reason, the importers are asked to enter into contracts for longer periods, wherever the market development allows.

And it's not all one-way. "Direct, long-term relations with suppliers allow [coffee] roasters to maintain the continuity that they need for their blends," says the report.

HOW LONG IS LONG-TERM?

How long is long-term in the fair trade system? Fairtrade Labelling Organisations International (FLO) does not define "long-term" precisely. Its standards for banana growers do make a suggestion. They state that importers should sign a contract of purchase for Fairtrade bananas with every producer/exporter, "for a period of at least one year and preferably for longer". Fairtrade-certified banana producers like Regina Joseph (see Reason 23) have only a twelve-month contract with Tesco.

On cocoa and coffee, no period is mentioned in FLO's standards. On cocoa they state that buyers and sellers will "establish a long-term and stable relationship in which the rights and interests of both are mutually respected". For small-farmer coffee growers, the standards state that buyer and seller "will sign contractual agreements for the first part of the season and a letter of intent for the rest of the season, to be confirmed by purchase contracts as the harvest progresses".

Some companies have maintained a relationship with growers over a long period. Green & Black's, for example, have bought cocoa beans from Mayan farmers since 1994 for their Maya Gold chocolate (Reason 44). "We now have a long-term contract with them, guaranteeing to buy all the cocoa they can produce. This security has helped them to improve the quality of life and provide a better education for their families," says Green & Black's.

Some "long-term" contracts could usefully be longer and more specific. At present they may not be long enough for producers to plan ahead and have stability. What the retailer may regard as 'long-term" may be seen differently by producers.

But shoppers too can buy into a longer-term relationship with fair trade products – and we can make our own choice about how long is long-term. Buying a product consistently over a long period – of course providing that it satisfies on quality – encourages retailers to keep on stocking it. They will soon take fair trade products off the shelves if they don't sell.

The Max Havelaar report, mentioned above, stresses that fair trade "is embedded in the entire operation of the organisations and their empowerment process, which develops gradually. The effect of fair trade is a long-term effect and cannot be isolated from other factors and influences."

Fair trade is long-term trade. When we buy fair trade we know that buying a product consistently over a long period of time gives the producer stability, and assurance of income and livelihood.

36. Show solidarity with Palestinian farmers

Both Palestinians and Israelis have suffered immensely from conflict in the Middle East. Palestinian farming communities have been among the worst-hit economically. Now there's a way to enjoy flavoursome food while acting in solidarity.

Cultivation of olive trees began thousands of years ago in the eastern Mediterranean, and some of the world's oldest olive groves are in Palestine. Their age, the local climate, fertile soils and traditional organic farming are said to give Palestinian olive oil a special quality.

With two-thirds of Palestinian families living in the countryside, farming is central to the local economy. Olive production provides essential income for more than 70,000 Palestinian farming households. But production has suffered drastically as a result of Israel's occupation of the West Bank, the Israeli settlements, the Palestinian *intifada* (uprising) and, most recently, construction of Israel's "security fence" or "separation wall".

Many farmers have had their lands confiscated, their groves destroyed, are refused access or have to seek authorisation from the Israeli military to tend their trees. Irrigation water has been shut off. Farmers have sometimes been attacked by settlers while picking their fruit. According to Jerusalem's Applied Research Institute, more than half a million olive trees have been uprooted, bulldozed and burned by Israeli soldiers and settlers since 2000.

To produce high-quality oil, olives need pressing within hours of being picked. With movement of people and goods so restricted, Palestinian farmers have found it increasingly hard to process and sell their oil. Local markets have shrunk as economic hardship has taken hold in the West Bank and Gaza, and prices have slumped. It's said that over half the West Bank's olive oil is currently thrown away for lack of markets. Yet Palestinians must harvest their crops, because the Israeli state confiscates unfarmed land.

Olive grower Nazeeh Hassan Shalabi, a 37-year-old father of seven, can no longer access the 400 trees his family has owned for generations. Lacking the right transit permit, Nazeeh farms 240 trees on rented land near his home instead. "We use olive oil for so many things," he says. "Cooking, soap, as medicine on the skin, wood from the olive trees for heating – everything. Olive oil is at the soul of this community."

Inam, Nazeeh's wife, adds, "There are so many things that I would like to buy for the children but cannot, like clothes. My dream is just to have a normal life." For Palestinian student Reem Ihmaid:

> It is obvious that poverty is all over the place – now more than ever before. People here are so desperate. Palestinian farmers are willing to sell olive oil, or whatever they have, for just about any price they can, so they can put food on the table.

WORKING TOWARDS FAIR TRADE

Solidarity organisations and groups in Israel, Europe and North America market Palestinian olive oil under fair trade terms, while formal Fairtrade certification is pending. Among these groups are the Palestinian Fair Trade Association and Palestinian Agricultural Relief Committees, Green Action Israel, Olive Co-operative (UK), Oxfam International, Zatoun Canada, Zaytoun UK, Jews for Justice for Palestinians, and Alter-Eco France.

Tel-Aviv-based and Oxfam-backed Green Action sells Palestinian olive oil in Israel. The oil is bottled in the West Bank to maximise the value retained locally. Green Action's director Avi Levi says, "We want to bring both Palestinians and Israelis together by making the most of this economic opportunity and gradually we will start to see the development of a closer understanding between the two sides."

Zaytoun is the leading UK supplier, set up in 2003 by Heather Gardener and Cathi Davis, with support from Edinburgh fair trade co-op Equal Exchange and the Triodos Bank. Working on a non-profit basis, Zaytoun (Arabic for "olives") buys olive oil at fair trade prices from 80 West Bank co-operatives representing thousands of family farms, and from women-led Israeli fair trade suppliers Sindyanna, who work with Arab Israeli growers. Proceeds are channelled back to the producer communities.

"One of the guiding principles of fair trade is early payment to producers. The finance from Triodos allowed us to pay Palestinian farmers for enough oil to meet fast-growing demand in the UK," says Zaytoun's Cathi Davis.

There have been setbacks, such as in 2004 when a shipment of oil intended for the UK Christmas market was diverted to Italy and arrived three months late. But in 2005 Zaytoun sold three times as much as the year before. Sales channels include fair trade shops and worldshops, churches and other faith groups, solidarity groups and distribution partners such as Olive Co-op, which promotes responsible travel (see Reason 26) during the olive harvest season as well as educational and solidarity links in Palestine and Israel.

Together, Zaytoun and Olive Co-op have launched an olive tree replanting and sponsorship programme under the title Trees for Life – Planting Peace in Palestine. The Palestine Fair Trade Association distributes the trees to farmers who follow fair trade guidelines, bringing the promise of better livelihoods.

"Our ancestors planted the trees so that we could eat. We protect the trees so that we may live. It's how we remember our past and how we safeguard our future," says Jehad Abdo, chair of the West Bank Al-Zaytouna farmers' co-operative, set up with support from Zaytoun, War on Want and others.

Zaytoun also supports producer communities in improving their processes and infrastructure. It hopes soon to get the olive oil into the Co-op and other UK supermarkets, and is starting to import other agricultural produce from Palestine such as dates, almonds and couscous.

Another way to support Palestinian olive farming families is to buy traditional natural olive oil soap made by women in the West Bank and Gaza, supplied in the UK by Ganesha.

37. Reach for the goals

The world has set itself the enormous challenge of halving poverty by 2015. Fair trade, our purchasing power, can help get us there.

A bold and historic commitment. At the United Nations Millennium Summit in September 2000, leaders of 189 countries unanimously agreed on goals that were bold, historic and visionary. Goals that were a fitting way to mark the start of a new millennium.

Leaders committed to eight Millennium Development Goals (MDGs), designed to rescue people from poverty and bring hope of a better life for all. Comprising 18 targets and 48 indicators, the goals provide a clear, unambiguous plan to reduce poverty, hunger and disease.

- Goal number 1 is to eradicate extreme poverty and hunger. "Reduce by half the proportion of people living on less than a dollar a day. Reduce by half the proportion of people who suffer from hunger."
- Goal 2 is to achieve universal primary education. "Ensure that all boys and girls complete a full course of primary schooling."
- Goal 3 is to promote gender equality and empower women. "Eliminate gender disparity in primary and secondary education preferably by 2005, and at all levels by 2015."
- Goal 4 is to reduce child mortality. "Reduce by two-thirds the mortality rate among children under five."
- Goal 5 is about improving maternal health. "Reduce by three-quarters the maternal mortality ratio."
- Goal 6 concerns the need to combat HIV/AIDS, malaria and other diseases. "Halt and begin to reverse the spread of HIV/AIDS. Halt and begin to reverse the incidence of malaria and other major diseases."
- Goal 7 aims to reverse the "loss of environmental resources. Reduce by half the proportion of people without sustainable access to safe drinking water. Achieve significant improvement in lives of at least 100 million slum dwellers, by 2020."
- And finally, Goal 8 is to "develop a global partnership for development".

[133]

But almost half way to 2015, progress in achieving the goals is painfully slow. They are not being given either enough priority or resources. At the present rate of progress, most developing countries are likely to miss most of the goals.

There has been little improvement in the number of people living in poverty. "Progress towards reducing the number of hungry people in developing countries by half by 2015 has been very slow and the international community is far from reaching its hunger reduction targets and commitments set by the MDGs," said Dr Jacques Diouf, director-general of the UN Food and Agriculture Organization, in 2005. The number of hungry people remains obstinately high at over 800 million.

According to a World Bank report, undernourishment increased in sub-Saharan Africa between 1992 and 2002. Over a billion people continue to scrape by on less than a dollar a day. At the present rate of progress it could take some countries over 100 years rather than ten years to meet the poverty goal.

On reducing child mortality by two-thirds, some regions have made substantial progress, says the World Bank – East Asia, Latin America, the Middle East and North Africa, for example.

On primary education, 51 countries have achieved the goal of complete enrolment of eligible children but progress is slow in parts of Africa and Asia. Worldwide, over 100 million children of primary-school age remain out of school, almost 60 per cent of them girls.

The goals will not be met unless there is action in a number of ways. More resources are needed.

"A substantial increase in official development assistance is required in order to achieve the MDGs by 2015," said G8 leaders at the end of their summit in July 2005. Yet they are not providing those resources. The Organisation for Economic Co-operation and Development predicts an increase in development aid of $50 billion a year by 2010 – from $79 billion in 2004 to around $130 billion in 2010. Oxfam points to United Nations estimates that $180 billion a year is needed by 2010 if the goals are to be reached. An additional $100 billion a year, rather than $50 billion, is therefore called for.

"If rich countries reach the internationally agreed target of 0.7 per cent of gross national income," estimates Jo Leadbeater of Oxfam, "this would mean $250 billion in aid each year by 2010."

Aid will have to increase substantially by 2010 if the MDGs are to be met, rising from the envisaged $130 billion a year to $180 billion a year. This would still be short of the 0.7 per cent aid target. But a world summit of leaders at the United Nations in September 2005 did little to advance the goals. No additional commitments were made.

An increase in aid would be an important advance, but not enough to achieve the MDGs. The goals will not be reached unless there is action on trade justice (see Reason 43), debt relief (Reason 29), good governance and climate change.

On governance there is progress. Democracies are increasing. The 2005 Africa Commission report spoke of improvements in governance in Africa. But on climate change the situation is literally deadly. "A staggering 182 million people in sub-Saharan Africa alone could die of disease directly attributable to climate change by the end of the century," said a Christian Aid report in May 2006. Climate-induced floods and drought are becoming more common. Climate change is reducing the area of land available for farming.

FAIR TRADE AND THE GOALS

The world's poor deserve better. We need to press governments – but not wait for them. Action is needed by consumers. An expansion in sales of fair trade products could help millions of people to overcome poverty and bring the Millennium Development Goals within reach for more countries and people.

Fair trade gives producers a fair deal, paying a proper and stable price for their products, thus raising their income and opportunities to escape from poverty. It helps more children to go to school and to get a better deal from society (Reason 14). The fair trade movement has been instrumental, for example, in building up consumer pressure on coffee and banana companies to stop using forced and child labour and to examine their business practices.

Again fair trade helps to promote gender equality and to empower women (Reason 8). It helps to improve people's health and to ensure environmental sustainability. And it does a great deal to "develop a global partnership for development".

Among organisations linking fair trade with the MDGs is Women of Reform Judaism. Its executive committee declared in 2006, "Fair trade rules are necessary to meet the development goals."

So in addition to aid, debt relief, trade justice, action on climate change and other measures, fair trade is needed to rescue the MDGs. Says Harriet Lamb, executive director of the Fairtrade Foundation:

> If we are to reverse the catastrophic trends on poverty and reach the Millennium Development Goals, a whole new global economics needs to take centre stage, focusing on increased aid flows and further debt cancellation but also, and most critically, a more just global trade regime which puts at its core and has as a declared aim, not liberalisation but sustainable development.

The Millennium Development Goals are too crucial to be missed.

38. Be a progressive coffee drinker

Our high streets are full of coffee shops. Most of the coffee chains will sell you a cup of fair trade. But only one of them is co-owned by the coffee growers. That's Progreso.

The world slump in coffee prices has seen incomes of most of the world's 25 million coffee growers fall to a quarter of their 1960 purchasing power. Farm-gate prices often don't even cover production costs (see Reasons 2 and 9). The lost income means less to eat for the family, poorer healthcare, children out of school (especially girls), some farmers turning to grow illegal crops like coca in Colombia, migration to the cities (Reason 48) and a host of other problems.

Yet it's obvious that the price crash has not hurt the transnational coffee brands and retailers. Quite the opposite. Their profits have increased year on year as their market dominance has grown. Coffee drinking has undergone a sea change in the global North with the spread of chains of coffee shops like Starbucks, Coffee Republic and Costa. Yet coffee farmers usually earn 1p or less when you buy an unfair-trade cup of coffee in one of these chains.

At least we can now buy fair trade coffee almost everywhere. And in some places, like Marks & Spencer's cafés, all the coffee is fair trade. It's an improvement, bringing a slightly better share to the growers. Let's not knock it.

But Starbucks, the world's leading coffee chain, sells only a small proportion of its coffee as Fairtrade certified – less than 4 per cent in 2005. Starbucks does have its own schemes supporting producers, and it buys and sells more fair trade coffee each year. Even so, as Harriet Lamb, Fairtrade Foundation director, puts it, "The effort to which Starbucks has gone in comparison with the potential difference it could make is very small."

MAKING PROGRESS

Progreso Cafés Ltd is a different sort of coffee chain. There are still just two cafés so far – in London's Portobello Road and, the first to open, in late 2004, Covent Garden. But it's a chain run for the coffee growers, not to make fat cats fatter.

Naturally, Progreso sells 100-per-cent high-quality Fairtrade-certified coffee, tea and drinking chocolate, along with Fairtrade banana smoothies and a range of tasty cakes, savouries, soups, salads and sandwiches, fair trade and organic wherever possible.

The biggest difference, though, is that the growers also own a share of the business and will profit from its success. The idea was thought up by Oxfam and La Central coffee producers' co-operative in Honduras. The concept is simple. Twenty-five per cent of the shares in Progreso belong to the producer co-ops that supply the coffee. Another 25 per cent of company shares are held in a trust fund to support development projects in poor coffee-producer communities. And Oxfam, which has worked with small-scale coffee farmers since the 1960s, holds the other half of the shares.

For now, profits are ploughed back into the business. The aim is to have 20 Progreso branches running as soon as possible. "Bohemian urban villages" in London, south-east England and central Scotland are targeted for expansion. With growth, shareholders will begin to receive dividend payments.

Currently Progreso's coffee comes from three main suppliers, two of which co-own the company: La Central in Honduras, a nationwide network of more than 10,000 farmers organised in 80 co-operatives, and Oromia Coffee Farmers Co-operative Union in Ethiopia, which represents 35 co-ops, about 23,000 members and 100,000 families. The third main supplier, the Gayo Organic Coffee Farmers' Association in Aceh, Indonesia, is not yet a shareholding member of the company. They're working on it.

Another key partner is Glasgow-based Matthew Algie & Co., the UK's largest independent coffee-roasting company.

Actor Colin Firth is on Progreso's board and has worked hard to support and promote the chain. During 2005 he learned about every stage of coffee production, visiting the Oromia co-op in Ethiopia, going to Glasgow to see the beans being roasted, and serving behind the counter in Portobello Road. Firth was impressed by the people he met in Ethiopia. "They are incredibly articulate, they have first-hand experience of everything," he said. "They're the people that should be speaking, but they don't get heard."

Progreso is also supporting another great idea: One water. When you buy a bottle of One water in a Progreso café, all the profit is used to fund a South African-based charity called Roundabout. Roundabout install "roundabout play-pumps" in African villages – fun roundabouts that harness children's energy when they play to drive a water pump, bringing clean water up from underground into storage tanks. Each roundabout – more than 650 installed so far – is sited near a school or crèche to ensure there are plenty of willing young workers available to keep the water flowing.

Progreso is establishing itself in a very competitive sector. "Our café at Covent Garden used to be a Starbucks. Anecdotally we're doing more business than they used to and the Portobello site is getting busier," board member David Williamson said in 2005. "The stores have to be successful because of the quality of the coffee, the staff and the atmosphere. And they are."

39. Send hope to a hungry country

How Fairtrade-certified mangos are making a huge difference to people's lives in West Africa.

Burkina Faso is one of sub-Saharan Africa's poorest and most malnourished countries. In the southwest of the country, Issaka Sommande grows mangos on five hectares of land. He is a member of a co-operative known as Association Ton, which is situated in Niangoloko, near the border of Cote d'Ivoire, and was set up in 1991. It's a large co-operative of 2,000 members, all living in the villages of the area.

Both women and men work on mango production. Men look after the pruning and harvesting of trees and planting of new stock, while women are responsible for cutting and drying the fruit. Farmers in the area intercrop food crops such as millet, maize, sorghum and beans with their mangos. The dried mangos can provide their only cash income.

Each week a different village supplies fresh organic mangoes to Ton's central drying station, which is operated by a team of 100 women from the villages – all of whom are also members of the co-operative. The women then slice and dry them ready for export.

In 2003 Association Ton came across Fairtrade Labelling Organisations International. There was already a spirit of democratic and good governance in the co-operative and this helped them to gain certification from FLO. "Fairtrade certification has enabled us to lift ourselves up. It has given us a higher price, about 30 per cent higher – around £3.50 per kilo – and a much bigger market," says Issaka. And it truly is a much bigger market – "double what it was before they gained certification". So he is selling twice as much – and getting 30 per cent more!

Before Fairtrade certification, there was a lot of waste, he says, as not all the producers could find markets. Some of his mangos were just left on the trees.

In addition to growing mangos, Issaka is also employed by the co-operative, working as a project manager. He trains people in literacy training, HIV/AIDS prevention, and helping people to combat malaria. Ton runs literacy campaigns for its members and promotes reafforestation and good agricultural practice among members. Trees are viewed as important in keeping the nearby desert at bay.

As Ton's members are completely organic, everything has to be mulched and composted. The higher returns that members now receive for their mangos enables them to plant new trees more often. And new trees are more productive than older trees.

ASSOCIATION WOUOL

Arsene Sourabie grows mangos on his seven hectares for another co-operative in Burkina Faso, Association Wouol. Set up in 1975, Association Wouol has 1,300 members, with landholdings averaging around five hectares in size.

Not all the members grow mangos. Some work for the co-operative at its mango cutting and drying station, which employs 170 women. About 70 per cent of Wouol's members are women. Arsene also works for his co-operative as quality control manager in the drying stations.

"Fair trade has given me the hope of a market and I've extended the area under mangos," he says.

Wouol promotes good agricultural practice amongst its members, actively training them in organic farming. Members are also encouraged to diversify into new activities such as hibiscus, cashew nut and sesame farming. Antoine Sombie, chairman of Wouol, describes the co-operative's mission as being "to work with the producers and elevate their condition".

Issaka and Arsene say that selling through the fair trade system has made a big difference to them personally and to their community as a whole. More children are now able to go to school and the rate of malnutrition has declined to very low levels.

The two co-operatives have only just begun to receive the Fairtrade premium. In both cases, the way the premium will be used is to be decided democratically by an assembly of the co-operative, elected by members.

The recent war and continuing unrest in Cote d'Ivoire has stifled traffic through the area where the co-operatives operate, meaning that all the restaurants and shops have lost their customary trade from passing lorries and cars. To add to this squeeze on resources, many refugees from Cote d'Ivoire have travelled into the area, looking for help from relatives living on the Burkina Faso side of the border. Especially in this difficult context, Fairtrade-certified mangos have been a lifeline for many people.

All the mangoes from Ton and Wouol are Fairtrade and organic (Soil Association) certified, and 100 per cent free from preservatives. The two co-operatives sell their dried mangos to a UK-based company Tropical Wholefoods which imports tropical foods. The company became involved in fair trade about 15 years ago. "We heard about Burkina Faso's mango producers through TwinTrading, one of the UK's first fair trade organisations," says Kate Sebag, a director of Tropical Wholefoods. "Fair trade gives people the confidence to believe there is a market for their goods."

Tropical Wholefoods sells through health food shops, fair trade shops and Oxfam shops throughout the UK, and through mail order. It also has a bakery which uses dried fruits to make Tropical Wholefoods Fairtrade-certified cereal bars.

Fairtrade certification is enabling Issaka and Arsene and the 3,000 plus members of their co-operatives to enjoy the fruits of their labours.

Most of Burkina Faso's mangos are not however sold under the fair trade system. Many producers are vulnerable to exploitation by traders who come to their villages to buy fruit. In the country as a whole, hunger and malnutrition are rife. This is in stark contrast to the area where Association Ton and Wouol operate.

An expansion in sales of Fairtrade-certified mangos could give more producers the chance to enter the system and the opportunity of a better life.

40. Co-operate with co-operatives

Co-operatives and fair trade belong together.

Today's international co-operative movement began when the Rochdale Pioneers – low-paid Lancashire cotton weavers – set up a co-op shop to sell household groceries to working families in 1844. The Pioneers meant their business to be different from other local shops that exploited them. Each customer would be a voting member, with a say in how the shop was run. When there was a profit, every member would get a share. The Rochdale co-op was not the first but became a model that many other groups of working people followed.

Of course, co-operative working was not "invented" in the nineteenth century or in the UK. Throughout the global South, traditional societies have managed natural resources and met their needs collectively since time immemorial.

Today millions of co-ops large and small around the world have an estimated 800 million members and 100 million employees. One in three Canadians, one in four Singaporeans, one in five Kenyans and one in ten Colombians is said to belong to a co-op. Co-ops are active in every sector, from agriculture and fisheries to housing and financial services, from manufacturing and crafts to child care and health, from education and sport to water supply and public transport.

CO-OPS AND FAIR TRADE

The principles behind co-operatives are close to those of fair trade. Co-ops are set up to meet shared needs, belong to their members, are democratically run, distribute profits fairly and aim to provide quality goods and services for a fair price. "Co-operatives ... foster economic fairness by ensuring equal access to markets and services for their members, with membership being free and open," says the International Labour Organization. It's no surprise that co-ops have been associated with fair trade since it began. Or that many – if not most – fair trade producers are co-operatives.

In the UK, the Co-operative Group helped pioneer fair trade. "The Fairtrade stance ... has the potential to combine all the elements of being a successful co-operative business," the Co-op says. "Fairtrade is obviously about business (not charity), but doing business in a co-operative spirit reflecting the values and principles of the co-operative movement."

The Co-op got into fair trade because "Many of our members and customers are concerned about the effects of world trading systems and about the people producing goods in developing countries." The Co-op has led Fairtrade-certified food and drink retailing in the UK. It was the first major chain to sell Cafédirect coffee, brought the first fair trade bananas and pineapples to the UK and launched the country's first supermarket fair trade wine.

In 2003 the Co-op's fair trade own-label coffee became the first sold at a lower price than the commercial brands. This was hugely significant. Until then, fair trade coffee had usually cost more than mainstream. The Co-op's move meant that customers who bought solely on price could now buy fair trade – it came within reach of a lot more people.

STRENGTH IN NUMBERS

Among fair trade producers, the link with co-operative working is equally strong. The first ever fair trade coffee was imported into the Netherlands in 1973 from Guatemalan farmer co-ops. Today nearly 200 coffee co-ops worldwide, representing 675,000 farmers, produce Fairtrade coffee.

In many producer countries co-operative principles have found fertile ground in traditional culture. Low-income coffee producers of indigenous Mayan descent in the Chiapas region of Mexico, for example, formed the Kulaktik co-op in 1991 and sell to the fair trade market. Being a co-op is important to them: "We have been unified by the organisation. ... The group helps us to be independent of some of the problems in the area."

Working with other co-ops is a key strategy. "We have been able to connect with six other indigenous coffee co-operatives," says Kulaktik's president Juan Girón Lopez. "A smaller group would be unable to apply for credit. With credit, we are paid throughout the harvest."

Many producer co-operatives working in fair trade are umbrella organisations representing smaller co-ops. The Organisation of Northern Coffee Cooperatives (Cecocafen) in Nicaragua, for example, is made up of eleven such members. And Coocafé in Costa Rica, one of the first Fairtrade coffee producer co-ops, represents nine others.

Well-organised co-ops can be a powerful force for change. Peruvian coffee growers' co-ops set up a national association that has lobbied their government for support for the coffee sector and led in the development of regional policy on coffee among Andean countries.

A co-op with a high profile in the fair trade sector is Kuapa Kokoo of Ghana. Established in 1993, Kuapa Kokoo (the name means "Good Cocoa Farmers Company") comprises a farmers' union run by elected representatives of regional groupings of village societies, a trading company, a trust that allocates the Fairtrade social premium to community projects, and a farmers' credit union and banking service.

By 2005 Kuapa had 45,000 cocoa farmer members – almost a third of them women – grouped in over 1,000 village societies. The organisation maintains a strong level of women's representation on its councils and committees. Kuapa Kokoo member Mary, aged 53, a widow with seven children, says:

> Life before the farmer co-operative was set up was extremely difficult. ... Now, people look at me and they cannot believe that I have money. ... Before I joined Kuapa I never had a voice. Now I am treasurer of my society and I can speak.

Kuapa's output represents about 8 per cent of total world cocoa sales. It's unique in Ghana as the only licensed cocoa buying company owned and run by farmers.

It has another claim to fame too. Kuapa owns 47 per cent of the Day Chocolate Company, the UK company it set up in 1998 with Twin Trading, supported by the Body Shop, Christian Aid, Comic Relief, the UK's Department for International Development and NatWest Bank, to launch Divine brand Fairtrade chocolate (see Reason 44). Two elected Kuapa representatives sit on the company's board.

Day Chocolate makes Dubble, the Fairtrade chocolate bar for children. Not surprisingly, it also supplies all the chocolate for the Co-op's own-label range.

YOUNG CO-OPERATIVES

An imaginative link between the co-operative and fair trade movements in the UK is Young Co-operatives. Run with support from Traidcraft and the Co-operative Group, the programme enables 14–17-year-olds to manage their own democratic co-operative, gain business skills and learn about fair trade.

Young Co-operatives groups range in size from 2 to 30 youngsters. Under adult supervision, they make a business plan, select and price stock, research markets, design promotions, sell fair trade products from stalls in schools, churches, shopping centres and at events, manage the money and take part in a range of other activities.

Young Co-operatives also provides nationally recognised training credits, with successful participants gaining a Certificate in Co-operative and Fair Trade Enterprise accredited by the Open College Network – probably the UK's first fair trade qualification for young people.

There are more than 200 registered Young Co-operatives groups in the country. "These Young Co-operatives may not recognise them-selves as leading a worldwide social revolution, but in a small way they are," says *Guardian* journalist John Vidal.

41. Prove the free trade eggheads wrong

Some free trade economists disagree with fair trade. They say it distorts world markets, making everybody worse off in the long run. Here's why they are wrong.

Fair trade is one of the great successes of our time. In 2002 around 100 Fairtrade-certified products were available in the UK. By 2006 there were 2,000. Thousands of low income farmers and other producers in developing counties have worked their way out of poverty because of fair trade.

Yet a small number of people don't like fair trade – chiefly econ-omists who believe in the dogma of the free play of market forces. They dislike anything that distorts an eighteenth-century theory of economists such as Adam Smith and David Ricardo that we would all be better off if nothing stands in the way of market forces.

It was Ricardo who developed a theory known as "comparative advantage". This maintains that everyone will gain when countries specialise in producing those goods and services in which they have an advantage – that they can produce at lower cost than other countries. They then exchange those goods with goods produced by other countries on the same principle – in other words, trade them freely, without restrictions or distortions.

The theory sounds good – in theory. There are at least three big problems with it.

First, "free" trade fails the poor.
The theory may work if trade takes place between countries at equal stages of economic development. When it takes place between rich countries selling industrial goods and much poorer countries selling primary products, like coffee and tea, the theory collapses. The stronger gain, the poorer lose. This happened throughout the twentieth century when the theory was given every chance to work – but failed. It failed especially the poor and the hungry.

"Free" trade has a price tag. And the price is paid by the poor. "Free" trade has plunged millions into destitution and bankruptcy. As trade has been liberalised, especially since the 1980s, so cheap, often subsidised, goods have surged into developing countries, costing millions of their farmers and industrial workers their livelihoods.

"Free" trade advocates believe that countries should increase trade in foodstuffs and that the money earned from the exports would enable people to buy more food than they could have produced themselves. This is not supported by the facts. Says environmentalist and international women's rights campaigner Vandana Shiva of India:

> We were told we would be able to buy more food by selling flowers than we grew for ourselves. But selling flowers destroys your food security – you can only buy a quarter of the food that you stopped producing. For every dollar earned by shrimp exports, more than ten dollars in local food security is being destroyed.

Second, "free" trade theory does not deal with power.
Transnational corporations (TNCs) have effectively captured the

international trading system. It is TNCs that distort the system, not fair trade. They have moulded the system in their image, to suit their purposes. They argue for "free" trade when it suits them and for protection when that suits them. It is the subsidies that TNCs demand and get from Western governments that distort the system. They exercise undue influence in the World Trade Organization to secure the rules they want, and are subject to no international regulation (see Reason 35).

Long-time fair trade campaigner Pauline Tiffen describes "free" trade as:

> a myth, an exercise in self-deception, a lie. The history of trade is the history of organised commercial groups conniving and lobbying for protection and preferential treatment for themselves. ... Regulating and controlling trade has generally been the prerogative of the rich and privileged.

Says NGO campaigner Peggy Antrobus:

> "Free" trade to uphold unfair practices between powerful and powerless countries is anything but free. It speaks of a "rules-based" trading system while leaving unregulated the largest corporations and financial flows of the wealthy. It claims to reduce poverty while exacerbating the impoverishment of increasing numbers of people. It claims to create a "level playing field" while denying the major structural imbalances – political, economic and technological – between countries.

Third, it's damaging the environment.
"Free" trade philosophy encourages quite similar products (apples, for example) to be flown thousands of miles across the world, causing carbon emissions and adding to global warming. "Free" trade is not consistent with sustainable development.

Some of the trade has led to severe local environmental damage. Take the case of intensive prawn farming in coastal areas of Asian countries, for example. Because it is capable of earning additional foreign exchange, this type of farming has been encouraged by the IMF and the World Bank. In Asia it has led to mangrove forests being destroyed, to make way for shrimp farms. Mangroves serve to protect coastlines. When the tsunami struck Asian coastlines in December 2004 it caused more damage in areas where the mangroves and natural protection had gone.

THE CHARGE

The charge against fair trade (specifically in coffee) was put in an Adam Smith Institute report in 2004. This claimed:

> Well intentioned, interventionist schemes to lift prices above market levels ignore ... market realities. Accordingly, they are doomed to end in failure – or to offer cures that are worse than the disease. There are constructive measures that can help to ease the plight of struggling coffee farmers, but they consist of efforts to improve the market's performance – not block it or demonize it. ... Symbolic victories are the only kind that the fair trade movement is likely to achieve.

It is not easy to imagine how a system that guarantees poor farmers a fair return for their crop could make the situation for coffee growers any worse.

The charge against fair trade was developed in a report by Nestlé – before one of its products was given the Fairtrade Mark (Reason 33):

> If coffee farmers were paid fair trade prices exceeding the market price the result would be to encourage those farmers to increase coffee production, further distorting the imbalance between supply and demand and, therefore, depressing prices for green coffee.

It is certainly the case that too much coffee has been produced around the world. But if the situation ever came about where all coffee was fair traded, many millions of producers would be far better off than they are today.

According to *Guardian* journalist John Vidal, the Adam Smith Institute's paper:

> recommends that the public does nothing to help the poorest, that developing countries open up more to world trade and that peasant farmers diversify. Considering that the [UK] Government ... the World Bank and UN accept that unfettered trade can have a dreadful human toll, this seems a particularly stupid piece of work.

"Free" trade economists claim that free trade will contribute to people's welfare in the long term. But this overlooks the kind of the world that free trade is leading to – a world of disposessed small farmers, where TNCs own the means of production and have economic control of the lives of the poor. In this situation, poverty is hardly likely to be alleviated. The poor cannot rely on the long term to solve problems the international trading system has created for them in the short term.

Western countries did not develop by "free" trade alone but with a combination of open markets and protectionism. In the nineteenth and twentieth centuries, Britain opened its markets for some products while protecting sectors of the economy that could not face competition. A two-track approach was pursued.

Fair trade is a viable economic option for the third millennium. It is a proven approach to trade that is helping the poor to develop. Says the Fairtrade Foundation:

> Free trade puts farmers and social and environmental concerns last, pushes prices down and monopolies up. Fairtrade works in and through the market but with new techniques: it puts farmers, their communities and environment first, prices are guaranteed, the disadvantaged are given access, and more control is put into the hands of producers.

Fair trade does not distort markets. It makes markets work for the poor (Reason 46). In today's international economy, what passes for "free" trade is unfair trade. By their attacks on fair trade, "free trade" economists push a dogma which is an insult to the many thousands whose lives have been transformed by fair trade.

But in the words of the Biblical book of Proverbs – "a wise person overlooks an insult".

42. Make tomorrow's business happen today

Tomorrow's best companies will make many of today's ruthless, short-sighted businesses look like dinosaurs. Fair trade is one of the best models we have for taking capitalism on to a new, higher level.

There's a struggle going on at the heart of business. Between yesterday and tomorrow. Yesterday's men – like those who ran Enron – have been top dogs for too long. Tomorrow's women and men are on the rise. Many of them work in fair trade.

What's wrong with yesterday's view of business is neatly summarised in an article by socially responsible business guru Terry Mollner. "Capitalism is not the end of history," he writes. "There are higher layers of maturity of thinking ... [that] will eventually result in more mature economic agreements."

Mollner criticises the *Economist* magazine, which preaches the cause of global free-market capitalism, for saying that managers of publicly owned companies have only one duty, which is to maximise the value of business owners' assets. "At one time it was assumed to be ethical to use slaves," Mollner comments. "At another time it was assumed to be ethical to discriminate against women and minorities when it came to promotions ... [or] to allow people downstream to die from pollution."

Times change, and so does awareness of what's important in business. "Co-operation, not competition, is fundamental in nature," argues Mollner. "This means that the true highest self-interest is the good of all as one." Yet much of the business world is still trapped in the past:

> many of the most powerful organizations on the planet are not being run by people but by contracts that are not giving highest priority to the good of all as one. We would not support our children to run a lemonade stand in this way and it is frightening to think that we are running the planet in this way.

Mollner's view that "the time of allowing a single child to be born into poverty is over" is shared by many of the most progressive business thinkers today. The UK's Institute of Business Ethics, for example, says:

> People expect companies to look after their staff and tell customers the truth. They also increasingly expect companies to address their environmental impacts and make sure that the people who make their products are treated fairly, wherever the company operates.

And ethics pays in the longer term. Research shows that companies with a code of ethics generally outperform those without.

The Co-operative Bank says it turned away potential business worth £10 million on ethical grounds in 2005. But this was easily outweighed by the 34 per cent of its £96.5 million pre-tax profit that it claims resulted from being known for its ethical and sustainability policies.

THE SHAPE OF BUSINESS TO COME?

As tomorrow's business model emerges, a lot of it looks like fair trade. A Costa Rican delegate at an international conference on social development in 2000 put it this way:

The fair trade movement has become a tool in the search for a new international economic order in that it expresses the desire to reach a greater balance and social equality in trade relations between industrialized and developing countries ... helping reduce the unfair exchange that is detrimental to and increasingly impoverishing developing countries.

He went on:

The fair trade movement is a clear example of a social initiative to reduce poverty that offsets the powerful exclusionary forces that are created by the current globalization process. The movement shows ... how private investment strategies can be changed to better meet the needs of the poor. ... Through fair trade, the poor have more opportunities to play more meaningful roles in political and economic processes, creating a safer environment, strengthening human rights and stimulating cultural diversity.

Corporate responsibility commentator Alice Owen is another advocate of tomorrow's kind of business who sees fair trade as a model. She writes that "links between business activity and poverty may seem obvious, but they are not obvious in how businesses currently make decisions. ... The model that underpins these business decisions is wrong." In Owen's view:

there is a role for each individual ... in making personal decisions that reflect the complexity of the world. We all need to get beyond the fragmented view of the world and consider ourselves connected in a myriad of ways to other people and to the rest of the world. ... Acting as a connected consumer is the basis of the fair trade movement.

Owen imagines fair trade expanding into new areas such as the renewable energy market:

> Even your choice of energy supply has an effect far beyond your energy bill or the climate change effects. ... There is an important connection between third-world poverty and the amount of money that developed countries spend on fossil fuels. ... Your choice to buy renewable energy makes a difference. The growth of small-scale renewable energy generation could enable developing countries to determine their own energy policies, rather than becoming dependent on the system that the developed world has established.

"Thinking in a connected way actually enables you to make better decisions," Owen concludes.

New approaches to business developed by fair trade entrepreneurs are gaining increasing recognition. In 2006 Traidcraft, one of the UK's leading fair trade companies, won a Queen's Award for Enterprise. Traidcraft's mission is to fight poverty through trade and to change the way business works.

"For more than a quarter of a century Traidcraft has pioneered an approach to business which challenges the mainstream to adopt ways of doing business that are both equitable and sustainable," said Traidcraft managing director Paul Chandler on receiving the award. "If a small organisation like Traidcraft can do it – and benefit from it – then so can everyone."

The idea that a business's environmental and social impacts are just as important as its financial results is the basis of Triple Bottom Line (TBL) accounting. Instead of just one bottom line – money – forward-thinking companies recognise two more: impacts on people and on the environment.

Many companies talk about TBL, but few take it as seriously as Traidcraft, which has published annual "social accounts" since the early 1990s. It was one of the UK's first plcs – if not the first – to do so. Traidcraft's social accounts describe how the company's actions have contributed to reducing poverty and to "mobilising public opinion behind fair trade" and "influencing the ways that private sector companies and governmental bodies think about trade and its impact on the developing world". The accounts also report on how Traidcraft has contributed to "more sustainable livelihoods for our producers" and on efforts to meet environmental targets and improve environmental monitoring.

Traidcraft's future plans include opening regional offices in Africa and Asia to scale up its impact on poverty. And its development charity, Traidcraft Exchange, has been voted one of the UK's most innovative (see Reason 46).

43. Vote for trade justice

The movement for trade justice is growing all around the world. Fair trade is part of the solution.

People all over the world are buying and enjoying fair trade goods and services – and showing that they want fairness in the international trading system. They want producers to get a fair return. The growth is particularly apparent in the worlds richest countries, the G7 – Canada, France, Germany, Italy, Japan, the UK and the USA. Says Fairtrade Foundation executive director Harriet Lamb:

> The public across the G7 countries seem to have an insatiable appetite for Fairtrade. The Fairtrade Foundation and other organisations in FLO are rushing to keep up with the demand for a greater volume and range of products. Ordinary people, in this way, are showing that they do care about trade, it is important to them and they want trade justice. They buy Fairtrade products as a practical demonstration of their demand for trade justice. The governments of the G8 countries should follow their lead and put trade justice at the heart of trade.

When we buy fair trade, we vote for trade justice. Because fair trade points the way to trade justice. The rules of fair trade could be a model for the mainstream trading system.

"We have begun to engage trade negotiators in a dialogue over what fair trade can offer as a model for good trade rules – ones that truly contribute to sustainable development and the elimination of poverty," says Mark Ritchie of the US-based Institute for Agriculture and Trade Policy.

But are the governments of the G8 countries (the G7 + Russia) putting trade justice at the heart of trade? Hardly. They continue to push trade liberalisation, "free" trade, apparently having difficulty with the idea of "justice". Slow to listen, they are even slower to act.

Campaigners are pressing for trade justice in a number of ways, not least through the Trade Justice Movement (TJM). Formed in 2000, TJM is a UK initiative supported by more than 70 organisations with over 9 million members, and "new organisations are joining every month," it says. The movement includes trade unions, aid agencies, environment and human rights campaigns, fair trade organisations, faith and consumer groups. The TJM wants radical changes in the rules of international trade, rules:

> weighted to benefit poor people and the environment. We believe that everyone has the right to feed their families, make a decent living and protect their environment. But the rich and powerful are pursuing trade policies that put profits before the needs of people and the planet. To end poverty and protect the environment we need trade justice not free trade.

In particular, the movement is urging Western country governments to:

- Ensure that poor countries can choose the best solutions to end poverty and protect the environment.
- End export dumping that damages the livelihoods of poor communities around the world.
- Make laws that stop big business profiting at the expense of people and the environment.

Let's consider these points one by one.

Allowing developing countries to choose their own solutions is a matter of the most basic justice. At the G8 summit in 2005, governments of leading Western countries recognised that right. "We agreed that poor countries must decide and lead their own development strategies and economic policies," they said.

Especially through the World Bank and the International Monetary Fund, however, the West continues to make aid and debt relief conditional on developing countries liberalising their trade system. It's all part of the myth that "free" trade is the answer to poverty. Poor countries everywhere are being forced to open their markets to foreign companies and cheap – often subsidised – imports, to stop helping vulnerable producers and to privatise essential services. The results are devastating, the cost heavy.

According to a Christian Aid report, the countries of sub-Saharan Africa are a massive US$272 billion worse off because of "free" trade policies forced on them as a condition of receiving aid and debt relief. The figure represents the income that poor countries there have lost over the past 20 years as a result of being forced to open their markets to imports. "In human terms it represents tens of thousands of destroyed lives and years of lost opportunity. Two decades of liberalisation have cost sub-Saharan Africa roughly what it has received in aid over the same period," the report says.

The European Union wants to impose free-trade Economic Partnership Agreements (EPAs) on African, Caribbean and Pacific (ACP) countries. It proposes the elimination of all barriers on 90 per cent of trade between the two blocs. This would mean that nearly all the tariffs and other barriers on European agricultural and industrial goods to ACP countries would be scrapped. It's survival of the fittest – the richest. EU countries have the funds to exploit the new market opportunities. They stand to benefit far more than the poorer countries. This is the very opposite of helping the poor out of poverty, the opposite of trade justice.

Dumping of agricultural produce damages the livelihoods of poor communities and should be stopped. Dumping – selling goods below the cost of producing them – happens because of the large subsidies the Western governments hand to their farmers. These encourage overproduction. Much of the surplus is then dumped in developing countries, often putting local farmers out of business.

Yet governments have moved at a snail's pace to reform their farm subsidy regimes in a way that would stop dumping. At the WTO's ministerial meeting in Hong Kong in December 2005, agreement was reached to end farm export subsidies by 2013. Western governments made much of this. But export subsidies are only one type of farm support – they account for less than 5 per cent of overall farm supports. Ending export subsidies is unlikely to stop most of the dumping. Other forms of support will continue. The injustice goes on.

The focus for the TJM in the first half of 2006 was a campaign for laws to stop business profiting at the expense of people and the environment. A Company Law Reform Bill passing through the UK Parliament in 2006 sought to modernise company law and included measures to give company directors new duties to act in the interests of workers and the environment. But it appeared to have too many loopholes that could allow directors to wriggle out of their obligations. Campaigners believed the Bill would deny justice to people in other countries whose livelihoods and environments are being harmed by companies that behave irresponsibly. So they pressed for it to be amended to include a new clause which states that company directors should be held accountable for the social and environmental impact of their company's activities (see Reason 5).

A growing number of people support fair trade and trade justice. They are challenging a system which is failing the poor. "The success of the Fairtrade model challenges the neo-liberal paradigm of free trade which has unequivocally failed the poorest communities in Africa," says Harriet Lamb.

Trade justice is about making trade work for everybody. And fair trade is a key part of the effort to secure trade justice.

44. Enjoy that sweeter taste

Whether you're an occasional nibbler or an out-and-out chocoholic, buying fair trade chocolate leaves a sweeter taste in the mouth.

The cocoa (or cacao) tree *Theobroma cacao* originated in South America. The Maya and Aztecs fermented its beans and consumed it as a bitter, spicy drink. For the Aztecs it was an aphrodisiac. Montezuma is said to have drunk it 50 times a day.

The Spanish conquistador Hernan Cortés brought chocolate – so called from the Mayan word *xocoatl* – to Europe, where with added sugar and vanilla it became a popular drink. European colonisers set up cocoa plantations in the Caribbean and South America using slave labour. Later, in the nineteenth century, large-scale production began in West Africa.

In the UK we eat and drink half a million tonnes of chocolate a year, spending close to £4 billion annually, an average of £1.20 per person each week. Europe and North America account for more than half of global consumption.

Once the cocoa pods are harvested, a process of extracting and fermenting the beans, drying, roasting, grinding and blending turns the raw cocoa into chocolate.

West Africa produces more than two-thirds of the world's cocoa. Côte d'Ivoire is the leading producer country, followed by Ghana. An estimated 14 million people work in cocoa production worldwide, mainly on small family farms.

Nestlé, Mars, Cadbury-Schweppes and a few other transnationals dominate the world chocolate business, making a great deal of money from it. So do players on the international futures market, whose speculations result in sudden price movements that can hit small-scale cocoa growers hard.

Producers' incomes have fallen sharply since the mid-1980s to a level of only about 6 per cent of the value of retail sales. In Ghana this means average earnings below £200 a year. Cocoa farming in Côte d'Ivoire has been linked to the use of illegal child labour (see Reason 28).

Luckily there's plenty of fair trade chocolate on the market, including Green & Black's, Divine, Dubble, Co-op own brand, Traidcraft and Chocaid. Cocoa is a fair trade crop for farmer co-operatives in Belize, Bolivia, Cameroon, Costa Rica, Dominican Republic, Ecuador, Ghana and Nicaragua.

Problem solved? Not quite. Fair trade demand, through growing pretty fast, still represents only a fraction of the total chocolate market. So producers still have to sell most of their cocoa on the open market, at unpredictable and often damagingly low prices.

THE FIRST FAIR TRADE PRODUCT

In 1994 Green & Black's Maya Gold organic chocolate became the first UK Fairtrade-certified product. It began when Craig Sams, founder of Whole Earth Foods, visited Belize's poor Toledo district and enjoyed the local cocoa- and spice-flavoured brew made by indigenous Mayan farmers. The community had a lot of cocoa to sell but little hope of a decent price. Sams offered to buy direct from the local growers' association, committing to a fair, stable price for the next five years.

Farmers supplying Green & Black's cultivate their cocoa trees organically under native shade trees and alongside other crops (Reason 27). Green & Black's buys all the cocoa produced by the Toledo growers' association, paying a good minimum price plus the Fairtrade social premium and the cost of organic certification. It helps train local extension officers in agronomy, IT and administration. Secondary school enrolment of local children has risen sevenfold since Green & Black's got involved, and families have upgraded their homes to solid-floored wooden bungalows. When Hurricane Iris hit southern Belize in 2001, Green & Black's and the UK government helped foot the bill for replacing damaged and destroyed cocoa trees.

The community are setting up a local-language radio station, and working in a producer co-op helped the Maya become strong enough politically to prevent 250,000 acres of rainforest being logged for timber.

Not everybody was pleased when Sams sold Green & Black's to transnational Cadbury-Schweppes in 2005. Tim Lang, professor of food policy at City University, saw "a tension and contradiction" between a small ethical company like Green & Black's and its transnational owner. But Cadbury's said it was committed to the fair trade arrangements with Belizean cocoa farmers, and to Green & Black's moving forward as a separate business within the company.

For Sams, although not all Green & Black's brands are Fairtrade-certified brand, "All our trading practices have been fair and ethical from the beginning." The tie-up with Cadbury's, he says, "has facilitated the planting of nearly one million new organic cacao trees ... to help smallholder farmers keep up with escalating demand".

BEST OF THE BEST

For another fair trade chocolate success story, look no further than Kuapa Kokoo. "Just a lovely idea. But it cannot be done," a Ghanaian government representative told fair traders Twin Trading in 1993. Their aim was to help small cocoa farmers in Ghana set up their own company and sell their cocoa to the fair trade market.

Kuapa Kokoo – "The Good Cocoa Farmers Company" – was born when Twin gave start-up loans to 22 founding villages to buy weighing scales and other essentials. Kuapa adopted the motto "Pa Pa Pa" ("best of the best"). Most of the farmers who joined produced less than 20 bags of cocoa a year each at the time.

Kuapa is now a democratic co-operative comprising 1,000 village societies and tens of thousands of farmers. Organised on three levels – village, regional and national – it runs a trading company, a credit union, a social development fund and mobile health clinics. It has financed water and sanitation projects, income generation schemes, schools, corn mills and more.

Kuapa sells about 650 tonnes of cocoa annually to the fair trade market – supplying cocoa to Traidcraft, which uses it in many of its chocolate products, such as the chocolate Geobar and gift-wrapped Belgian chocolates.

Uniquely, Kuapa's members also own 47 per cent of the Day

Chocolate Company in the UK. Day makes Divine Chocolate (launched in 1998) and Dubble (launched with Comic Relief in 2000). With fast-rising sales, Divine and Dubble now offer a popular Fairtrade alternative to the big brands.

Dubble – a mixture of chocolate and puffed rice – is named after the double benefits of purchasing the product: the buyer gets good chocolate, and the cocoa growers get a better price. "Cocoa farmers feel really proud," says Kwabena Ohemeng-Tinyase, managing director of Kuapa Kokoo Limited and Day Chocolate board member. Day's managing director Sophi Tranchell believes Fairtrade chocolate can help raise standards industry-wide:

> It makes other companies look at their supply chains. ... We never expected everyone to turn into fair trade companies, but we hoped that they would ... do business better. It's worked in environmental terms – people have put pressure on companies and companies have had to change.

In mid 2006 Dubble, Comic Relief and educational charity Trading Visions held a series of "cocoa summits" for young people across the UK, to "bring alive the connection between the chocolate we all love and the not-so-sweet issues facing cocoa farmers in the developing world". The outcome was a "Chocolate Challenge Manifesto" presented by a Ghanaian–British youth delegation to UK International Development Secretary Hilary Benn, calling for a better deal for all cocoa farmers everywhere. Thirteen-year-old Isaac Owusu told Hilary Benn:

> We want the UK government to continue to support Fairtrade. ... My grandfather is a cocoa farmer and has been for a long time. Before, our lives were hard. Then my uncle read a book about Fairtrade and now my grandfather sends his cocoa beans to Fairtrade companies such as the Kuapa Kokoo and he gets a fair price for his products.

Accepting the manifesto, Mr Benn said:

Buying Fairtrade products is a way for everyone to make a difference in the lives of people living in poor countries. But we can all do more. We need to keep reminding people about Fairtrade, to keep talking about it.

45. Celebrate in March – and again in May

On the first two weeks in March and the second Saturday of May each year, fair trade organisations, campaigners and shoppers celebrate a better way of doing business.

And in March 2006 it was some celebration! Fairtrade Fortnight, traditionally held each year in the UK in first two weeks of March, was celebrated in 9,000 to 10,000 activities around the country. In workplaces, clubs, universities, cafes and restaurants, shops and supermarkets, churches and other venues, people gathered to taste the food and the fashions, drink the wine and the fruit juice – and do all sorts of different things. Fair trade parades, concerts and debates, to tea dances, fiestas and family days were among them. Activists were able to explain how a small change in shopping habits brings big changes for farmers and their communities in developing countries.

Fairtrade Fortnight is the brainchild of the Fairtrade Foundation but the events are organised locally. Every year has a different theme. The theme in 2006 was "Make Fairtrade Your Habit". The aim was to encourage people to become part of the "quiet revolution" which has seen such great Fairtrade success in the UK. And to persuade consumers who have purchased products carrying the Fairtrade Mark to buy a more varied selection from the wide range of products.

"So many people in the UK are won over by the idea of Fairtrade and want to shop with respect. Our challenge now is to make it easy to get the Fairtrade habit and switch to buying Fairtrade-certified goods," says the Fairtrade Foundation.

The biggest concentration of activities was in the 150 Fairtrade Towns, where Fairtrade is bringing together networks of supporters from local councillors to schoolchildren, retailers to faith groups (see Reason 16). More than 20 more cities, boroughs and towns achieved and announced Fairtrade Town status by the end of Fairtrade Fortnight (see Appendix 2).

A small number of fair trade growers are invited to the UK in the fortnight, and travel around the UK, taking in as many events as they can. Says Harriet Lamb of the Fairtrade Foundation:

> The thousands of Fairtrade Fortnight events bring Fairtrade alive because people can hear from the growers and workers themselves about the benefits of Fairtrade and taste-test products they have not tried before. Our experience is that when people understand the difference Fairtrade can make they are all too willing to choose the products, especially when they realise how good they are.

In 2007 the theme of Fairtrade Fortnight will be Change Today Choose Fairtrade.

WORLD FAIR TRADE DAY

World Fair Trade Day is an international celebration of fair trade, held each year on the second Saturday in May. Events take place worldwide and some of them continue throughout the whole of May.

World Fair Trade Day started as a European movement of over 2,000 world shops and fair trade shops, working together through NEWS! Movements to celebrate the same day and to campaign for fair trade in Japan and the USA joined them. "World Fair Trade Day" was initiated by Safia Minney, founder of People Tree, and adopted by IFAT members at a meeting in 2001.

The annual day has been raising the profile of fair trade ever since. IFAT member organisations in 70 countries, together with fair trade shops and networks, host events such as fair trade breakfasts, talks, music concerts, fashion shows and (again) a range of activities to promote fair trade and campaign for justice in trade. Fair trade products from marginalised communities, including coffee and tea, clothes, jewellery and handicrafts, are traditionally showcased on this day.

Fair trade shops and organisations have been crucial to the development of internationally agreed fair trade standards. With their knowledge and supply chain relationships, they have often led the way in launching new products.

Like Fairtrade Fortnight, World Fair Trade Day takes a different theme each year. In 2006 the theme was: Fair Trade Organisations NOW!

The day focused on the unique role of fair trade organisations, ranging from producer groups and fair trade companies, to retailers, and also the fair trade network. This is now huge, consisting of producer and consumer co-operatives, shops, collectives, advocacy groups, unions, producer groups, family workshops, fair trade shops, Internet stores, catalogue companies, religious institutions, NGOs, regional networks, national networks and many more.

Celebrating the day is again an opportunity to encourage conventional companies to sell more fair trade products. Said IFAT of the 2006 day:

> We call on 65 nations to push fair trade to the front of the political agenda. This year's World Fair Trade Day will showcase IFAT's dynamic network of FTOs around the world, proving what excellent role models for Business Sustainability they are, and highlighting their pioneering work in alleviating poverty through trade.

As developing countries face falling prices, subsidies and dumping, increased poverty and income disparities, and globalisation rules that are written by the rich countries, said IFAT, "there is a need for poverty alleviation through trade, and through campaigning to level the playing field. Fair Trade Organisations pioneer this international movement."

One of the messages for World Fair Trade Day 2006, received from Norma Velasquez Traverso, director of Peruvian producer group Minka Fair Trade, read:

We, as all southern poor producers, need more than better prices for our production. We need fair trade terms, we need equal partners, we need friends who can trust in us. We want to participate, with better roles, in changes of our unfair situation. We know that all together through joined actions can be built a better world. We know the way but we need that you are on our side.

By raising the profile of fair trade, the activities in March and May each year give a boost to poorer producers throughout the developing world.

46. Make markets really work for the poor

Fair trade organisations know more than most about the impacts markets have on poor people. And they have a pretty good record of delivering support and assistance where they're most needed.

It's official: MMW4P.

That's jargon for "Making Markets Work for the Poor", and at last governments are recognising the need to do this. Government aid agencies like the UK's Department for International Development and Sweden's International Development Cooperation Agency now recognise that globalised markets all too often work *against* poor people and the environment. So they're adopting the MMW4P approach. That means looking at ways to achieve "pro-poor growth" by reforming "market imperfections".

This would be fine if the same governments – and intergovernmental organisations like the European Union, World Bank, International Monetary Fund and World Trade Organization – were not also pushing international trade policies that keep making markets work *against* the poor and in favour of big business.

Western governments talk about the globalised market as if it's basically sound, with just a few "imperfections" that need fine-tuning. But with poverty killing 30,000-plus people a day, global income and wealth inequality growing year on year, and many environmental problems getting worse not better, the problems clearly go deeper.

To quote Nobel Prize-winning economist Joseph Stiglitz: "Critics of globalization accuse Western countries of hypocrisy, and the critics are right."

ANTIDOTE

The antidote to hypocrisy is putting your money where your mouth is. The fair trade movement does this in more ways than one. Traidcraft, for example, well known as the UK's largest fair trade organisation, also runs a successful international development programme, working through its charity Traidcraft Exchange – "the UK's only development charity specialising in making trade work for the poor".

The two sides of Traidcraft's work are complementary but independently financed. Traidcraft Plc ploughs back most of its surplus into growing the business, whereas Traidcraft Exchange runs mainly on grants and donations. Traidcraft Exchange promotes pro-poor trade approaches, fairer terms of trade and market access. It links fair trade buyers with suppliers and helps local organisations working with low-income people in some of the world's poorest countries build practical business skills and capacity.

DEVELOPMENT MODEL

Drawing on 25 years' experience, Traidcraft Exchange's "development model" concentrates on working with small and medium-sized enterprises in four regions where poverty and hardship are rife: East Africa, Southern Africa, South Asia and South-east Asia.

[167]

Take Kenya, where an estimated 80,000 people rely on wood-carving for a livelihood. As a result of markets not working for the poor, Kenyan woodcarvers have lost most of their international sales due to changing consumer trends, poor-quality finishing, lack of new designs and tough international competition. Traidcraft Exchange has been running a programme of product development support, helping Kenyan craftspeople develop products that are more suitable for export markets.

In neighbouring Tanzania, beekeeping and organic honey production have supported many low-income and landless households in the forested mid-west Tabora region. But again, market forces have had negative impacts. Responding to the collapse of the regionwide beekeepers' co-operative, Traidcraft Exchange has joined Tanzanian non-profit organisations in providing business support and employment opportunities to 900 beekeepers.

In Orissa, one of India's poorest states, many people struggle to earn a living through traditional crafts production but are often badly exploited by local traders. Traidcraft Exchange and its partners are running a capacity-building programme here for local business support organisations, with training workshops, mentoring and other forms of help.

Orissa's large indigenous population includes many communities that depend for their livelihood on production of non-timber forest products such as cashew nuts, tamarind, and medicinal and herbal extracts. Unregulated private traders rule the market. Traidcraft Exchange's Trade Justice for Tribal Communities project helps producers find alternative markets, improve terms of trade and have a say in decision making that affects their lives.

Traidcraft Exchange is also active in Bangladesh, helping develop income-generation projects among low-income villagers who live on the *chars* – temporary sandbanks in the river Brahmaputra. And in South-east Asia it has programmes in Cambodia, Laos, the Philippines and Viet Nam.

SHOELESS TECHNICIANS

Traidcraft is not the only fair trade organisation that runs and supports development programmes. Oxfam, Tearfund and other non-governmental organisations that played a key role in the early years of fair trade have been doing it for decades.

Training is often the key, with far-reaching impacts for individuals and communities. Elvia Marroquin Corea received training in organic coffee production as a member of the COMUCAP coffee co-op in an Oxfam-supported programme in Honduras:

> We received one year of training, then follow-up training. ... We were given the title *tecnicas descalzas* [shoeless technicians]. Shoeless because we were going to work very hard, so hard that we would have no shoes at the end of it! They chose me and two other women.
>
> The first year they sent us to the fields with the different groups, and we taught the other women what we had learned about organic coffee production – how to survey the land, prepare the earth, dig the holes, and apply the fertilizer. We started to put our learning into practice – and to learn by doing, because that's how you learn. With the little salary that we are starting to receive, I have been able to buy a little plot of land, and last year I grew five *quintales* [500 lb] of cherry coffee. This year I still haven't cut my coffee, so we will see how much I will get.

Fairtrade Labelling Organisations International (FLO), the umbrella certification body based in Germany, has set up in partnership with Netherlands-based international development organisation SNV to work with disadvantaged workers and producers in developing countries and support them in gaining access to international markets under fair conditions.

AgroFair, the Netherlands-based fair trade tropical fruit importer with sales across Western Europe including the UK, has its own development arm. AgroFair Assistance and Development works with local partners to help topical fruit producers with conversion to fair trade and organic production, certification and export promotion.

Buying fair trade – especially from dedicated fair trade suppliers – helps strengthen the movement. And the stronger the movement, the more it can do to ensure that markets really do benefit poor people.

47. Invest in fair trade

You can invest in the future by investing in fair trade

Buying fair trade goods is one thing – but there's more, much more. You can buy into fair trade by putting your money into enterprises that help fund the trade – Shared interest, the Co-operative Bank, and Triodos Bank, for example. Shared Interest is "the world's leading fair trade finance organisation". A co-operative, it aims to reduce poverty in the world by providing fair and just financial services. It started in 1990 and now has around 8,300 members who have invested more than £20 million. Owned and controlled by its members, it pools their savings to facilitate fair trade.

Shared Interest finances fair trade by:

• lending to and working with producer and buyer organisations who are committed to using fair trade principles
• promoting a North–South partnership
• enabling investors in the UK to share risk and take positive action to direct funds to borrowers working in poorer parts of the world
• listening to and promoting Southern voices and views
• strengthening the fair trade movement so that it continues to present a more just model of trade.

Shared Interest works with fair trade businesses all over the world, both producers and buyers, providing credit to enable producers to be paid in advance and to help fair trade develop. In 2005 it provided credit to 43 fair trade producers' organisations in 25 countries, and to 38 fair trade buyer organisations in 16 countries.

Shared Interest is a member of the International Fair Trade Association (IFAT), the Trade Justice Movement and the Fairtrade Foundation. It provides credit to fair trade organisations through its Clearing House. Like for example to Yayasan Mitra Bali (Mitra Bali Foundation) in Indonesia.

BALI

Yayasan Mitra Bali was established in 1993 with the support of local Oxfam representatives. Adhering to fair trade principles, it acts as a market and export facilitator for small craft producers who are missing out to large, well-established, businesses in the Bali tourism bonanza.

Without direct access to the tourist centres, it was difficult for those producers to access orders or even local trade. Yet, the contribution of these artisans to the development of the island is substantial. Their artistic output represents the visible face of Balinese Culture, which, ironically, helps to draw tourists and buyers to Bali.

A member of IFAT, Yayasan Mitra Bali works with around 100 producer groups employing over 1,000 men and women. To counter the marginalisation of these producers, it markets their products both locally and internationally, and exports internationally to both alternative and commercial buyers. Shared Interest and Yayasan Mitra Bali began working together in 2001. Shared Interest provides trade finance for their orders from several large buyer organisations.

Due to the terrorist bomb in October 2002, Bali has suffered a dramatic downturn in tourism and this has affected the livelihoods of many craftspeople on the island. But because of the relationships that Yayasan Mitra Bali has established with international fair trade buyers, the small producers they work with have been able to survive this difficult period and are now looking forward as the tourist trade picks up slowly.

Membership of Shared Interest's Clearing House is open to both buyer and producer members of IFAT, and to producers certified by FLO who have satisfied the credit criteria.

In addition to putting money into Shared Interest, investors are also offered the chance of becoming an "ambassador", speaking at local events and generating media interest, for example.

The Co-operative Bank advocates support for International Labour Organization Conventions, supporting businesses which take a responsible position with "regard to fair trade [and] labour rights in their own operations and through their supply chains in developing countries".

Triodos Bank lends only to charities, community groups, social businesses and environmental initiatives, from welfare to wind farms, health to housing, and organic food to fair trade organisations such as Cafédirect. The bank runs partnership accounts which connect people's money with "the causes closest to their hearts". It works, for example, with the Fairtrade Foundation, Friends of the Earth, the Soil Association, Amnesty International and the World Development Movement. Triodos offers a Fairtrade Saver Account and an ethical Individual Savings Account (ISA).

Jupiter Asset Management favours companies that ensure that the materials they use are "from organic or fair trade sources".

You can also invest in fair trade companies when they make a share issue. Cafédirect and Traidcraft have both done this. Investing in fair trade co-operatives, banks and companies may yield savers a lower interest rate but a high rate of satisfaction, knowing that you are helping to spread the benefits of fair trade to more people.

It is also worth looking at your mortgage and your pension. "Ask your provider whether they support Fairtrade companies. Let them know that you want returns but not at the cost of people's livelihoods," suggests *New Consumer* magazine.

Governments could be encouraged to invest in fair trade. The Commission for Africa, which reported in March 2005, said that increased funding from developed countries:

would help increase the participation of producer groups in

"fairtrade". The demand for products carrying the "fair-trade" mark is growing but investment is needed in building the capacity of producer groups in Africa to meet the rigorous demands of developed country markets.

Encourage governments yes, but also take a good look at your savings and ask – how can my money help to change the world?

48. Keep families and communities together

Family farms and rural communities are under threat everywhere from global economic forces. Fair trade helps them survive and thrive.

"To leave our land is to suffer," says Eduardo Verdugo, a coffee producer from Chiapas, southern Mexico.

For some, migration may be an act of choice, the pursuit of opportunity. But for many, little choice is left when earning a decent living at home becomes impossible. Within countries, says the UN, 180,000 rural people migrate to towns and cities daily. Internationally, 86 million workers are migrants. Some take family with them. Millions migrate alone.

Causes are complex, but the global economy plays a central role. "Actions of transnational corporations, international development and financial institutions ... heighten inequality among and within states, increas[ing] pressure to migrate," delegates at the World Conference Against Racism in 2000 concluded.

Because rural communities are often tied to a single commodity, migration can be seasonal. Haitian coffee producer Mercius Aristil told Oxfam:

When the coffee season is over, men tend to cross the border and leave the women at home with all the responsibilities of the house and the children. The money the men send home doesn't make up for this absence.

Worse happens when cash crop prices fall. When coffee prices collapsed in the late 1990s, millions of coffee farmers in Haiti, Mexico, Tanzania and other Southern countries were badly hit, and many were forced to migrate in search of work.

Interviews by Oxfam with Caribbean banana and coffee producers in 2002–04 told the same story:

- "Now farmers are leaving the industry. ... People are migrating or growing drugs," said St Vincent banana grower Nioka Abbott. Most of the farmers left locally were women.
- "We're not seeing young people coming into farming now," Amos Wiltshire, a Dominica banana farmer, told Oxfam. "Kids leave school and they don't want to work on the family farm. They're not interested in farming. ... Family life starts to disintegrate."
- "Young women are not so interested in staying in the countryside. There isn't much for them here," said Soutene Jean Baptise, a Haitian coffee producer.

Quality of life for migrants is notoriously bad. Millions who seek a new life in the cities of the global South cannot find decent work and get trapped in the shantytowns. "People [who] leave the countryside and migrate to the city," says Bernardo Jaén, a pineapple farmer in Costa Rica, "come into contact with serious problems such as unemployment, drug addiction and prostitution. They have no jobs to go to and no training to help them."

Much of world commodity production centres on large estates and plantations using migrant labour.

Whether rural-to-urban or international, migration disrupts families and communities, separating spouses and generations, often forever.

RIGHT TO REMAIN

The scale of the problem is huge, but fair trade makes a difference for individuals, families and communities.

Rural people in developing countries have a right to remain in their community if they choose. Fair trade offers decent livelihoods in place of poverty, dignity and hope in the face of humiliation and despair, staying put as an alternative to migration.

An important strategy is help for small-scale producers to diversify sources of income and reduce their dependency on a single market or crop. More labour-intensive organic and environmentally sensitive production (see Reason 27) helps create jobs, and farmers who receive a better price can in turn create better jobs for even poorer people who have no land of their own but survive as harvest labourers. Besides, fair trade's support for democratic structures (Reason 5) and community development projects promotes solidarity, collective decision making and hands-on solutions.

Many fair trade producers see it that way too.

Comments Nicaraguan coffee farmer Vincent Hernandez:

> The Fairtrade premium is absolutely critical to our survival as a community. Without it, we would be with the 21,000 unemployed coffee workers and their families camped out in the streets having lost their livelihoods and their homes.

Merling Preza, another Nicaraguan coffee grower, agrees: "Thanks to fair trade, the 2,400 families in our co-operative are staying on the land. ... They are eating fairly well at a time when hunger is a reality for many of their neighbours." Jorge Reina Aguilar of the ISMAM coffee co-op in Mexico says the same: "The more Fairtrade coffee we sell, the more stability we have in our community, and the less we have to migrate." And for St Vincent banana grower Denise Sutherland, "As long as I am selling in Fairtrade, I can earn enough to support my family. It is a vicious circle when you are not selling the Fairtrade bananas."

A small family farm in a developing country may support between six and eight people – working adults, children and grandparents. Fair trade offers hope to future generations too, as Haitian coffee farmer Luckson Bastien. points out:

> There are some younger people joining the co-op. ... By involving them in the training we motivated them to take part. ... I think that the co-op will continue into the next generation.

Reporting on its fair trade organic cotton initiative in India, Traidcraft found that, besides farmer incomes rising, "There is evidence that young people in the area are making a choice to get into agriculture rather than migrate to cities in search of employment. Migration to urban areas from the project area has decreased."

Going further, the Fairtrade Foundation reports a study in India that links fair trade cotton production to the first signs of migration *back to* the villages from urban centres. Alternative clothing company Bishopston Trading puts it well in the context of Bangladesh:

> Fair trade clothing has provided thousands of jobs for handweavers, hand embroiderers, block printers and tailors in the rural areas ... Fair trade provides an alternative to urban migration, enabling families to stay together, avoid the appalling living conditions of life in Dhaka slums.

Fair trade's recognition of the social importance of women is another important element in keeping families and communities together (Reason 8).

And let's not forget the multiplier effect. US faith-based NGO Lutheran World Relief provides this persuasive scenario:

> Someone, somewhere in North America buys a fair trade product. Because it's fair trade, more of the purchase price reaches the family who produced it. The extra income helps that family buy a hen it could never afford before. The family sells some eggs for income, supplements its meager diet with the remainder and raises some of the chicks to sell, generating more income.

Repeating the process, the family uses part of the income to pay school fees that they were unable to pay before. Because she returns to school instead of leaving the family to look for work in the city, the eldest daughter isn't lured into a lifestyle that puts her at risk of contracting HIV/AIDS. The math and literacy skills she gains in school come in handy when she starts her own small handcrafts business, generating further income and employing her brother.

Because this family is part of a fair trade co-operative, success stories like this are repeated dozens of times within this small community. Using profits re-invested by the co-op, the community makes quality-of-life improvements such as digging wells, upgrading sanitation systems and building schools and churches. Gradually, the economic, educational and healthcare systems of several communities improve, which begin to be felt at regional and even national levels.

It's a story too good to ignore.

49. Defend diversity

Everybody's in favour of diversity these days. Fair trade's commitment runs deeper than most.

Margaret Thatcher's 1980s catchphrase "There is no alternative" was supposed to justify rising inequality and social dislocation caused by hard-line neo-liberal policies. The "Iron Lady" even applied the phrase to Africa. Was the world's poorest continent meant to embrace full economic globalisation or fall off the map?

When it comes to trade and development, one size does not fit all, and there are alternatives, as this book shows. In 2001 "Another world is possible" became the motto of the World Social Forum's annual gatherings of social movements and networks opposed to corporate globalisation and committed to justice and sustainability.

Fair trade shares this alternative vision, one that celebrates human diversity and embraces partnerships with people the mainstream economy often rejects, such as indigenous peoples and people affected by disabilities. It's a vision of one world with space for many different worlds.

PEOPLE WITH DISABILITIES

One in five of the world's poorest people has a disability. Poverty will never be history until such people have a place in the economic system.

Ganesha and People Tree are among the UK's most successful suppliers of fair trade clothes, accessories and gifts, and both have active partnerships with disabled producers' organisations. Among People's Tree's suppliers are Assisi Garments in India and the Bombolu Workshop in Kenya. Assisi employs deaf and mute women in Tamil Nadu in the manufacture and supply of cotton clothing. Bombolu, one of Kenya's largest jewellery workshops, employs blind and visually impaired people, as well as people affected by other disabilities, in making famously beautiful jewellery.

Ganesha sells items made by disabled people's organisations in India, and its leather and felt bags and handicrafts are supplied by the Nepal Leprosy Trust, where sheltered workshops train and employ people affected by leprosy and other disabling conditions.

Other notable fair trade suppliers whose work by people with disabilities is sold in fair trade and worldshops in the UK include Jacaranda of Kenya and Reaching Out Handicrafts of Viet Nam. Jacaranda employs ex-students of a Nairobi school for children with learning difficulties. Its workshop produces fashion jewellery for export and local sale, using mainly local clay, ceramic beads and brass. Pay is costed to ensure a living wage.

Reaching Out Handicrafts works with disabled artisans across Viet Nam and hires them at its workshop in Hoi An. Currently supplying Silkwood Traders in the UK and Global Village in Canada, it provides training, advice and support programmes for its disabled workforce. Reaching Out takes pride in the fact that unlike other handicraft businesses in the country it retained all its workers during the 2003 SARS-induced slump in tourism.

INDIGENOUS PEOPLES

Three to four hundred million people worldwide belong to indigenous peoples (sometimes known as Aboriginal, First Nations, Native or Tribal peoples). With unique ancestral land-based cultures, they rely more directly than the rest of us on natural resources. Throughout the global South they are among the poorest of the poor.

Fair trade's fine record of working with indigenous peoples has earned it praise from the European Parliament: "Fair Trade has proven to be an effective tool to support indigenous people by giving them the opportunity to sell their goods directly to European markets while pursuing traditional ways of life and production."

The first growers to sell organic fair trade coffee were indigenous farmers in Oaxaca, Mexico. After a visit in 1985 from Dutch and German agronomists and fair traders, their organisation Union of Indigenous Communities in the Isthmus Region (UCIRI) switched to organic production and began selling to Gepa in Germany and Max Havelaar in the Netherlands.

Income among UCIRI's 2,000-plus member families is said to have doubled since then, and the farmers have set up the region's first public bus line. UCIRI's impressive website states: "We try to maintain our culture and wisdom ... and to value the good things given to us by our ancestors. We encourage our compatriots to speak their own languages, because it is our culture."

In Honduras, COMUCAP, an indigenous women's organisation, has developed from next to nothing to become another producer group exporting fair trade coffee to Europe. Dulce Marlen Contreras, COMUCAP's co-ordinator, tells the story:

In this region the majority of people are Lenca. The Lenca people have lost their language. It is believed that when the Spanish arrived and found the 'Indians', as they called us,

[179]

there were many more of us. It is thought that a great fight began. The only Indians left alive were those who emigrated to the mountains, and that is where we are found today. ...

We have a very special, deep respect for nature and for the land. ... Our ancestors were forced to exchange their land ... because they were very poor. After many years, the peasant groups got organised to recover their land, and that created conflict. During the 1980s many indigenous leaders were killed.

COMUCAP was formed in 1993, initially to promote women's rights, later moving into income generation:

Coffee is the main product grown in this area. Women used to go to work on other people's *fincas* [estates], and we realised that they already knew a lot about coffee. So we decided to start training them in organic coffee production – that was in 1999. ...

We trained the women in surveying, terracing, soil protection, making organic fertiliser, drilling the holes, and organic seedbed maintenance. Then we gave training on managing a tree nursery, planting trees, looking after the coffee. ... When Oxfam saw what we had done with the *manzana* [1.7 hectare plot] they had funded, they gave us the money to buy another 40. ...

Last year we sold our coffee for the first time. ... This year will be our first real harvest, and we hope to produce 400 *quintales* [1 *quintale* = 100 lb].

For the Advisais (indigenous peoples) of India, fair trade tea may prove equally important. Tea plantation workers and small producers include many Adivasi people.

Just Change is one of the most original approaches to working with Adivasi tea growers. Describing itself as "Fair Trade Plus", it was set up by activists and social entrepreneurs Mari and Stan Thekaekara with the idea of "taking fair trade further" by linking poor communities and encouraging them to trade among themselves.

Just Change India Producer Company is a co-operative founded by four Adivasi, women's and community groups. It has trading links with consumer groups in the UK and Germany. While currently trading internationally only in tea – grown by Adivasis in the Gudalur valley of the Nilgiri Hills, southern India – community groups involved in India also trade in rice, coconut oil, honey, soaps and umbrellas among themselves.

UK trading partners of Just Change include Unicorn and Eighth Day Co-op in Manchester, Out of This World in Newcastle, Soundbites in Derbyshire, and The Greenhouse in Norwich. Volunteers in London and Manchester are seeking links with like-minded community groups, co-ops, schools and faith groups.

Indigenous peoples also sell traditional crafts through fair trade. Minka Fair Trade in Peru, for example, markets the work of thousands of rural indigenous producers. People Tree, Traidcraft and others sell its hand-knitted woollen garments and other handicrafts. Minka was the first organisation based in the global South to become a member of the International Fair Trade Association (see Reason 3) and now runs ethical tourism projects in partnership with local communities (Reason 26).

50. Change the world!

Step by step ... we can change the world when we shop.

Start with a day in your life. See how far fair trade goods can be part of your life – and then identify the gaps. You can do something about those gaps.

You get out of bed in the morning and get dressed. There is no reason at all why you should not dress yourself from head to toe in fair trade clothes. If you're in doubt, take a good look at the People Tree and Traidcraft catalogues.

You eat breakfast. Wow! Take your pick from a vast range. Fruit juice, muesli, bananas, mangoes, pineapples and other fruits, nuts and raisins, coffee, tea, cocoa, marmalade and much more. Any gaps in the fair trade range? Well it could be the bread, and the wheat that makes it.

You go to work, wearing if it's appropriate your fair trade trainers. If you walk there, fine. But if you use public transport, cycle or drive, the fair trade trail goes cold.

If you work in an office, you may switch on your computer. Problems again (more below). You have a midmorning snack with a delicious Fairtrade Geobar. Lunch – again take your pick from the wide range of fair trade fruits, cook some rice or pasta and maybe spread a little jam or honey on the bread.

If everything stops for tea, you could add a piece of cake made with fairly traded sultanas from South Africa and sugar from Malawi.

Want a gift on your way home for someone? How about a box of Traidcraft's fair trade Belgium chocolates, or the Chocolate Lover's Gift Set?

For dinner, the rice and pasta again looks attractive, also a glass of delicious fair trade wine. For vegetables there are peppers and green beans. There are herbs and spices, chutney and sauces. There are gaps with meat and fish, but you could end with a fair trade yoghurt.

Should you fancy kicking a ball about in the evening, pick up a fair trade football. Maybe you want to read, watch television or listen to the radio – and again there are gaps. If you are planning ahead, consider a fair trade holiday for next year.

And so to bed. You pull on your fair trade pyjamas, take your pick from fair trade cotton sheets or duvet covers, until finally your head hits the fair trade pillow case.

You have a dream. You dream that you would like everything you buy, everything you use, to have been fairly traded. Can the dream be turned into reality? Let's start by asking questions.

Why can't our bread be fair traded? Traidcraft's pasta is made from durum wheat. Bread is of course more perishable, but let's press the case for a way to be found for fair trade bread.

FAIR TRADE MANUFACTURES? EVEN COMPONENTS?

"There is a very powerful message behind fair trade," says Harriet Lamb, executive director of the Fairtrade Foundation. "You can intervene successfully in markets. So logically, then, why not roll it out on a much larger scale?" Lamb expects more manufactured products coming from developing countries to carry the Fairtrade Mark so that more income is earned by the poor.

It's in the mechanical world that the biggest challenges lie. Products such as vehicles or computers – how could they be fairly traded when they are made up of components that probably come from many countries? So there is a need to go beyond finished products – most fair trade goods at present – and take a look at components. And ask – why cannot the components of manufactured goods be fairly traded?

Many manufactured goods are produced in conditions that are a long way from delivering justice to the people who make them. Take computers, for example. More than a third of computers are made in developing countries. The Catholic aid agency CAFOD has uncovered evidence that workers making computers in Thailand, Mexico and China are being exploited.

In China, workers are paid well below the minimum wage of £30 a month. They have to do illegal amounts of overtime to earn enough to live on, alleges CAFOD, and "can be hired and fired easily. They can't get social security benefits like food vouchers, maternity leave, holidays or pension."

The need for improvements is clear. Fair trade manufactured goods and components are worth pursuing. Otherwise too many people will be locked into an unfair system and locked into poverty.

If we ask the difficult questions, raise the unthinkable, then fair trade is ripe for huge expansion.

Sales of fair trade goods and services are already growing every day. The system may still be small compared with the mainstream trading system – an infant among giants, "but the future lies with the infant", says *New Internationalist* journalist David Ransom.

Can the future be fair trade? Could the fair trade system replace the present mainstream trading system as the chief way in which goods are traded? It could, if enough people want it to happen, if enough people insist that they want everything they buy and use to give the producer a fair return. The more fair trade goods we buy, the more we clamour for the range of goods to be increased, the sooner that becomes reality. Says Harriet Lamb:

> I hope that Fairtrade in five years time will be as much a part of British life as fish and chips – enjoyed with a cup of Fairtrade tea! We expect Fairtrade to become the norm – albeit a very special norm – so that products without the Mark are collecting dust on the shops' bottom shelves. And that more and more people in developing countries are getting the chance to build new and exciting Fairtrade businesses – from Colombian small-scale gold miners to rubber tappers in Sri Lanka, small-scale fishermen to silk cultivators.

Paul Chandler, chief executive of Traidcraft, believes that the rapid growth in sales of "fairly traded food and the range of food products will continue". He sees a new emphasis on increasing the proportion of added value generated in the South, "with fair trade producers moving beyond fair trade ingredient supply to supplying a greater range of finished products". Non-food products will be flowing through into the mainstream on a bigger scale "although this will have required new approaches to fair trade production to cope with the quantities, consistency of quality and sufficiently competitive prices required to break through".

Developing countries can be expected to exchange more fair trade goods between them in the coming years. At present, most fair trade is between South and North. But South–South trade in general has been growing rapidly in recent years; fair trade products are well placed to share in this growth.

"We expect that you'll be able to buy products with the Fairtrade Mark when you travel to India, South Africa or Brazil too as the global movement keeps on expanding," says Harriet Lamb, who goes on:

> My hope is that making Fairtrade our habit will become

plain common sense. People who grow our tea, bananas, sugar and cotton deserve the basic dignities of life just as much as we do, and just like us, want their kids to go to school and be treated when they get ill and have clean water to drink and enough food to eat. And they want the chance to sell their great products to us and our children – and show us every day that the future is Fairtrade.

During the next five years we can expect to see "increasing consumer recognition of the differences between Fairtrade-marked products coming from commercial players and those that are from dedicated fair trade organisations ... committed to pioneering new frontiers in fair trade", believes Paul Chandler.

So let's buy and live fair trade. For fair trade is consumer power, our power, in action. When we open our purses, our wallets, when we press for more fair trade, we can change the world for the poor, we can help people out of poverty. What an opportunity!

Notes and sources

The notes below give sources for almost every quotation included in the book, generally in the same order that the quotations appear in each Reason. Some notes give additional information and/or mention a key published or web resource.

INTRODUCTION

Martin Luther King, widely quoted, original source unknown.
Shah Abdus Salam, "Only fair trade can", World Fair Trade Day,
    www.wftday.org/english/messages/sub/articles/index06.htm.
Harriet Lamb, "Better than fair", *Developments*, (25), 2004,
    www.developments.org.uk/data/issue25/behind-fair-trade.htm.
Fairtrade Foundation: www.fairtrade.org.uk.
(Websites accessed 28 July 2006.)

1. BACK A SYSTEM THAT BENEFITS THE POOR

Renato Ruggiero, speech at the Royal Institute of International Affairs,
    London, 16 January 1998.
Ha-Joon Chang, in John Madeley, *A People's World*, 2003, London, Zed
    Books, 2003, pp. 40–1.
Make Poverty History: www.makepovertyhistory.com (accessed 4 May 2006).
David Korten, *When Corporations Rule the World*, 1995, London, Earthscan,
    1995, p. 12.

2. PAY SMALL-SCALE FARMERS A FAIRER PRICE

Oxfam GB, *Global Partners: Fairtrade and Local Authorities – How to
    Support Global Sustainable Development in your Locality*, 2001,
    www.fairtrade.org.uk/downloads/pdf/local_authority_guide.pdf.
Fairtrade Foundation, "Fairtrade bananas impact study", 2004,
    www.fairtrade.org.uk/downloads/pdf/dominica_profile.pdf.
Fairtrade Foundation, *Spilling the Beans on the Coffee Trade*, 1997, revised
    2002,
    www.fairtrade.org.uk/downloads/pdf/spilling.pdf.
(Websites accessed 14 July 2006.)

3. BUY PRODUCTS YOU CAN TRUST

FLO: www.fairtrade.net.
IFAT: www.ifat.org/joinifat.shtml.
Traidcraft: www.traidcraft.co.uk.
(Websites accessed 1 August 2006.)

4. HELP PRODUCERS BELIEVE IN TOMORROW

Fairtrade Foundation, *Highlights 2003*,
    www.fairtrade.org.uk/downloads/pdf/Fairtrade_highlights_2003.pdf.
Fairtrade Foundation,
    www.fairtrade.org.uk/suppliers_growers_tea_sivapackiam.htm.
Fairtrade Labelling Organisations International, "Have a nice cup of tea!",
    www.fairtrade.net/sites/impact/story2.html.
Tear Fund, "Fairtrade bananas",
    www.tearfund.org/webdocs/Website/Campaigning/Fairtrade%20bananas
    %20.pdf.
(Websites accessed 14 July 2006.)

5. MAKE TRADE MORE DEMOCRATIC

World Investment Report, 2005, New York and Geneva, UNCTAD.
Institute for Policy Studies: www.ips-dc.org.
FLO: www.fairtrade.net/standards.html
Right Corporate Wrongs: www.tjm.org.uk/action/corporate240106.shtml.
(Websites accessed 1 August 2006.)

6. PUT A HUMAN FACE ON DEVELOPMENT

Interview with Joel Uribe and Luis Villaroel of COASBA (Cooperativa
    Campesina Apícola Santa Bárbara), Santa Bárbara, Chile, 29 December
    2005.

7. ENSURE PLANTATION WORKERS EARN A LIVING WAGE

International Tea Committee: www.intteacomm.co.uk.
UK Tea Council: www.tea.co.uk.
Indian People's Tribunal report: www.oneworld.net/article/view/82821/1/.
Fairtrade Foundation: www.fairtrade.org.
(Websites accessed 1 August 2006.)

8. EMPOWER WOMEN AND GIRLS

Oxfam Make Trade Fair campaign, quoted at www.hattitrading.co.uk/fair_trade.php. Fairtrade Foundation, "Cotton on to Fairtrade", www.fairtrade.org.uk/pr171105.htm.
Fairtrade Foundation, "100 world food producers meet in London as world leaders talk trade in Cancun",
www.fairtrade.org.uk/pr050903.htm.
Traidcraft, "It's a new order – thanks to fair trade",
www.traidcraft.co.uk/template2.asp?pageID=1818.
(Websites accessed 14 July 2006.)

9. BRING HOPE TO COFFEE GROWERS

Interview with Blanca Rosa Molina, Reading International Solidarity Centre, UK, March 2003.

10. SAVE A COTTON FARMER'S LIFE

GM Watch, www.gmwatch.org/archive2.asp?arcid=6055.
India Together, www.indiatogether.org/2005/jan/agr-vidarbha2.htm.
Share the World's Resources, www.stwr.net/content/view/696/37.
Interview with Shailesh Patel during Fairtrade Fortnight, London, March 2006.
Agrocel Industries Ltd: www.agrocel-cotton.com.
(Websites accessed 14 July 2006.)

11. BE PART OF A GROWING GLOBAL MOVEMENT

FLO Annual Reports, 2004 and 2005: www.fairtrade.net.

Global Journey: www.ifat.org/globaljourney.

Fair Trade in Europe 2005: Facts and Figures on Fair Trade in 25 European countries, survey by Marie Krier, Brussels, Fair Trade Advocacy Office, www.ifat.org/downloads/marketing/FairTradeinEurope 2005.pdf.

(Websites accessed 1 August 2006.)

12. SAY "NUTS!" TO UNFAIR TRADE

Twin Trading, "Go nuts for Fairtrade!",
www.fairtradecookbook.org.uk/downloads/060525_twin_fairtrade_
nuts.doc.

"Fairtrade nuts reach UK despite Amazon floods",
www.peopleandplanet.net/doc.php?id=2704.

(Websites accessed 14 July 2006.)

13. ENJOY REAL QUALITY, PRODUCED WITH PRIDE

Fairtrade Foundation: www.fairtrade.org.uk/pr190306.htm, www.fairtrade.
org.uk/fc-spr00a.htm.

Harrogate Fairtrade campaign: www.harrogatefairtrade.co.uk.

John Vidal, "If you eat chocolate then you can make a difference", *Guardian*,
7 December 1999.

(Websites accessed 1 August 2006.)

14. SEND A CHILD TO SCHOOL

Oxfam Australia, "Coffee farmers' stories", www.oxfam.org.au/campaigns/
mtf/coffee/stories/index.html.

Oxfam GB, *Global Partners: Fairtrade and Local Authorities – How to Support Global Sustainable Development in your Locality*, 2001,
www.fairtrade.org.uk/downloads/pdf/local_authority_guide.pdf.

Cafédirect, "Day in the life of Cecilia Mwambebule", www.cafedirect.co.uk/
news.php/000074.html.

(Websites accessed 14 July 2006.)

15. KEEP ON MAKING POVERTY HISTORY

Caroline Maria de Jesus, *Child of the Dark*, diary of a Brazilian slum dweller, New York, Dutton, 1962, quoted at http://inic.utexas.edu/hemispheres/units/migration/Brazil.pdf.

Make Poverty History report, 28 December 2005: www.makepoverty history.org.

Reading Campaign to Make Poverty History, communication with authors, June 2006.

Harriet Lamb and Raymond Kimaro, www.fairtrade.org.uk/pr300705.htm.

Tony Blair, quoted at www.fairtrade.org.uk/pr080705.htm.

(Websites accessed 6 and 7 June 2006.)

16. MAKE YOUR TOWN A FAIRTRADE TOWN

George Foulkes, Bruce Crowther and Liaquat Ali Amod, quoted at www.fairtrade.org.uk.

Warwick University, quoted at www.peopleandplanet.org.

Information about becoming a Fairtrade town, city, country, borough, village, island, zone, university, college, school or place of worship is available from the Fairtrade Foundation: www.fairtrade.org.uk/get_involved.htm.

By mid-2006 there were 200 Fairtrade towns and other areas in the UK, with well over 200 more working towards Fairtrade status; 2,845 Fairtrade Churches, Cathedrals, Chapels and Quaker Meetings; 13 Fairtrade Synagogues; at least one Fairtrade Mosque; and 34 Fairtrade Colleges and Universities. See Appendix 2.

(Websites accessed 14 July 2006.)

17. BUILD CONFIDENCE, REDUCE RISK

International Coffee Organization, composite indicator price of arabica and robusta coffee, rounded to nearest cent: www.ico.org.

FLO International: www.fairtrade.net.

(Websites accessed 1 August 2006.)

18. GIVE SOMEONE'S HEALTH A BOOST

Fairtrade Foundation, *Unpeeling the Banana Trade*, 2000,
    www.fairtrade.org.uk/downloads/pdf/unpeeling.pdf.
Fairtrade Foundation, "Fairtrade bananas impact study", 2004,
    www.fairtrade.org.uk/downloads/pdf/dominica_profile.pdf.
Tearfund, "Fairtrade coffee",
    www.tearfund.org/webdocs/Website/Campaigning/Fairtrade% 20coffee
    %20.pdf.
(Websites accessed 14 July 2006.)
Nicaragua Solidarity Campaign,
    www.nicaraguasc.org.uk/partners/index.htm (accessed 14 March 2006).

19. PROMOTE HUMAN RIGHTS

United Nations: www.un.org/Overview/rights.html.
Traidcraft: www.traidcraft.co.uk/template2.asp?pageID=1780.
Amnesty International: www.amnesty.org/pages/ec-unnorms_2-eng.
Corporate Europe Observatory: www.corporateeurope.org/norms.html.
Fairtrade Foundation: www.fairtrade.org.uk/fc-spr00a.htm.
(Websites accessed 10 May 2006.)

20. FREE CHILD CARPET WORKERS

Rugmark: www.rugmark.net.
For a list of Rugmark suppliers, see Appendix 1, Where to buy fair trade.
Rugmark Germany, "A tough job on the bike",
    www.rugmark.de/english/navi/frnakg.htm.
Tanya Roberts-Davis "Leaving a 'rug' mark on child labour",
    www.equalitytoday.org/edition5/leaving.html.
(Websites accessed 14 July 2006.)

21. BYPASS THE INTERMEDIARIES

Juan Valverde Sánchez .
    www.fairtrade.org.uk/suppliers_growers_sugar_juan.htm.
Renson, www.fairtrade.org.uk/suppliers_growers_bananas_renson.htm.

Guillermo Vargas Leiton: www.fairtrade.org.uk/suppliers_growers_coffee_
   guillermo.htm.
(Websites accessed 29 March 2006.)

22. DRINK TO A BETTER WORLD

Interview with Sergio Allard, export director, Vinos Los Robles, Santiago,
   Chile, 22 December 2005.
Co-op Fairtrade website: www.co-opfairtrade.co.uk/pages/producers_
   beerwinespirits2.asp (accessed 18 July 2006).
Los Robles and many other fair trade wines are available in the UK from
   Traidcraft, independent stores and supermarkets. See Appendix 1 Where
   to buy fair trade.

23. TRANSFORM LIVES

Interview with Regina Joseph, Oxford, March 2005.
Windward Islands Fairtrade-certified bananas are available at all the big
   supermarket chains.

24. GIVE BAD BALLS THE BOOT

Fair trade sportsballs are available in the UK from Oxfam shops, Save the Children shops and fair trade shops, the Co-op and Fair Deal Trading. See
   Appendix 1, Where to buy fair trade.

25. STAMP OUT PESTICIDE POISONING

FAO press release, "New code on pesticides adopted", 4 November 2002,
   www.fao.org/english/newsroom/news/2002/10525-en.html.
J. Jeyaratnam, "Acute pesticide poisoning: a major global health problem",
   World Health Statistics Quarterly, 1990 43(3), pp. 139–44.
Annual Report of the Pesticide Residues Committee, 2002,
   www.pan-uk.org/poster.htm.
Friends of the Earth, "Do we really know what pesticides are in our food?",
   www.foe.co.uk/pubsinfo/briefings/html/20020111082053.htm.
Nicaraguan producer: www.nicaraguasc.org.uk/campaigns/index.htm.
(Websites accessed 26 and 27 April 2006.)

26. TRAVEL WITH RESPECT

Polly Pattullo with Orely Minelli, *The Ethical Travel Guide: Your Passport To Alternative Holidays*, London, Tourism Concern/Earthscan, 2006.

27. BE A FRIEND OF THE EARTH

Fairtrade Foundation, "Fairtrade standards",
    www.fairtrade.org.uk/about_standards.htm.
Soil Association: www.soilassociation.org.
Fairtrade Foundation, "Benefits of Fairtrade: a cleaner environment",
    www.fairtrade.org.uk/about_benefits_environment.htm.
TransFair USA: "Environmental benefits of fair trade coffee, cocoa & tea",
    www.transfairusa.org/pdfs/env.ben_coffee.cocoa.tea.pdf.
(Websites accessed 4 August 2006.)

28. END CHILD EXPLOITATION

British Association for Fair Trade Shops, "Stand up for their rights", campaign leaflet, 2005.
Brooke Shelby Biggs, "Slavery free chocolate?", 2002,
    www.alternet.org/story/12373/.
Human Rights Watch 2002 report, quoted in A. Nicholls and C. Opal, *Fair Trade: Market-Driven Ethical Consumption*, London, Sage, 2005, p. 39.
"Ecuador's banana fields, child labor is key to profits", *New York Times*, 13 July 2002,
    www.organicconsumers.org/Starbucks/0828_fair_trade.cfm.
(Websites accessed 18 July 2006.)

29. LIFT THE DEBT BURDEN

Fairtrade Foundation,
    www.fairtrade.org.uk/suppliers_growers_coffee_isabel.htm, and
    www.fairtrade.org.uk/fc-spr99.htm.
Christian Aid, "The damage done: aid, death and dogma", 2005,
    www.christianaid.org.uk.
Tara Projects: www.taraprojects.com
(Websites accessed 11 May 2006.)

30. SAY NO TO GMOs

Christian Aid, "Genetically modified crops: Christian Aid's concerns",
www.christian-aid.org.uk/indepth/0206gm/gmcrops.htm.

ActionAid, "Robbing coffee's cradle: GM coffee and its threat to poor farmers",
www.risc.org.uk/readingroom/coffee/GMcoffee.pdf.

"GM coffee 'threatens farmers'",
http://news.bbc.co.uk/1/hi/sci/tech/1332477.stm.

Fairtrade Foundation, "Redressing a global imbalance: the case for Fairtrade
certified cotton",
www.fairtrade.org.uk/downloads/pdf/cotton_briefing.pdf.

Friends of the Earth, "EU states must reject GM rice",
www.foe.co.uk/resource/press_releases/eu_states_must_reject_gm_r_
24032004.html.

Institute of Science in Society, "Mass deaths in sheep grazing on Bt cotton",
www.i-sis.org.uk/MDSGBTC.php.

On Dr Arpad Pusztai, see Andrew Rowell, *Don't Worry (It's Safe to Eat): The
True Story of GM Food, BSE and Foot and Mouth*, London, Earthscan,
2003.

(Websites accessed 18 July 2006.)

31. DO SOMETHING FUNKY WITH YOUR FURNITURE

Tara Projects: www.taraprojects.com.

Traidcraft: www.traidcraft.org.

New Overseas Traders: www.theindiashop.co.uk/acatalog/Furniture_ Range.
html.

Urchin: www.urchin.co.uk/articles/urchin-fairtrade-kids.html.

Bali Spirit: www.balispirit.com/products/bali_fairtrade_handicraft.html.

Anjuna: www.anjunaonline.com.

London Metropolitan University: www.londonmet.ac.uk/library/k49772_3.pdf.

(Websites accessed 29 and 30 May 2006.)

32. REBUILD LIVES AND LIVELIHOODS

"Thomas Fricke and Sylvia Blanchet: ForesTrade".
www.forestrade.com/images/ForesTade%20Profile%20-%20Fricke%20
&%20Blanchet%20(Mar-05).pdf.

Café Campesino, "Hurricane Stan ravages our Guatemalan friends",
www.cafecampesino.com/fairgrounds/0510/hurricane.html.

Sustainable Harvest, "First report in from APOCS leader Raniero Lec",
www.fairtrade.com/coffeefund/guatemala_2.htm.

Equal Exchange, "Hurricane Stan wreaks havoc on Central America and southern Mexico", www.equalexchange.com/hurricane-stan.

TransFair USA, "Three Seattle companies join to aid coffee co-operative destroyed by Hurricane Stan",
www.transfairusa.org/content/Downloads/UDEPOM_Donation_Release.doc?ndmViewId=news_view&newsId=20051021005051&newsLang=en.

(Websites accessed 18 July 2006.)

33. MAKE TRANSNATIONALS TRADE MORE FAIRLY

Banana Link:
www.bananalink.org.uk/images/walmart_banana_price_cuts_160306.pdf.

Baby Milk Action:
www.babymilkaction.org/press/press6oct05.html.

WDM:
www.wdm.org.uk/news/presrel/current/nestle.htm.

Fairtrade Foundation:
www.fairtrade.org.uk/pr071005.htm.

Nestlé:
www.news.bbc.co.uk/1/hi/business/4788662.stm.

Oxfam:
www.maketradefair.com/en/index.php?file=coffee_pr04.htm.

WI:
www.nfwi.org.uk/newsfile/newsitem.shtml?newsitem=051007-125912.

People and Planet:
www.peopleandplanet.org/news/story540.

Guardian:
www.guardian.co.uk/guardianweekly/outlook/story/0,,1580916,00.html.
www.guardian.co.uk/uk_news/story/0,3604,1356599,00.html.

Paul Chandler, correspondence with authors, July 2006.

34. PUT PAID TO SWEATSHOPS

Oxfam International, *Offside! Labour rights and sportswear production in Asia*, May 2006, www.oxfam.org.uk/what_we_do/issues/trade/offside_ sportswear.htm (accessed 18 July 2006).

For fair trade clothes suppliers, see Appendix 1, Where to buy fair trade.

35. BUY INTO A LONGER-TERM RELATIONSHIP

Traidcraft,www.traidcraft.org.uk/template2.asp?pageID=1650&fromID=1276.

Gossypium, www.gossypium.co.uk/x10170.html.

"Making trade work for the producers: 15 years of Fairtrade labelled coffee in the Netherlands", 2003, www.fairtrade.org.uk/resources_reports.htm.

FLO: www.fairtrade.net.

Green & Black's: www.greenandblacks.com/chocolate.php.

(Websites accessed 23 and 26 May 2006.)

36. SHOW SOLIDARITY WITH PALESTINIAN FARMERS

Oxfam GB, "Palestinian olive oil trickles to market", www.oxfam.org.uk/what_we_do/where_we_work/palterr_israel/oliveoil. htm.

Oxfam GB, "Palestinian and Israeli students take action to Make Trade Fair", www.oxfam.org.uk/what_we_do/where_we_work/palterr_israel/mtf_launch.htm.

Triodos Bank, "Slick oil", *Triodosnews*, spring 2006, p. 7, www.triodos.co.uk/uk/whats_new/triodos_news/?lang=.

(Websites accessed 18 July 2006.)

37. REACH FOR THE GOALS

MDGs: www.un.org/millenniumgoals.

FAO, www.fao.org/newsroom/en/news/2005/.

World Development Indicators, 2005: www.worldbank.org.

Oxfam International press release, 8 July 2005, www.oxfam.org/en/news/pressreleases2005.

Christian Aid, "The climate of poverty: facts, fears and hope", www.christian-aid.org.uk.

Women of Reform Judaism: www.wrj.rj.org/reso/ending_poverty.html.
Fairtrade Foundation, July 2005, www.fairtrade.org.uk/pr300705.htm.
(Websites accessed 1 June 06.)

38. BE A PROGRESSIVE COFFEE DRINKER

"Fair dunk'em", *Guardian*, 9 February 2006, http://business.guardian.co.uk/
economicdispatch/story/0,,1706406,00.html.
"Why Mark Darcy is full of beans for the latest fair-trade coffee venture",
Sunday Herald (Scotland), 19 June 2005.
www.sundayherald.com/50367.
(Websites accessed 18 July 2006.)

39. SEND HOPE TO A HUNGRY COUNTRY

Interview with Issaka Sommande, Arsene Sourabie and Kate Sebag, Reading
International Solidarity Centre, UK, March 2006.
Fairtrade mango products from Burkina Faso are sold under the brands Trop-
ical Wholefoods and Traidcraft and also used in the Day Chocolate
Company's Mango Divine Delights.

40. CO-OPERATE WITH CO-OPERATIVES

Working Out of Poverty, Geneva, ILO, 2003, quoted in Commonwealth
Secretariat, *Chains of Fortune: Linking Women Producers and Workers
with Global Markets*, London, 2004,
www.divinechocolate.com/shared_asp_files/uploadedfiles/
F7284775-DFCD-447D-B79F-0CCE784FD654_ChainsofFortune.pdf.
Co-operative Wholesale Society, "Co-op Fairtrade",
www.babymilkaction.org/pdfs/spinpdfs/appendices/Coop_
fairtrade.pdf.
Fairtrade Foundation, *Spilling the Beans on the Coffee Trade*, London, 1997,
revised 2002, www.fairtrade.org.uk/downloads/pdf/spilling.pdf.
Young Co-operatives: www.youngcooperatives.org.uk.
(Websites accessed 8 June 2006.)

41. PROVE THE FREE TRADE EGGHEADS WRONG

Vandana Shiva, speech to a meeting at the Royal Commonwealth Society, London, 14 October 1999.

Pauline Tiffen, speech to Fair Trade Futures Conference, Chicago, October 2005,
www.fairtradefederation.org/2005ftconference/pdf/workshops/Keynote_Pauline.pdf.

Peggy Antrobus, quoted in John Madeley, *A People's World*, London, Zed Books, 2003.

Adam Smith Institute, "Grounds for complaint? 'Fair trade' and the coffee crisis", 2004.

Nestlé report quoted in Oliver Balch, "A bitter pill to swallow", *Guardian*, 22 March 2004,
www.guardian.co.uk/fairtrade/story/0,,1175192,00.html.

John Vidal, "Eco soundings", *Guardian*, 24 March 2004,
http://society.guardian.co.uk/environment/story/0,,1176046,00.html.

Fairtrade Foundation, "Fair comment", autumn 2001,
www.fairtrade.org.uk/fc-aut01a.htm.

Proverbs 12-16b.

(Websites accessed 24 and 25 May 2006.)

42. MAKE TOMORROW'S BUSINESS HAPPEN TODAY

Terry Mollner, "The *Economist*'s thinking is yesterday, CSR thinking is today",www.via3.net/pooled/articles/BF_DOCART/view.asp?Q=BF_DOCART_131655.

Institute of Business Ethics, www.ibe.org.uk/faq.htm#diff.

Hernando Monje Granados, "Fair Trade: a social innovation for reducing poverty", www.icsw.org/copenhagen_implementation/copenhagen_papers/paper10/granados.htm.

Anne Owen, "Poverty, governance and individual action: how can the smallest of cogs turn the biggest of wheels?", www.article13.com/A13_ContentList.asp?strAction=GetPublication&PNID=1038.

International Fair Trade Association, "Alternative approach gains royal accolade", www.ifat.org/current/traidcraftqa.shtml.

Traidcraft, "Traidcraft's 2005 social accounts",
www.traidcraft.co.uk/socialaccounts.

(Websites accessed 18 July 2006.)

43. VOTE FOR TRADE JUSTICE

Fairtrade Foundation, July 2005, www.fairtrade.org.uk/pr300705.htm.
Mark Ritchie, "Fair trade and the WTO ministerial at Cancun", *Landmark*, January/February 2004.
Trade Justice Movement: www.tjm.org.uk.
Christian Aid, "The economics of failure: the real cost of 'free' trade for poor countries", June 2005,
    www.christianaid.org.uk/indepth/506liberalisation/index.htm.
G8 Gleanagles 2005, Chair's summary, 8 July.
(Websites accessed 5 and 6 May 2006.)

44. ENJOY THAT SWEETER TASTE

"When big business bites", *Guardian*, 8 June 2006,
    http://business.guardian.co.uk/story/0,,1792511,00.html.
"How a £1.50 chocolate bar saved a Mayan community from destruction", *Observer*, 28 May 2006,
    http://observer.guardian.co.uk/foodmonthly/story/0,,1781908,00.html.
Divine Chocolate: www.divinechocolate.com.
"Raising the bar", *Developments* (25), 2004,
    www.developments.org.uk/data/issue25/chocolate-save-world.htm.
Divine Chocolate, "Young Fairtraders from UK and Ghana present 'Chocolate Challenge' to International Development Secretary", June 2006,
    www.divinechocolate.com/Templates/Internal.asp?NodeID=90736&strAreaColor=.
Craig Sams, *Guardian* letters page, 12 June 2006.
(Websites accessed 18 July 2006.)

45. CELEBRATE IN MARCH – AND AGAIN IN MAY

Fairtrade Foundation, www.fairtrade.org.uk/pr060306.htm.
World Fair Trade Day: www.wftday.org/english/about_wftday/this_yrs_theme/index.htm.
Norma Velasquez Traverso, quoted at www.wftday.org/english/messages/sub/articles/index04.htm.
(Websites accessed 3 July and 1 August 2006.)

46. MAKE MARKETS REALLY WORK FOR THE POOR

Joseph Stiglitz, *Globalization and Its Discontents*, London, Penguin 2004.
Interview with Elvia Marroquin Corea, Honduras, 2003, kindly provided by
   Oxfam GB.

47. INVEST IN FAIR TRADE

Shared Interest: www.shared-interest.com/files/soc_ac_sum.pdf.
Co-operative Bank: www.co-operativebank.co.uk/s ... CoopBank/Page/
   tplPageStandard&c=Page.
Triodos Bank: www.triodos.co.uk/uk/personal_banking/savings/140289/
   ?version=1&lang=en.
Jupiter Asset Management: www.jupiteronline.co.uk.
New Consumer: www.newconsumer.org/index2.php?pageId=267.
Commission for Africa, qoted at www.fairtrade.org.uk/pr300705.htm.
(Websites accessed 3, 4 and 31 July 2006.)

48. KEEP FAMILIES AND COMMUNITIES TOGETHER

Oxfam interviews kindly provided by Oxfam GB.
Columban Fathers, www.columban.org/jpic/Migration/BorderIssues/July%
   2016%20-%20economic%20factors.PDF.
Dallas Peace Center, "The debate you're not hearing: immigration and trade",
   http://dallaspeacecenter.org/?q=node/847.
Fairtrade Foundation, "The world's first Fairtrade pineapples arrive in the
   UK", *Fair Comment*, spring 2003,
   www.fairtrade.org.uk/fc-spr03.htm.
Tearfund, "Uncovered: the lowdown – fairtrade", http://youth.tearfund.org/
   webdocs/Website/Youth/Bible%20study%20Fairtrade.pdf.
Claire Stoscheck, "The growing fair trade movement", Committee on
   US–Latin America Relations *Newsletter*, spring 2003,
   www.rso.cornell.edu/cuslar/newsletter/spring03/fairtrade.htm.
TransFair USA, www.transfairusa.org/content/about/global_reach.php#.
Wales Fair Trade Forum, *Newsletter*, spring 2003,
   www.walesfairtradeforum.org.uk/Newsletter4.html.
Traidcraft, Social Accounts 2004/5,
   www.traidcraft.co.uk/socialaccounts/sa_a6.html.

Bishopston Trading Company, www.bishopstontrading.co.uk/fair.htm.
Lutheran World Relief, "Fair trade and human rights: the perfect combination",
    www.lwr.org/toto/FT_HR.pdf.
(Websites accessed 18 July 2006.)

49. DEFEND DIVERSITY

Interview with Dulce Marlen Contreras, Honduras, kindly provided by
    Oxfam GB.
European Parliament, *Report on Fair Trade and Development*, rapporteur
    Frithjof Schmidt, 2006,
    www.europarl.europa.eu/omk/sipade3?PUBREF=-//EP//NONGML+
    REPORT+A6-2006-0207+0+DOC+PDF+V0//EN&L=EN&LEVEL=
    0& NAV=S&LSTDOC=Y (accessed 18 July 2006).

50. CHANGE THE WORLD!

CAFOD, "Clean up your computer" campaign, www.cafod.org.uk/get_
    involved/campaigning/clean_up_your_computer/what_s_wrong_
    with_my_computer.
David Ransom, *The No-Nonsense Guide to Fair Trade*, Oxford, New
    Internationalist, 2001.
"Better than fair", *Developments* (25), first quarter 2004,
    www.developments.org.uk/data/issue25/behind-fair-trade.htm.
Fairtrade Foundation press release, July 2005,
    www.fairtrade.org.uk/pr080705 .htm.
Paul Chandler and Harriet Lamb, correspondence with authors, July 2006.
(Websites accessed 12 July 2006.)

Appendix 1:
Where to buy fair trade

CONTENTS

Hundreds of Oxfam shops sell fair trade products. Find your nearest shop at: www.oxfam.org.uk/shop/online/index.htm.

All major supermarkets and most coffee-shop chains now sell Fairtrade-certified food and drink. For details of these and other retailers see the lists on the Fairtrade Foundation website at www.fairtrade.org.uk/suppliers_retailers.htm.

For the full range of Fairtrade-certified products, visit www.fairtrade.org.uk/products.htm.

1. FAIR TRADE AND WORLD SHOPS (BRITISH ASSOCIATION FOR FAIR TRADE SHOPS – BAFTS)

Channel Isles
mondomundi
Unit 4
St Martin's Court
St Martin's
Guernsey GY4 6AA
Tel: 07781 132686
phil.soulsby@fairtradeci.com
www.mondomundi.com

East Anglia
Art Gecko
15 Rose Crescent
Cambridge
Cambridgeshire CB2 3LL
Tel: 01223 367483
artgecko6@hotmail.com
www.Artgecko.co.uk

Just Sharing
The Free Church (URC)
Market Hill
St Ives, Huntingdon
Cambs PE27 5AL
Tel: 01480 496570
jsharing@fish.co.uk
www.stivesfreechurch.org

The Fair Trade Shop
15 Orwell Place
Ipswich IP4 1BD
Tel: 01473 288225
mlfish@fish.co.uk

Traders Fair World Shop
12 Museum Street
Colchester
Essex CO1 1TN
Tel: 01206 763380
tradersfair@fish.co.uk

The World Shop, Norwich
NEAD, 38 Exchange Street
Norwich
Norfolk NR2 1AX
Tel: 01603 610993
teresa@nead.org.uk
www.worldshop.org.uk

Midlands
Ethos
Little Tarrington Farm
Little Tarrington
Herefordshire HR1 4JA
Tel: 01432 890423
annie@hopline.farmcom.net
fairtrade@stmichaels

The Fair Trading Place
28 Market Place
Melbourne
Derbyshire DE73 8DS
Tel: 0845 458 5078
leesderby@aol.com

The Fairtrading Post
8a Burton Street
Melton Mowbray
Leicestershire LE13 1AE
Tel: 01664 503027
dolores.harvey@ntlworld.com

Just Fair Trade
10 Bishop Street
Town Hall Square
Leicester
Leicestershire LE1 6AF
Tel: 0116 2559123
sarah@justfairtrade.com
www.justfairtrade.com

St Michael at the Northgate
Cornmarket Street
Oxford
Oxfordshire OX1 3EY
Tel: 01865 722505
claretegla@hotmail.com

Shared Earth
87 New Street
Birmingham B2 4BA
Tel: 0121 633 0151
jp@sharedearth.co.uk
www.sharedearth.co.uk

Traid Links
20 Market Place

Wirksworth
Derbyshire DE4 4ET
Tel: 01629 824393
info@traid-links.co.uk
www.traid-links.co.uk

Wikijum
61 High Street
Stone
Staffs ST15 8AD
Tel: 01785 819508
wikijum@aol.com

World of Difference
20 High St
Rugby
Warks CV21 3BG
Tel: 01788 579191
info@worldofdifference.org.uk

North East
3W Trading
St Mary's Court Shopping Arca
North Bar Within
Beverley
Yorkshire HU17 8DG
Tel: 01482-888020
info@3wtrading.com
www.3wtrading.com

Elemental
8 Main Street
Ingleton
Via Carnforth
N Yorks LA6 3EB
Tel: 015242 42626
heather@elementallife.co.uk
www.elementallife.co.uk

Fair Trade Parties
13 Farnley Lane, Otley
West Yorkshire LS21 2AB
Tel: 01943 850645
sima@fairtradeparties.co.uk
www.fairtradeparties.co.uk

Fairer World
84 Gillygate
York YO31 7EQ
Tel: 01904 655116
fairerwrld@aol.com

Gateway World Shop
Market Place
Durham DH1 3NJ
Tel: 0191 384 7173
info@gatewayworldshop.co.uk

Hull One World Shop
c/o Methodist Central Hall
Waltham St, King Edward Street
Hull HU1 3SQ
Tel: 01482 327727
info@oneworldhull.co.uk
www.oneworldhull.co.uk

Just Bazaar
Unit 20, The Colonnade
Piece Hall
Halifax
West Yorkshire HX1 1RE
Tel: 01422 832248
philippateal@ukonline.co.uk
www.justbazaar.co.uk

Radish
128 Harrogate Road
Chapel Allerton

Leeds
Yorks LS7 4NZ
Tel: 0113 2694241
info@radishweb.co.uk
www.radishweb.co.uk

Shared Earth
1 Minster Gates
York
Yorkshire YO1 7HL
Tel: 01904 655314
jp@sharedearth.co.uk
www.sharedearth.co.uk

Sonia's Smile
85 Main street
Haworth, West Yorks BD22 8DA
Tel: 01535 647776
rita@soniassmile.com
www.soniassmile.com

Traidcraft shop
(different location each Christmas)
Middlesbrough
Teesside TS21 1DR
Tel: 01740 630475
medhurst@clara.co.uk

North West
Carlisle World Shop
1 Lowthian's Lane, English Street
Carlisle CA3 8JR
Tel: 01228 550385
l.strong@rattenrow.co.uk

Chester Fair Trading
Wesley Methodist Church
St.John's Street
Chester CH1 1DA

Tel: 01829 770847
info@bafts.org.uk

Fair 4 All
Stall 38/39, Retail Market
Academy Way
Warrington WA1 2EN
Tel: 01925 415121
afthomson@ntlworld.com

Fairground
Wesley Hall Methodist Church
Paradise Lane
Blackburn BB2 1LQ
Tel: 01254 682210
info@bafts.org.uk

Fairly Goods
4 Woodfield Road
Chorley
Lancashire PR7 1QT
Tel: 01257 271216
info@fairlygoods.co.uk
www.fairlygoods.co.uk

Justicia
81 Knowsley Street
Bolton
Lancs BL1 2BJ
Tel: 01204 363308
shop@justicia.greenisp.org

Shakti Man
68 Parliament Street
Ramsey
Isle of Man IM8 1AJ
Tel: 01624 815060
shaktinepal@hotmail.com

Shared Earth
86 The Merrion Centre
Leeds
Yorkshire LS2 8PJ
Tel: 0113 2426424
jp@sharedearth.co.uk
www.sharedearth.co.uk

Shared Earth
51 Piccadilly
Manchester M1 2AP
Tel: 0161 236 1014
jp@sharedearth.co.uk
www.sharedearth.co.uk

Tierra Canela
60 Dickens Lane
Poynton
Cheshire SK12 1NT
Tel: 01625 850160
info@tierracanela.com
www.tierracanela.com

World Museum Liverpool Shop
World Museum Liverpool
William Brown Street
Liverpool L3 8EN
Tel: 0151 478 4025
karen.grant@liverpoolmuseums.
org.uk
worldmuseumliverpool.org.uk

Northern Ireland
Anjuna
79 Union Street
Lurgan
Craigavon
County Armagh BT66 8EB
Tel: 02838 344299

info@anjunaonline.com
www.anjunaonline.com

Scotland
Earth Matters
67 High Street
North Berwick EH39 4 HG
Tel: 01620 895401
earthmattersltd@fsmail.co.uk
www.earthmatters.co.uk

Fair Shares
128 High Street
Burntisland
Fife KY3 9AP
Tel: 01592 870071/07952/161305
info@fairshares-shop.co.uk
www.fairshares-shop.co.uk

Fayre Trade Limited
7 Newton Street
Greenock PA16 8UH
Tel: 01475 787876
eve@fayretrade.co.uk
www.fayretrade.co.uk

Hadeel
St George's West Church
58 Shandwick Place
Edinburgh EH2 4RT
Tel: 0131 225 1922
palcrafts@fish.co.uk
www.hadeel.org

One World Shop (Edinburgh)
St.John's Church
Princes Street
Edinburgh EH2 4BJ
Tel: 0131 229 4541

rfarey@oneworldshop.co.uk
www.oneworldshop.co.uk

Rainbow Turtle
28 The Vennel, Linlithgow
West Lothian EH49 7EX
Tel: 01506 840348
info@rainbowturtle.org.uk
www.rainbowturtle.org.uk

Rainbow Turtle
7 Gauze Street
Paisley PA1 1EP
Tel: 0141 887 1881
info@rainbowturtle.org.uk
www.rainbowturtle.org.uk

The Coach House
Balmore
Torrance
Glasgow G64 4AE
Tel: 01360 620742
info@bafts.org.uk

Third World Centre
St Mary's Chapel, Church of St
Correction Wynd
Aberdeen
Aberdeenshire AB10 1JZ
Tel: 01224 645650
sue.good101@btopenworld.com
http://beehive.thisisnorthscot

Trenabies
16 Albert Street
Kirkwall
Orkney KW15 1HP
Tel: 01856 874336
leannerendall@hotmail.com

Wrap Around
84 Queensbury Street
Dumfries DG1 1BH
Tel: 01387 250053
nettie@alternativedumfries.co.uk
www.dumfries-gifts.co.uk

South East and London
Bread of Life Fair Trade Centre
Christchurch URC and Methodist
263 Barry Road
East Dulwich
London SE22 0JT
Tel: 020 8693 4170
breadoflifecentre@hotmail.co.uk
www.cced.org.uk

Chandni Chowk
13 Marmion Road
Southsea
Hants PO5 2AT
Tel: 02392 751576
mail@chandnichowk.co.uk
www.chandnichowk.co.uk

Fair Enough
136 Church Street
Croydon
Surrey CR0 1RF
Tel: 020 8688 9213
Nigel.Eltringham@ntlworld.com

Fair Share
102 Berwick Street
London W1F 0QP
Tel: 020 7287 8827
fairshare@tiscali.co.uk
www.fairshare-soho.org

Fair Trade Fairies
2 Runnalow
Letchworth
Hertfordshire SG6 4DT
Tel: 07951 758294
info@fairtradefairies.com
www.fairtradefairies.com

Fairwind
47 Park Road
Crouch End
London N8 8TE
Tel: 020 8374 6254
info@fairwindonline.com
www.fairwindonline.com

Ganesha
3 Gabriel's Wharf
56 Upper Ground
London SE1 9PP
Tel: 020 7928 3444
shop@ganesha.co.uk
www.ganesha.co.uk

Lovethatstuff
29 Coleman Street
Brighton
East Sussex BN2 9SQ
Tel: 01273 675778
kipp.wilson@virgin.net
www.lovethatstuff.co.uk

Natural Flow Direct
Unit 11, Mews Business Centre
Clifford Road
Bexhill-on-Sea
East Sussex TN40 3QA
Tel: 01424 220688

enquiries@naturalflowdirect.
com
www.NaturalFlowDirect.com

One Village
(On A44 Woodstock-Oxford)
Charlbury
OX7 3SQ
Tel: 01608 811811
progress@onevillage.org
www.onevillage.com

One World Shop (Waterloo)
St John's Church
Waterloo Road
London SE1 8TY
Tel: 020 7450 4601
ehamilton9@hotmail.com

Paper High
Flat 4, 30 Elmbourne Road
Balham, London SW17 8JR
Tel: 020 8675 2794
mark@paperhigh.com
www.paperhigh.com

Siesta
1 Palace Street
Canterbury
Kent CT1 2DY
Tel: 01227 464614
siesta@btconnect.com
www.siestacrafts.co.uk

Sust!
Food Centre
Secklow Gate
Milton Keynes MK9 3NE
Tel: 01908 232255

sust@phonecoop.coop
www.sustmk.co.uk

Ta-lmari
High Street
Ventnor
Isle of Wight PO38 1RZ
Tel: 01983 857707
enigmisle@onetel.com

The Fair Trade Shop Southampton
106 Shirley High Street
Shirley
Southampton
Hampshire SO16 4FB
Tel: 02380513344
clem.elaine@tesco.net

The World Shop, Reading
RISC, 35–39 London Street
Reading
Berks RG1 4PS
Tel: 0118 9586692
catherine@risc.org.uk
www.risc.org.uk

South West

Bishopston Trading Company
8A High Street
Glastonbury
Somerset BA6 9DU
Tel: 0145 883 5386
mail@bishopstontrading.fsnet.
co.uk

Bishopston Trading Company
79 High Street
Totnes
Devon TQ9 5PB

Tel: 0180 386 8488
mail@bishopstontrading.fsnet.
co.uk

Bishopston Trading Company
33 Silver St
Bradford-on-Avon
Wilts BA15 1JX
Tel: 01225 867485
mail@bishopstontrading.fsnet.
co.uk

Bishopston Trading Company
33 High Street, Stroud
Glos GL5 1AJ
Tel: 0145 3766355
mail@bishopstontrading.fsnet.
co.uk

Bishopston Trading Company
193 Gloucester Rd
Bishopston, Bristol
Avon & Bristol BS7 8BG
Tel: 0117 9245598
mail@bishopstontrading.co.uk
www.bishopstontrading.co.uk

Chandni Chowk
102 Boutport St
Barnstaple
Devon EX31 1SY
Tel: 01271 374714
mail@chandnichowk.co.uk
www.chandnichowk.co.uk

Chandni Chowk
6 New Bond St
Bath
Bath and Bristol BA1 1BH

Tel: 01225 484700
mail@chandnichowk.co.uk
www.chandnichowk.co.uk

Chandni Chowk
66 Park St
Bristol
Bath and Bristol BS1 5JN
Tel: 0117 9300059
mail@chandnichowk.co.uk
www.chandnichowk.co.uk

Chandni Chowk
1 Harlequins
Paul Street
Exeter
Devon EX4 3TT
Tel: 01392 410201
mail@chandnichowk.co.uk
www.chandnichowk.co.uk

Chandni Chowk
14a The Bridge
Riverside Place
Taunton
Somerset TA1 1UG
Tel: 01823 327377
mail@chandnichowk.co.uk
www.chandnichowk.co.uk

fair's fair
17 Bear Street
Barnstaple
North Devon EX32 7BX
Tel: 01271 370877
herad@fish.co.uk

Moon Dragon
Fraziers Yard, East Wharf

Mevagissey
Cornwall PL26 6QQ
Tel: 01726 844555
moon_dragon@madasafish.com

Quipu
Brewers Quay, Hope Square
Weymouth
Dorset DT4 8TP
Tel: 01305 788474
quipu@tiscali.co.uk
www.quipucrafts.co.uk

The India Shop
35 Duke Street
Henley-on-Thames
Oxon RG9 1VR
Tel: 01491 579315
info@theindiashop.co.uk
www.theindiashop.co.uk

The India Shop
5 Hilliers Yard
Marlborough
Wilts SN8 1BE
Tel: 01672 515585
info@theindiashop.co.uk
www.theindiashop.co.uk

The India Shop
35 High Street
Salisbury
Wilts SP1 2JD
Tel: 01722 321421
info@theindiashop.co.uk
www.theindiashop.co.uk

The India Shop
39 Market Place

Wantage
Oxon OX12 8AW
Tel: 01235 771040
info@theindiashop.co.uk
www.theindiashop.co.uk

Tumi
8/9 New Bond St Place
Bath BA1 1BH
Tel: 01225 446025
info@tumi.co.uk
www.tumi.co.uk

Tumi
1/2 Little Clarendon St
Oxford
Oxfordshire OX1 2HP
Tel: 01865 512307
info@tumi.co.uk
www.tumi.co.uk

Uneeka
Lemon Street Market
Lemon Street
Truro
Cornwall TR1 2PN
Tel: 01872 242276
jodi@uneeka.com
www.uneeka.com

Utani-UK
6 Richmond Gate
160 Charminster Road
Bournemouth
Dorset BH8 8UX
Tel: 01202 528262
joy@utani-uk.com
www.utani-uk.com

Wales
Fair Do's/Siopa Teg
10 Llandaff Road
Canton
Cardiff
Glamorgan CF11 9NJ
Tel: 029 2022 2066
jtucker@fairdos.com
www.fairdos.com

Jo Pott, Mercer
127 High Street, Bangor
Gwynedd LL57 1NT
Tel: 01248 362434
jo.pott@virgin.net
www.jopott.com

Just Shopping/Cynnyrch Cyfiawn
13 Bangor Road
Conwy LL32 8NG
Tel: 01492 593500
lis@fish.co.uk
www.justshopping.co.uk

Oyster
28 Castle Arcade
Cardiff
S. Wales CF10 1BW
Tel: 02920 644107
info@oysterclothing.co.uk
www.oysterclothing.co.uk

Shared Earth
14–16 Royal Arcade
Cardiff CF10 1AE
Tel: 02920 396900
jp@sharedearth.co.uk
www.sharedearth.co.uk

Siop Clare
Ty Ebrill
Y Sgwar
Crymych
Pembrokeshire SA41 3RJ

Tel: 01239 831666
clarebutler@crymych.fsworld.
co.uk

2. OTHER DEDICATED FAIR TRADE RETAILERS, MAIL ORDER AND INTERNET SUPPLIERS

Art Gecko
15 Rose Crescent
Cambridge
Cambridgeshire CB2 3LL
Tel: 01223 367483
artgecko6@hotmail.com
www.Artgecko.co.uk

Clean Slate
19 Dig Street, Ashbourne
Derbyshire DE6 1GF
Tel: 0845 3372963
enquiries@cleanslateclothing.co.uk
www.cleanslateclothing.co.uk

Concepts of Peru
87 Genesta Road
London SE18 3EX
Tel: 020 8855 3282
concepts.peru@virgin.net
www.conceptsofperu.co.uk

Epona
Unit 5, Lilford Business Centre
61 Lilford Road
London SE5 9HR
Tel: 020 7095 1222
info@eponasport.com
www.eponasport.com

Equal Exchange Trading Ltd
Suite 1, 2 Commercial Street
Edinburgh EH6 6JA
Tel. 031 554 5912
info@equalexchange.co.uk
www.equalexchange.co.uk

Ethical Junction
info@ethicaljunction.org.uk
www.ethical-
junction.org/contact.html

Ethical Shopper
4 Windsor Terrace
City Road, Islington
London N1 7TF
Tel: 020 7490 7952
ian@ethicalshopper.co.uk
www.ethicalshopper.co.uk

Ethical Threads
Tel: 020 7241 1717 / 07939 250108
info@ethicalthreads.co.uk
www.ethicalthreads.co.uk

Fair Deal Trading
m.kunz@fairdealtrading.co.uk
www.fairdealtrading.com

[213]

Fair Trade Design
440 Lichfeld Road
Sutton Coldfield
West Midlands B74 4BL
Tel: 0121 308 0387
sales@fairtradedesign.co.uk
www.fairtradedesign.co.uk

Fairs Fayre
Workshop 8, Fairground Craft
Weyhill
Andover
Hants SP11 0QN
Tel: 01264 771112
fairsfayre@tiscali.co.uk

Fair Trade Media
Tel: 0191 211 1934.
info@fairtrademedia.co.uk
www.fairtrademedia.co.uk

Get Ethical
Unit 3n, Leroy House
436 Essex Road
London N1 3QP
sales@getethical.com
www.getethical.com

Go Fair
Pump Works (AUTOOL)
Padiham Road, Sabden
Clitheroe
Lancashire BB7 9EW
Tel: 01200 440300
info@gofair.co.uk
www.gofair.co.uk

Gossypium
210 High Street

Lewes BN7 2NH
Tel: 0800 085 65 49
info@gossypium.co.uk
www.gossypium.co.uk

Hire Education Ltd
Unit 8, Navigation Way
Ripon Business Park, Ripon
N. Yorks HG4 1AB
Tel: 01765 607 815
peter@starbeck.com
www.starbeck.com

Hug
Unit 5, Lilford Business Centre
61 Lilford Rd
London SE5 9HR
Tel: 0845 130 15 25
info@hug.co.uk
www.hug.co.uk

Jungle Berry Trading
19 Lethaby House
Rubens Place
London SW4 7RB
Tel: 020 7274 4800
info@jungleberry.co.uk
www.jungleberry.co.uk

Just Change
john@justchangeuk.org
manchester@justchangeuk.org
justchangelondon@yahoo.co.uk
www.justchangeuk.org
www.justchangeindia.com

Manumit Fair Trade Limited
PO Box 6097
Newbury

Berkshire RG14 9BL
Tel: 01635 231211
info@manumituk.com
www.manumituk.com

New Consumer Shop
6–8 Charlotte Square
Newcastle-upon-Tyne
Tyne and Wear NE1 4XF
Tel: 0191 211 1934
shop@newconsumershop.org
www.newconsumershop.org/shop

Nomads Clothing
Priory Yard
Launceston
Cornwall PL15 8HU
Tel: 0845 1306633
enquiresaw05@nomadsclothing.com
www.nomadsclothing.com

Olive Co-operative
Bridge 5 Mill
22a Beswick Street
Manchester M4 7HR
Tel: 0161 273 1970
info@olivecoop.com
www.olivecoop.com

One World Is Enough
18 Ronald Rolph Court
Wadloes Road
Cambridge CB5 9PX
Tel: 0845 1661212
mail@one-world-is-enough.net
www.one-world-is-enough.net

Orchid Trading
131 Alstone Lane

Cheltenham
Gloucestershire GL51 8HX
Tel: 01242 282191
info@orchid-trading.co.uk
www.orchid-trading.co.uk

Oxfam
www.oxfam.org.uk/shop/online/
index.htm
Search for your nearest Oxfam shop at
www.multimap.com/clients/places.c
gi?client=oxfam3&searchtype=shop
&SUBMIT=Search

Pachacuti
19 Dig Street
Ashbourne,
Derbyshire DE6 1GF.
Tel: 01335 300003
hats@panamas.co.uk
www.pachacuti.co.uk

People Tree
Unit 7
8–13 New Inn Street
London EC2A 3PY
Tel: 020 7739 0660
support@ptree.co.uk
www.peopletree.co.uk

PointOV
6-8 Charlotte Square
Newcastle NE1 4XF
Tel: 0191 2111934
andy@pointov.com
www.newconsumershop.org

Progreso coffee bars
156 Portobello Road

London W11 2EB
Tel: 020 7985 0304
portobello@progreso.org.uk
and
Downstairs, Tomas Neal's Centre
35 Earlham Street,
London WC2H 9LD
Tel: 020 7379 3608
neals@progreso.org.uk
www.progreso.org.uk

Ralper
64 Rosamond Road
Bedford MK40 3UQ
Tel: 0845 226 1040
enquiries@ralper.co.uk
www.ralper.co.uk

Rugmark
www.rugmark.net
For a list of Rugmark suppliers in the
UK see http://rugmarkuk.mysite.wan
adoo-members.co.uk/page4.html

Sacred Lotus
54 Hamilton Square
Birkenhead
Wirral CH41 5AS
Tel: 0151 6508757
ayesha@sacredlotus.co.uk
www.sacredlotus.co.uk

Schmidt Natural Clothing
Tel: 0845 345 0498
catalogue@naturalclothing.co.uk
www.naturalclothing.co.uk

Silkwood Traders
The Old Main Post Office

Ship Street, Brighton
Tel: 01273 884587
info@silkwoodtraders.com
www.silkwoodtraders.com

Silverchilli.com
Tel: 0208 342 8883
directors@silverchilli.com
www.silverchilli.com

Simply Fair
Tel: 0191 491 5400
helpdesk@simplyfair.co.uk
www.simplyfair.co.uk

Sunlover
Leigh Farm Buildings
Standerwick, Frome
Somerset BA11 2PR
Tel: 01373 831153
sales@sunlover-gifts.co.uk
www.sunlover-gifts.co.uk

SuSuMaMa World Wear
2 Brambletyne Avenue
Saltdean, Brighton BN2 8EJ
Tel: 01273 300606
carli@susumama.co.uk
www.susumama.co.uk

Tearcraft
PO Box 5050
Annesley
Nottingham NG15 0DL
Tel: 0870 2404896
tearcraft@prolog.uk.com
www.tearcraft.org/cgi-bin/tcraft

The Fair Trade Stand
164 Hardy Mill Road
Bolton
Lancs BL2 3PW
Tel: 01204 528409
sales@fartradestand.net
www.fairtradestand.net

The Pink Planet Company
107 Hollywood Lane
Wainscott
Rochester
Kent ME3 8AT
Tel: 01634 313112
claire.greenway@pink-planet.co.uk
www.pink-planet.co.uk

Think Clothing
2nd Floor, 145–157 St John Street

London EC1V 4PY
info@thinkfairtrade.com
www.thinkfairtrade.com

Traidcraft
Kingsway, Gateshead
Tyne & Wear NE11 0NE
Tel: 0191 491 0591
comms@traidcraft.co.uk
www.traidcraft.co.uk
Search for the nearest retailers selling
products from the Traidcraft range at
www.traidcraft.co.uk/template2.asp?
pageID=1895

Zaytoun
Tel: 0845 345 4887
order@zaytoun.org
http://zaytoun.org

3. CATERING DISTRIBUTORS AND WHOLESALERS OF FAIRTRADE-CERTIFIED PRODUCE

Links to lists of catering distributors and wholesalers of Fairtrade-certified produce on the Fairtrade Foundation website:

Catering distributors: www.fairtrade.org.uk/suppliers_caterers.htm
Wholesalers: www.fairtrade.org.uk/suppliers_wholesalers.htm

4. ETHICAL TRAVEL

www.responsibletravel.com

Tourism Concern
Stapleton House
277-281 Holloway Road
London N7 8HN
Tel: 020 7133 3330
info@tourismconcern.org.uk
www.tourismconcern.org.uk

Ethical tourism links:
www.tourismconcern.org.uk/links/
ethical-links.html

A wide range of ethical holidays are
listed in Tourism Concern's book:
Polly Pattullo with Orely Minelli,
*The Ethical Travel Guide: Your
Passport To Alternative Holidays,*

London, Tourism Concern/Earth-
scan, 2006

Traidcraft Meet the People Tours
www.traidcraftinteractive.co.uk/
calendar.php?9701

5. FAIR TRADE FINANCE

Shared Interest
No.2 Cathedral Square
The Groat Market
Newcastle upon Tyne NE1 1EH
Tel: 0191 233 9100
enquirer@shared-interest.com
www.shared-interest.com

Triodos Fairtrade Saver Account
Triodos Bank
Brunel House
11 The Promenade
Bristol
BS8 3NN
Tel: 0117 973 9339
mail@triodos.co.uk
www.triodos.co.uk/uk/personal_
banking/savings/our_accounts/
fairtrade_saver/

Appendix 2: Fairtrade Towns and other areas in the UK

By mid 2006 there were 200 declared Fairtrade Towns, Cities, Boroughs etc., with well over 200 more working towards Fairtrade status – all listed below. There were also 2,845 Fairtrade Churches, Cathedrals, Chapels and Quaker Meetings; 13 Fairtrade Synagogues; at least one Fairtrade Mosque; and 34 Fairtrade Colleges and Universities. According to the Fairtrade Foundation, new applications come in every week.

Information kindly provided by the Fairtrade Foundation (and see www.fairtrade.org.uk/get_involved_ fairtrade_towns.htm).

FAIRTRADE TOWNS, CITIES, BOROUGHS, VILLAGES, ZONES, ISLANDS, COUNTIES AND DISTRICTS

Key: T = Town, C = City, B = Borough, V = Village, Z = Zone, I = Island, Co = County, D = District

1. Aberdeen (C)
2. Aberfeldy (T)
3. Aberystwyth (T)
4. Altrincham (T)
5. Ammanford (T)
6. Arundel (T)
7. Ashbourne (T)
8. Baildon (T)
9. Banbury (T)
10. Barnstaple (T)
11. Bath & NE Somerset (Z)
12. Belfast (C)
13. Bewdley (T)
14. Bideford (T)
15. Bingley (T)
16. Birmingham (C)
17. Bolton (T)
18. Bradford (Z)
19. Bradford-on-Avon (V)
20. Brampton (T)
21. Brecon (T)
22. Bridgnorth (T)
23. Brighton & Hove (C)
24. Bristol (C)
25. Burgess Hill (T)
26. Burntisland (T)
27. Cam & Dursley (T)
28. Cambridge (C)
29. Canterbury (C)
30. Cardiff (C)
31. Carlisle (C)
32. Castle Cary (T)
33. Charnwood (B)
34. Chelmsford (T)
35. Cherry Burton (V)
36. Chesham (T)

37. Chester (C)
38. Chorlton-cum-Hardy (Z)
39. Colchester (C)
40. Conwy (Co)
41. Coventry (C)
42. Criccieth, N. Wales (V)
43. Cumbria (Co)
44. Denbighshire (Co)
45. Derby (C)
46. Doncaster (T)
47. Dorchester (T)
48. Dorking (T)
49. Dornoch (T)
50. Dundee (C)
51. Dunoon (T)
52. Dyfi Valley (Z)
53. East Grinstead (T)
54. Edenbridge (T)
55. Eden Valley (Z)
56. Edinburgh (C)
57. Exeter (C)
58. Fairlie (V)
59. Fair Isle (I)
60. Falkirk (T)
61. Falmouth (T)
62. Faringdon (T)
63. Faversham (C)
64. Flintshire (Co)
65. Frome (T)
66. Garstang (T)
67. Glasgow (C)
68. Glastonbury (T)
69. Guernsey (I)
70. Guildford (C)
71. Guisborough (T)
72. Hamilton (T)
73. Hartlepool (T)
74. Harrogate (B)
75. Haworth (V)
76. Hebden Bridge (Z)
77. Hereford (C)
78. Herefordshire (C)
79. Hitchin (T)
80. Holme Valley (T)
81. Horsham (T)
82. Hornsea (T)
83. Horwich (T)
84. Hull (C)
85. Isle of Wight (I)
86. Ilkley (T)
87. Jersey (I)
88. Kendal (T)
89. Keswick (T)
90. Keynsham (T)
91. Kilmacolm & Quarriers (V)
92. Kinross-shire (Co)
93. Knighton (T)
94. Lakes Parish (Z)
95. Lampeter (T)
96. Lancaster (C)
97. Largs (T)
98. Ledbury (T)
99. Leeds (C)
100. Leicester (C)
101. Leighton Linslade (T)
102. Leominster (T)
103. Lewes (T)
104. Lingfield & Dormansland (Z)
105. Linlithgow (T)
106. Liverpool (C)
107. Livingston (T)
108. Llanidloes (T)
109. Lochgelly (T)
110. London, Camden (B)
111. London, Croydon (B)
112. London, Greenwich (B)
113. London, Hammersmith & Fulham (B)

114. London, Islington (B)
115. London, Kingston (B)
116. London, Lambeth (B)
117. London, Lewisham (B)
118. London, Richmond (B)
119. Lowestoft (T)
120. Ludlow (T)
121. Macclesfield (T)
122. Malvern (T)
123. Manchester (C)
124. Market Harborough (T)
125. Matlock & District (T)
126. Milford Haven (T)
127. Millom (T)
128. Milton Keynes (B)
129. Minehead (T)
130. Mirfield (T)
131. Monmouth (T)
132. Morpeth (T)
133. Nailsworth (T)
134. Newbury (T)
135. Newcastle-upon-Tyne (C)
136. Newton Abbot (T)
137. Northallerton (T)
138. Norwich (C)
139. Nottingham (C)
140. Oswestry (T)
141. Oxford (C)
142. Paisley (T)
143. Peebles & Tweeddale (Z)
144. Penarth (T)
145. Pendle (B)
146. Perth (C)
147. Plymouth (C)
148. Porthcawl (T)
149. Portsmouth (C)
150. Preston (C)
151. Purbeck (D)
152. Reading (T)

153. Rochdale (B)
154. Romsey (T)
155. Rotherham (T)
156. Royal Leamington Spa (T)
157. Salford (C)
158. Sevenoaks (T)
159. Sheffield (C)
160. Shetland Islands (I)
161. Shipley (T)
162. Somerset (Co)
163. Southampton (C)
164. Southwell (T)
165. St Albans (C)
166. St Andrews (T)
167. St Neots (T)
168. Stafford (T)
169. Stirling (C)
170. Stockport (B)
171. Stoke-on-Trent (C)
172. Stourport-on-Severn (T)
173. Strathaven (T)
174. Stroud (T)
175. Swanage (T)
176. Swansea (C & Co)
177. Swindon (B)
178. Taunton (T)
179. Tavistock (T)
180. Teignmouth (T)
181. Thornbury (T)
182. Uckfield (T)
183. Vale Royal Borough (B)
184. Wareham (T)
185. Warrington (B)
186. Wells (C)
187. Weymouth and Portland (Z)
188. Wimborne Minster (T)
189. Wiveliscombe (T)
190. Windermere and Bowness (T)
191. Windsor and Maidenhead (B)

192. Wirral (B)
193. Worcester (T)
194. Woking (B)
195. Wolverhampton (C)
196. Worthing (T)
197. Wotton-under-Edge (T)
198. Wrexham (Z)
199. York (C)
200. Yatton & Claverham (Z)

TOWNS AND OTHER AREAS WORKING TOWARDS FAIRTRADE STATUS

1. Abingdon, Oxfordshire
2. Addlestone, Surrey
3. Adlington
4. Allerdale
5. Andover
6. Anglesey
7. Arbroath
8. Ashburton
9. Ashford
10. Aylesbury
11. Ayr
12. Balfron
13. Ballymoney
14. Bangor
15. Barrow-in-Furness
16. Basingstoke
17. Bathrone
18. Batley and Spen
19. Beaconsfield
20. Beccles
21. Bedford
22. Berwick
23. Beverley
24. Bexhill-on-Sea
25. Billericay
26. Bishopton
27. Blackpool
28. Bognor
29. Bournemouth
30. Braintree District
31. Bridgend
32. Broseley
33. Broxtowe
34. Burscough
35. Burton upon Trent
36. Bury St Edmunds
37. Buxton
38. Caernarfon
39. Caerphilly
40. Caradon District
41. Castle Douglas
42. Castle Point
43. Chapel Allerton
44. Chesterfield
45. Chester-le-Street
46. Chew Magna
47. Chorley
48. Chichester
49. Cleckheaton
50. Clitheroe
51. Cockermouth
52. Coleraine
53. Congleton
54. Coniston & Torver
55. Coupar
56. Crawley
57. Dacorum
58. Darlington
59. Dawlish
60. Devizes

61. Dinas Powys
62. Deal
63. Droitwich Spa
64. Dundonald
65. Durham
66. East Dunbartonshire
67. East Renfrewshire
68. East Staffordshire
69. East Sussex
70. Eastbourne
71. Eastleigh
72. Eden Valley
73. Egremont
74. Ellesmere Port and Neston
75. Ellon
76. Elmbridge
77. Epsom
78. Evesham & District
79. Fareham
80. Farnham
81. Ferndown
82. Fylde
83. Gateshead
84. Glossop
85. Gloucester
86. Grange-over-Sands
87. Grove, Oxfordshire
88. Gwynedd
89. Hadleigh
90. Harlow
91. Hastings and St Leonards
92. Havant
93. Heathfield
94. Heswall, Wirral
95. Hinckley & Bosworth
96. Honiton & Sidmouth
97. Hope Valley, Derbyshire
98. Hornchurch
99. Huntingdon

100. Hyndburn
101. Inverclyde
102. Inverness
103. Ipswich
104. Isle of Man
105. Isle of Arran
106. Kent
107. Kidderminster
108. Kilwinning
109. Knaresborough and Harrogate
110. Knutsford
111. Lancashire
112. Larkhall
113. Lavenham
114. Leek
115. Letchworth
116. Lichfield
117. Limpsfield
118. Llandrindod and Builth Wells
119. London, Barking and Dagenham
120. London, Barnet
121. London, Bexley
122. London, Brent
123. London, Bromley
124. London, Ealing
125. London, Enfield
126. London, Haringey
127. London, Harrow
128. London, Havering
129. London, Hounslow
130. London, Merton
131. London, Newham
132. London, Redbridge
133. London, Southwark
134. London, Sutton
135. London, Tower Hamlets
136. London, Waltham Forest
137. Longniddry, Scotland

138. Louth
139. Lydney
140. Lymington
141. Lyndhurst
142. Malton
143. Mansfield
144. Marlborough
145. Medway
146. Melton Mowbray
147. Middlesbrough
148. Milnthorpe
149. Moreton-in-Marsh
150. Newcastle-under-Lyme
151. Newmarket
152. Norfolk
153. North Ayrshire
154. North Yorkshire
155. Northampton
156. Nottinghamshire
157. Oban and District
158. Ormskirk
159. Orpington
160. Otley
161. Ottershaw
162. Oundle
163. Oxted
164. Painswick
165. Penistone
166. Penwortham
167. Penzance
168. Polesworth
169. Pontypridd
170. Poole
171. Powys
172. Redditch
173. Retford
174. Richmond, Yorkshire
175. Rutland
176. Salisbury

177. Sandhurst, Berkshire
178. Seaford
179. Scarborough
180. Sefton
181. Shaftesbury
182. Sherbourne
183. Shrewsbury
184. Shropshire
185. Skipton
186. Slough
187. Southend-on-Sea
188. South Holland
189. South Tyneside
190. Southwell, Nottinghamshire
191. St Bees
192. St Helens
193. St Leonards on Sea
194. Stamford
195. Stevenage
196. Stockton
197. Stourbridge
198. Strathblane and Blanefield
199. Sunderland
200. Tarporley
201. Tenby
202. Thanet
203. Three Rivers
204. Todmorden
205. Torbay
206. Trafford
207. Tring
208. Ullapool
209. Wakefield
210. Ware
211. Warminster
212. Waterside Area
213. Watford
214. Welwyn Garden City
215. West Lothian

Appendix 3:
Where to find out more

CONTENTS

1. LEADING UK FAIR TRADE ORGANISATIONS AND INFORMATION SOURCES

British Association for Fair Trade
Shops (BAFTS)
Unit 7, 8–13 New Inn Street
London EC2A 3PY
Tel: 07796 050045
info@bafts.org.uk
www.bafts.org.uk

Ethical Consumer magazine and
research services
Unit 21, 41 Old Birtley Street
Manchester M15 5RF
Tel: 0161 226 2929
mail@ethicalconsumer.org
www.ethicalconsumer.org

Fairtrade Foundation
Room 204
16 Baldwin's Gardens
London EC1N 7RJ
Tel: 020 7405 5942
mail@fairtrade.org.uk

www.fairtrade.org.uk

New Consumer magazine
51 Timberbush
Edinburgh EH6 6QH
Tel: 0131 561 1780
editorial@newconsumer.org
www.newconsumer.org

Trading Visions
4 Gainsford Street
London SE1 2NE
www.tradingvisions.org

Traidcraft
Kingsway
Gateshead
Tyne & Wear NE11 0NE
Tel: 0191 491 0591
comms@traidcraft.co.uk
www.traidcraft.org

Twin Trading
1 Curtain Road
London EC2A 3LT
Tel: 020 7375 1221
info@twin.org.uk
www.twin.org.uk

2. TRADE-RELATED CAMPAIGNS

Banana Link
www.bananalink.org.uk

Clean Clothes Campaign
www.cleanclothes.org

CORE, the Corporate Responsibility
Coalition
www.corporate-responsibility.org

Labour Behind the Label
www.labourbehindthelabel.org

Make Trade Fair
www.maketradefair.com

No Sweat
www.nosweat.org.uk

People & Planet fair trade campaign
www.peopleandplanet.org/fairtrade

Trade Justice Movement
www.tjm.org.uk

3. INTERNATIONAL FAIR TRADE ORGANISATIONS

European Fair Trade Association
(EFTA)
Kerkewegje 1
6305 BC Schin op Geul
The Netherlands
Tel: +31 43 325 69 17
efta@antenna.nl
www.european-fair-trade-
association.org

Fairtrade Labelling Organisations
International (FLO)
FLO International
Bonner Talweg 177

53129 Bonn
Germany
Tel: +49 228 949230
info@fairtrade.net
www.fairtrade.net

Fair Trade Advocacy Office (FINE)
43 Rue de la Charite
1210 Brussels
Belgium
Tel: +32 02 217 36 17
osterhaus@fairtrade-advocacy.org

International Fair Trade Association
(IFAT)
Prijssestraat 24
4101 CR Culemborg
The Netherlands
Tel: +31 0345 53 59 14
info@ifat.org
www.ifat.org

Network of European Worldshops
(NEWS)
Christofsstrasse 13
55116 Mainz
Germany
Tel: +49 6131 9066 410
office@worldshops.org
www.worldshops.org

4. FAIR TRADE AROUND THE WORLD

Full members of Fairtrade Labelling
Organisations International (FLO):

Fairtrade Labelling Australia &
New Zealand
PO Box 306
Flinders Lane PO
8009 Victoria
Australia
Tel: +61 3966 22919
admin@fta.org.au
www.fta.org.au
www.fta.org.nz

Fairtrade Austria
Wohllebengasse 12–14
1040 Wien
Austria
Tel: +43 1 533 0956
office@fairtrade.at
www.fairtrade.at

Max Havelaar Belgium
Troonstraat 173
Rue du Trone
B 1050, Bruxelles
Belgium
Tel: +32 2 500 1060

info@maxhavelaar.be
www.maxhavelaar.be

Transfair Canada
302-251 Bank Street
Ottawa, ON K2P 1X3
Canada
Tel: +1 613 563 3351
fairtrade@transfair.ca
www.transfair.ca

Max Havelaar Denmark
c/o WWF, Ryesgade 3F
2200 København N
Denmark
Tel: +45 70231345
info@maxhavelaar.dk
www.maxhavelaar.dk

Reilun kaupan edistämisyhdistys ry
Finland
Kolmes Linja 4
00530 Helsinki
Finland
Tel: +358 9 5658680
reilukauppa@reilukauppa.fi
www.reilukauppa.fi

Max Havelaar France
Immeuble le Méliès
261 rue de Paris
93100 Montreuil
France
Tel: +33 1 42877021
info@maxhavelaarfrance.org
www.maxhavelaarfrance.org

TransFair Germany
Remigiusstrasse 21
50937 Köln
Germany
Tel: +49 221 942 040 0
info@transfair.org
www.transfair.org

Fairtrade Mark Ireland
Carmichael Centre
North Brunswick Street
Dublin 7
Ireland
Tel: +353 1 475 3515
info@fairtrade.ie
www.fairtrade.ie

Fairtrade TransFair Italy
Passagio De Gasperi 3
35131 Padova
Italy
Tel: +39 049 8750 823
info@fairtradeitalia.it
www.fairtradeitalia.it

Fairtrade Label Japan
c/o St. Paul Lutheran Church of the
JELC
5-3-1-Koutoubashi, Sumida-ku
Tokyo 130

Japan
Tel: +81 3 3634 7867
info@fairtrade-jp.org
www.fairtrade-jp.org

TransFair Minka Luxemburg
2a Rue de la Gare
6910 Roodt sur Syre
Luxemburg
Tel: +352 35 07 62
info@transfair.lu
www.transfair.lu

Stichting Max Havelaar
Netherlands
Lucasbolwerk 7
3512 EG Utrecht
the Netherlands
Tel: +31 30 2337070
vanderijke@maxhavelaar.nl
www.maxhavelaar.nl

Max Havelaar Norge
Storgata 11
0155 Oslo
Norway
Tel: +47 23010330
maxhavelaar@maxhavelaar.no
www.maxhavelaar.no

Asociación para el Sello de
Comercio Justo España
Gaztambide 50
28015 Madrid
Spain
Tel: +34 91 543 33 99
info@sellocomerciojusto.org
www.sellocomerciojusto.org

Rättvisemärkt Sweden
Pustegränd 1-3
11820 Stockholm
Sweden
Tel: +46 8 505 756 90
info@rattvisemarkt.se
www.rattvisemarkt.se

Max Havelaar Stiftung Schweiz
Malzgasse 25
4052 Basel
Switzerland
Tel: +41 61 2717500
postmaster@maxhavelaar.ch
www.maxhavelaar.ch

TransFair USA
1611 Telegraph Ave, Suite 900

Oakland
CA 94612
USA
Tel: +1 510 663 5260
info@transfairusa.org
www.transfairusa.org

Associate FLO member:

Comercio Justo México
Guanajuato 131, Desp. 302
Colonia Roma Norte
Delegación Cuauhtémoc
06700 México DF
Mexico
Tel: +52 55 55 74 71 16
info@comerciojusto.com.mx
www.comerciojusto.com.mx

Acronyms

ACP	African, Caribbean and Pacific
AFTF	Asia Fair Trade Forum
BAFTS	British Association of Fair Trade Shops
CAFOD	Catholic Agency for Overseas Development
CECOCAFEN	Organisation of Northern Coffee Cooperatives, Nicaragua
COASBA	Cooperativa Campesina Apícola Santa Bárbara (beekeepers' co-operative, Santa Bárbara, Chile)
COFTA	Cooperation for Fair Trade in Africa
COMUCAP	indigenous women's coffee co-op, Honduras
Coocafé	Fairtrade coffee producer co-op, Costa Rica
COSURCA	coffee co-operative, Colombia
EFTA	European Fair Trade Association
EPA	Economic Partnership Agreement
FIFA	Fédération Internationale de Football Association
FINE	collaboration between FLO International, IFAT, NEWS! and EFTA
FLO	Fairtrade Labelling Organisations International
FTO	Fair Trade Organisation
GM/GMO	genetically modified/genetically modified organism
HIV/AIDS	Human Immuno-Deficiency Virus/Acquired Immuno-Deficiency Syndrome
HRW	Human Rights Watch
IFAT	International Fair Trade Association
ILO	International Labour Organization
ISA	individual savings account
I-SIS	Institute of Science in Society, London
ISMAM	coffee co-op, Mexico
KNCU	coffee co-operative, Tanzania
MDGs	Millennium Development Goals
NEWS!	Network of European World Shops
NGO	non-governmental organisation
PRODECOOP	Cafédirect partner, Nicaragua
SARS	Severe Acute Respiratory Syndrome
SCIAF	Scottish Catholic International Aid Fund
SNV	Netherlands-based international development organisation
SOPPEXCCA	fair trade coffee co-operative in Nicaragua

Tara	Trade Alternative Reform Action
TJM	Trade Justice Movement
TNC	transnational corporation
Ton	mango growers co-operative, Burkina Faso
TBL	Triple Bottom Line
TRIM	trade-related investment measure
TRIP	trade-related intellectual property right
UCIRI	Union of Indigenous Communities in the Isthmus Region, Mexico
UNCTAD	United Nations Conference on Trade and Development
UNICEF	United Nations Children's Fund
WTO	World Trade Organization
WWF	Worldwide Fund for Nature
YMCA	Y Development Co-operative Co Ltd

The Green Economics Institute exists to promote change, through both academic and non-academic channels. At the centre of Green Economics are connections – between cultures and between generations, between natural and social sciences and between people and the planet.

Traditional economic models ignore the value and real wealth created by a large segment of the Earth's population – those engaged in "women's work", subsistence farming and small rural crafts production – and in fact ignore all activities and existing values that are not measurable in direct monetary terms. Like our natural resources, the people at the bottom of the poverty pyramid are regarded as expendable inputs to the system – without intrinsic value and of interest only as a target market.

Green economics seeks to change the way we look at the world. The new models it proposes listen to what natural scientists tell us, emphasising climate change over business cycles, long-term responsibility over short-term profit. It favours local goals in decision making, and attention to cultural difference, against the interests of globalisation, defined as rolling out one limited concept everywhere in the world.

Green economics is about connectedness. It recognises overall well-being and happiness as key values by which economic development should be assessed – while acknowledging that these cannot be achieved without addressing claims of justice, global poverty, and the biosphere.

The Green Economics Institute brings people together through events, conferences and publications, with the aim of developing an ethical and just view of the world we can change.

Green Economics Institute
6 Strachey Close
Tidmarsh
Reading RG8 8EP
UK
www.greeneconomics.org.uk
greeneconomicsinstitute@yahoo.com

Index